Fragments of Identity

A JOURNEY OF RESILIENCE, DISCOVERY, AND REDEMPTION

JENNY TOUSSAINT

MILTON & HUGO L.L.C.
4407 Park Ave., Suite 5
Union City, NJ 07087, USA

Website: *www. miltonandhugo.com*
Hotline: *1- 888-778-0033*
Email: *info@miltonandhugo.com*

Ordering Information:
Quantity sales. Special discounts are granted to corporations, associations, and other organizations. For more information on these discounts, please reach out to the publisher using the contact information provided above.

Library of Congress Control Number: 2024902698
ISBN-13:   979-8-89285-031-5   [Paperback Edition]
                979-8-89285-032-2   [Digital Edition]

Rev. date: 02/23/2024

DEDICATIONS

"Dedicated to Papa Wemba,

A musical icon, a fashion trailblazer, and a source of inspiration. Your legacy lives on in the rhythms of my life, guiding me through challenges and moments of self-discovery. This book is a tribute to your influence on my journey".

"To my mentor and life partner,

Your guidance and unwavering support have been instrumental in shaping not only my artistic journey but also the narrative of my life. This book stands as a tribute to your love, influence and the profound impact you've had on my path. Thank you for being a beacon of inspiration".

"To my dearest daughter,

You are the heartbeat of this story, the source of my strength, and the embodiment of Love's enduring power. May these words reflect the resilience and joy you've brought into my life. This book is dedicated to you, my greatest inspiration".

"To all my supporters,

Your unwavering encouragement, love, and belief in my journey have been the pillars of strength that sustained me through every twist and turn. This book is dedicated to each of you who stood by me, offering kindness and support. Your impact on my life is immeasurable. With heartfelt gratitude".

"To all survivors of adversity,

In recognition of your strength, resilience, and the indomitable human spirit that prevails over darkness. This book is dedicated to you, brave souls who have faced unimaginable challenges. May your stories inspire courage and bring about positive change. With deepest respect".

CONTENTS

CHAPTER

1

Introduction: Finding an Old Photograph

"In the quiet solitude of the old chimney adjacent amidst forgotten old and dusty bookshelf relics, I stumbled upon an artifact frozen in time, a photograph that whispered of untold stories. The faded hues and sepia tones held a silent promise of unraveling mysteries and little did I know that this chance encounter would set in motion a journey to discover the profound truth of my own identity." As I held the dusty photograph in my hands, its image seemed to beckon me into a forgotten chapter of my history. As the dust settled on the colored photograph, a shiver of anticipation crept down my spine, signaling the profound impact this chance discovery would wield on the tapestry of my existence. Little did I know that this singular photograph would become the key, unlocking the door to a realm where the past and present danced in intricate harmony, urging me to embark on a journey of self-discovery.

Discovering evidence on a photo suggesting its use for witchcraft or a spell was unsettling, yet it ignited a deeper curiosity to explore further into my bloodline. The evolution of my name from Lokango Shungu to Jenny Shungu and later Jenny Toussaint, coupled with the uncertainty surrounding my birth and biological parents. I found myself standing at the intersection of curiosity and nostalgia, ready to embark on a personal quest to decode the secrets of the SHUNGU family, a journey that would lead me to uncover the profound truths hidden in the layers of time. As I delved deeper into the enigma of my identity, I unearthed a pivotal moment, my arrival in the United States alongside the diplomate and his wife. Being brought to the states with a political title you'd think my world would be filled with the corridors of power and privilege intertwined, however, it was filled with the complexities of my personal history, adding an extra layer of intrigue to my quest to understand my true identity, along with growing up in American, or should I say, "African American Culture".

According to my birth certificate, I was born in The Democratic Republic of Congo (DRC) (Congo) on June 6th, 1986. Congo, situated in the heart of Africa, has a rich and complex history marked by both cultural diversity and political turmoil. Its history is intertwined with colonialism, independence struggles, and post-colonial challenges. The cultural tapestry of Congo is woven with vibrant traditions, music, and art. Renowned Congolese artists like Papa Wemba have significantly contributed to the global music scene, showcasing the nation's cultural richness. Papa Wemba, a prominent figure in the Congolese music scene, not only contributed to the world of music but also played roles in films. This artistic legacy has become a source of pride and connection for me while exploring my roots. The region has faced periods of conflict, including civil wars. The impact of these conflicts on families and individuals, as well as their subsequent search for safety and asylum. The reality for many conflict-ridden regions in Congo is the challenges of starting anew in a different cultural context. The diaspora is often left with questions of identity and belonging. In the 1980s, Congo (then known as Zaire) was under the rule of President Mobutu Sese Seko.

Mobutu's presidency, which spanned several decades, was characterized by autocratic rule, corruption, and a cult of personality. He maintained a strong grip on power through a combination of political maneuvering and the suppression of opposition. Mobutu' leadership was widely criticized for human rights abuses and economic mismanagement, leading to a challenging socio-political climate in the country. The government's functioning during this period was marked by a centralized and authoritarian system that stifled dissent. This unexpected intersection of political displacement and international diplomacy was a consequence of political turmoil in Congo and laid the foundation for the international intrigue that shrouded my introduction to the United States. Little did I anticipate the complexities that awaited me in this new land as the echoes of Congo's unrest reverberated through the corridors of my American experience. Papa Wemba, a prominent musician, and cultural icon was known for his influence in the entertainment industry and his contributions to the Congolese music scene. However, it's crucial to note that the government's focus during that time was not typically on issues related to missing persons, especially those linked to private familial matters. In my narrative, the significance of my maiden name, SHUNGU, implies a connection to family ties and adds weight to labeling my displacement as a familial matter. While the philosophy "we are all family" is readily rooted and embraced in African culture, the nuances of those who dwell in riches, especially in American culture highlight that not everyone sharing common last names necessarily belongs to the same lineage. For instance, the surname Smith does not universally unite individuals into a single-family group. However, no historical evidence or documentation suggests that Papa Wemba notified government officials about a missing princess. During Mobutu's regime, the Government's priorities were strictly centered around political stability, control, and maintaining the existing power structure. Curiosity now extended beyond familial ties, encompassing the diplomatic world that once cradled my introduction to the United States. With this newfound revelation, my journey unfolded as a tapestry woven with threads of personal history and international intrigue, each knot holding a piece of the truth waiting to be unraveled.

CHAPTER

2

The Promenade of Broken Dreams

"From early on, my journey was marked by the absence of parental guidance, a void that echoed with the challenges of adaptation and self-discovery. The landscape of America, though filled with opportunities, often cast long shadows of stereotypes upon me. The labels imposed by society seemed to weave themselves into the very fabric of my existence, presenting obstacles that required resilience and strength to overcome. As an African-born individual, the clash of cultures was palpable, creating a mosaic of identity that demanded constant negotiation. I struggle to reconcile the richness of my heritage with the expectations and biases of my surroundings. Yet, amid the hardships, there emerged a story of overcoming adversity, dismantling stereotypes, and reclaiming my true self. Each stride through the labyrinth of identity brought with it a lesson, a triumph over preconceptions, and a step closer to embracing the uniqueness of my journey.

Through the struggles, I forged an identity that transcended labels, celebrating the richness of my African roots and the resilience cultivated in the melting pot of America. The threat of being brought to the United States with an old diplomat couple unraveled abruptly in 1996 when fate dealt a harsh blow of the passing of the diplomat. Suddenly, the stability of my world crumbled, and I found myself tossed from the care of one relative to another, from uncles to aunts. The loss of the diplomat, who had been a tether to a world of privilege and influence, marked a profound shift in my journey. The uncertainties of life without parental figures intensified, and the challenges of adaptation took on a new gravity. Each transition between relatives became not only a change in living arrangements but a shift in the landscape of my identity."

"Living On a Prayer" & "The Purpose of Prayer"

"Jesus set the perfect example of obedience in prayer, although His day was filled from morning to night with many pressures and responsibilities - addressing crowds healing the sick, granting private interviews, traveling, and training His disciples – He made prayer a top priority. If Jesus was so dependent upon this fellowship in prayer alone with His Father, how much more you and I should spend time alone with God".

OBJECTIVE = To understand the importance of prayer to your life.

"Why are we to pray?

God commands us to pray, watch and pray (Luke 21:36; Mark 14:38)

Pray thanksgiving (Philippians 4:6, Col 4:2)

Pray in the Spirit (1 Corinthians 14:15)

Always pray and not give up (Luke 18:1)

"We also pray to have fellowship with God. Prayer is not just an 'escape hatch' for us to get out of trouble and please ourselves or gain our selfish ends. It is our "Hotline" of communication and fellowship with God in the process, we receive spiritual nurture, and strength to live a victorious life, and we maintain the boldness necessary for a vital witness for Christ".

"To whom do we pray?

We pray to the Father in heaven - through the name of the Lord and through the ministry of the Holy Spirit. When we pray to the Father, our prayers are accepted by Jesus Chest and interpreted to God the Father by the Holy Spirit. Because God is one God manifested Himself in three forms and sense, there is no jealousy, between the three of the trinity it is perfectly acceptable to pray to Jesus or the Holy Spirit. As we pray both Jesus and the Holy Spirit are interceding on our behalf. Paul records in (Romans 8:34), Christ Jesus who died more than so, was raised to Life at the right hand of God and is also interceding for us. Paul wrote, "The Spirit helps us in our weakness and he who searches our hearts knows the mind of the Spirit, because the Spirit intercedes for the saints in accordance with God's will.

When should we pray?

God's word commands us to pray continually (1 Thessalonians 5:17) Charles Spurgeon said prayer pulls the rape down below, and the great bell rings above in the ears of God, some scarcely stir the bell some give only an occasional jerk or two at the rape, but he who communicates with heaven is the woman who grasps the rape badly and pulls continuously with all his/her might. We can be in prayer frequently throughout the day, demonstrating our devotion to God as we go about our daily task. Morning in prayer, as you get out of bed, fall on your knees to worship Him as a way of saying, Lord, I bow before you and acknowledge you as my master. Throughout the day, I focus my thoughts on the Lord, often talking to Him, praising Him, and thanking Him for His goodness, love, and grace.

UNLOCKING THE SECRETS OF A SUCCESSFUL PRAYER

What is Prayer?

Simply put, prayer is communicating with God. As a child of God, you are invited to come boldly before His Throne. Prayer is the creator as well as the channel of devotion. The spirit of devotion is the spirit of prayer. Prayer and devotion are united as soul and body are united, as life and heart are connected. Real prayer is expressing our devotion to our Heavenly Father, inviting Him to talk to us as we talk to Him. Who can pray? Anyone can pray. The key is praying a clean heart also is vital to successful prayer if I had cherished sin in my heart, the Lord would not have listened (Psalm 66:18). We cannot expect God to answer our prayers if there is any unconfessed sin in our life. One of the most frequent hindrances to prayer is an unforgiving spirit. When you stand praying, if you hold anything against anyone, forgive him/her, so that your Father in Heaven may forgive you your sins (Mark 11:25) No prayer except the prayer of confession can be answered by God unless it comes from a heart that is free of unforgiveness and bitterness.

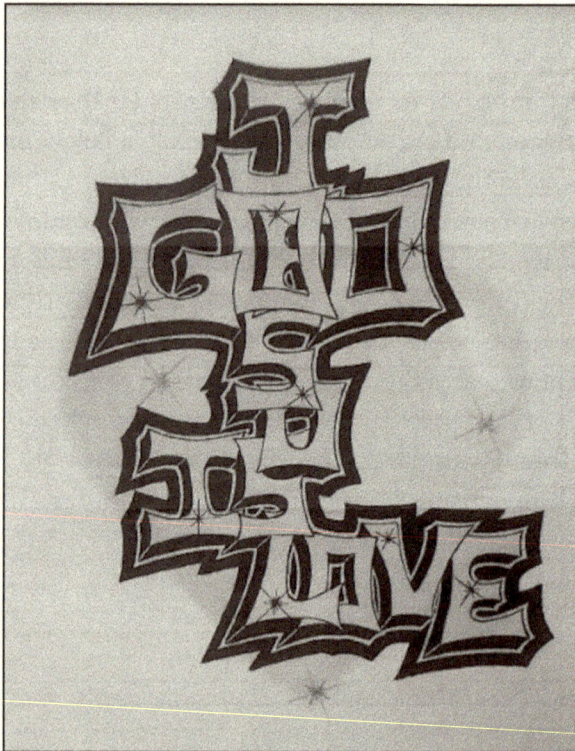

In the evening, I ask the Lord is there anything in me that is displeasing to you, anything I need to confess? If the Holy Spirit reveals any sins or weakness, I confess them and claim by faith God's victory for my life.

God wants us to be in touch with Him (constantly wherever we are. We can pray in the car, while washing the dishes, or while walking, faking a shower, cooking, on your job site etc.

What should we include in our prayer?

Although prayer cannot be reduced to a formula, certain basic elements should be included in our communication with God: **A.C.T.S.**

A = doration - to adore God is to worship and praise Him to honor and exalt Him in our heart and mind and with our lips.

C = confession - when our discipline of prayer begins with adoration, the Holy Spirit has the opportunity to reveal any sins in our life that need to be confessed, by seeing God in His purity, His holiness, and His love, we become aware of our sinfulness and unworthiness. Confessing our sins and receiving His forgiveness restores us to fellowship with Him and clear the channel from God to hear and answer our prayer (1 John 1: 7-9).

T = thanksgiving - nothing pleases God more than our consistent expression of Faith. What better way to do this than to tell Him Thank You for Gods Words, Commands, give thanks in all circumstances because this is God's will for you in Christ Jesus (1 Thes 5:18).

An attitude of thanksgiving enables us to recognize that God controls all things – not just the blessings, but the problems and adversities as well.

S = Supplication - Includes petition for our own needs and intercession for others. We are to pray for everything and specific terms. As you talk to God, for example, pray that your inner person may be renewed, always sensitive to and empowered by the Holy Spirit. Pray about your problems, pray for wisdom and guidance, pray for strength to resist temptation, pray for comfort in time of sorrow, pray for everything (Phil 4:6). Then pray for others - your spouse, your children, faith, your parents, neighbors, and friends. Pray for your pastors, church, pray for those in authority (1 Timothy 2: 1-2)

ACTS - have helped many people to develop a more well-rounded prayer Life

TYPES OF PRAYER

1. The prayer of agreement: To use the prayer of agreement, you must be sure that the person with whom you are agreeing is in line with what you are asking for. If someone asks me to pray in agreement with them, ask, what specifically do you want me to pray for? You absolutely must make sure you are in perfect agreement about what your prayer request is before you join with another believer in the prayer of agreement.

2. The Prayer of Faith is also known as petition pray - is the prayer, that most people think of when they use the term petition prayer is between you and God and it is asking God for a particular outcome. The key verse from the prayer of faith is Mark 11:24 in which Jesus says, "therefore I say to you, whatever things you ask when you pray, believe that you receive them, and you will have them. The Rule to consider here is when you pray - not after you pray, not when you pray, not when you feel something. When you pray (the moment). The moment that you pray you must believe that you receive what you asked for. When you pray in faith, God immediately gives you what you prayed for - in the Spirit realm, but in the natural world, due to several factors, it may take time for the answer to manifest itself. God answers prayers and He will answer your specific prayer in line with His Word, but it is your faith that brings that answer out of the Spiritual World and the physical world.

3. The prayer of Consecration and Dedication: In Luke 22: 41-42, we see outlined, the prayer of consecration and dedication. And He Jesus withdrew from them. (Peter, James, and John) about a stone throw and He knelt and prayed, saying, "Father if it is your will, take this cup away from me, nevertheless not my will, but yours, be done". He was praying,

in effort if there is any other way to do this, let's do it that way; The key for Jesus and for us, is nevertheless not my will, but yours, be done.

4. The prayer of praise and worship: In this prayer, you are not asking God to do something for you or to give you something, you are not even asking for direction, nevertheless, dedicating your life to whatever it is God has called you to do. Rather, you just want to praise the Lord, to thank Him for His many blessings and mercy, you want to tell Him how much you love Him.

5. The prayer of intercession: Intercession means you are interceding - acting in prayer on behalf of someone else. The person maybe, incapable of praying for themself. Perhaps he/she is confused by doctrines or perhaps the individual is too sick to muster up the strength to pray. Intercession involves praying for others.

6. The prayer of binding and losing: This prayer is found in Matthew 18: 18-19. Jesus says assuredly I say to you, whatever you bind on earth will be bound in Heaven and whatever you lose on earth will be lost in heaven again. I say to you that if two of you agree on earth concerning anything that they ask, it will be done for them by my Father in Heaven. There are several important nuggets in Jesus statements here is the first, being that we have authority here on this earth by virtue of our covenant rights, through Jesus. The second thing we notice is the direction of the action. Things do not begin in Heaven and come to earth rather the action starts here on earth. Notice that it says whatever you bind on earth will be bound in heaven, and whatever you lose on Earth will be lost in heaven. Like all things in God's system, this type of prayer works only in line with God's word and His laws. You can, however, bind foul spirits that are at work, in people's lives or loose angelic spirits to work on your behalf in those areas where God has already promised you results. When you pray in this manner God affirms it in heaven and puts His seal of approval on your prayer. Winning and losing have to be based on the authority God has granted you in scripture, not on some desire you have. God has provided each type of prayer for a specific purpose. Though you may use more than one at any given time, it is

important to be clear about which type you are using and why, and to be aware of its limitations. Knowing what type of prayer to pray and when to pray is very important!

- Toussaint
February 2, 2014 (Time: 8:45am)

———◆———

The shift from a private school setting to a low to middle-class American lifestyle after the passing of the diplomat introduced a significant change in my upbringing. The low to middle-class American lifestyle handed to me in America not only shaped my early experiences but also sparked questions about the circumstances surrounding my journey to a new land. Aunt Betty-Ann embodies the essence of a Southern woman, radiating warmth and hospitality that wraps around you like a comforting embrace. Her vivacious personality exudes a genuine charm, creating an inviting atmosphere wherever she goes. A master of the art of hospitality, Aunt Betty-Ann effortlessly weaves a tapestry of Southern grace, making everyone feel like an honored guest. Beneath the sweet tea and magnolia-scented air, there's a refreshing touch of bluntness in Aunt Betty-Ann's outward expression. She wears honesty like a badge, with a straightforward demeanor that cuts through pretense. Her words, though direct, are infused with a sincere candor that adds authenticity to every interaction.

Amid the Southern charm, Aunt Betty-Ann's straightforwardness serves as a reminder that true hospitality includes a genuine connection, even if it means embracing the unvarnished truth. Aunt Betty-Ann was married to one of the sons of the deceased diplomat, however, she was made aware of the fact that the diplomat's name is the one printed on my birth certificate as my father. I was never clearly aware of the diplomat's exact age and was told by her to "stay in a child's place". Aunt Betty knew figured that the Diplomat could not possibly be my biological father because of her involvement and marriage to his oldest son and the age spans involved were already extraordinary. Aunt Betty

Ann was astonished and blessed that fate had made her a guardian, especially since she did not have any children of her own, nevertheless she loved me like her own.

*"Walking Through the Light Darkness: Discovering God's
Guidance in an Age of Spiritual Counterfeits"*

Why does God lead us down faith-testing paths?

The life led by the Spirit of God is marvellous sensing His presence, living victoriously, and knowing the truth. But what if you couldn't sense His presence, and God suspended His blessings? Job faced such a trial, losing health, wealth, and family. In our dark moments, questions arise:

- ✓ "What did I do to deserve this?"
- ✓ "Did I miss a turn in the road?"
- ✓ "Is this the cost of a righteous life?"
- ✓ "Where is God?"
- ✓ "Why is this happening?"

Like Job, we may feel like cursing our existence. In my family's two dark periods, Isaiah 50:10-11 guided us. It addresses believers walking in uncertainty, urging trust in the Lord during spiritual darkness. The narrative explores how to navigate faith-testing paths, emphasizing the importance of continuous faith, even in the darkest times.

One key lesson is to never stop walking, even when darkness obscures the path. Trusting the previous revelation, even if subtle, is crucial. I share a personal experience of a church-building project where God's guidance was evident. However, after its completion, I faced uncertainties, including financial struggles and doubts about God's leading. In the darkest hour, a profound realization of walking by faith occurred, leading to unexpected opportunities and blessings.

The narrative delves into the consequences of attempting to "light your own fire" during dark times, emphasizing the importance of resisting the urge to create artificial light.

Examples from biblical figures like Abraham and Moses illustrate the pitfalls of deviating from God's guidance.

A second dark period involves my wife's health challenges. Isaiah 21:11-12's theme of enduring through the night echoes the hope that morning follows darkness. Personal struggles, medical bills, and emotional trials became opportunities for spiritual growth and dependence on God.

The narrative explores the purpose of dark times—learning compassion, waiting patiently, and understanding true resources. Brokenness and relying on God's vastness emerge as essential aspects. The account concludes by highlighting the significance of spiritual maturity, postponing rewards, and acknowledging that God makes everything right in the end.

In times of darkness, trusting in the Lord's guidance becomes paramount. The narrative concludes with a prayer for the reader's heart to be filled with expressions of praise, pain, commitment, and understanding of God's truth and will in the New Age.

"P.S. I, my dear, hope to encourage you, strengthen you, and enlighten you with these words by Dr. Neil Anderson. My prayer for you is that you believe in yourself and your electrifying potential along with your magnifying capabilities. Every experience in life is essential to your being to ensure that you grow. Learning to have patience."

CHAPTER

3

The Puzzle of Identity

Aunt Betty-Ann from Valdosta, Georgia, played a significant role in my life, becoming a guiding presence after the passing of the diplomat. As I reminisced about Aunt Betty-Ann from Valdosta, Georgia, it struck me how certain individuals step into our lives like unexpected guiding stars, providing solace and direction when we need it the most. The shift from the name Lokango to Jenny S-H-U-N-G-U reflects the names I was known by, emphasizing the influence of community and societal perceptions in shaping my identity. As I navigated these twists of fate, the specter of stereotypes and labels persisted. The realization that my name had transformed wasn't just a change in letters; it was a metamorphosis of identity sculpted by the hands of community perceptions. The name preference assertions sparked contemplation on the powerful impact of names and the weight of societal expectations, prompting reflection on how these factors shape individuals lives and perceptions. The name Lokango is a pronoun of the phase Luká yango meaning "look for it" in the native language Lingala. The assertion of the name preference Jenny stirred deeper contemplation but also served as a poignant hint to Aunt Betty that my identity at that age had yet to be fully established. In American culture Jenny means "ass" or "God is gracious".

"Take the Power"

"This life is yours
take the power
to choose what you want to do
and do it well
Take the power
to love what you want in life
and love it honestly
Take the power
to walk in the forest and be a part of nature
Take the power
to control your own life
no one else can do it for you
Take the power
to make your life happy" - Susan Polis Schutz

In "The Secret of Happiness by Mother - The Teaching of Mother Rytasha 'The Angel of Bengal." The passage explores the pursuit of true happiness, emphasizing the importance of an internal spiritual connection with God. Mother Rytasha's insights, illustrated through a story, highlight the futility of seeking happiness in external possessions. The secret of happiness is revealed through chanting the Holy Names of God. The summary also introduces The Servants of Charity-Food Relief International, founded by Mother Rytasha, dedicated to humanitarian efforts.

- Toussaint
February 11, 2015

The intersections of being an African-born child, now grappling with the upheavals of familial loss and displacement, made the journey all the more complex. Yet, amid adversity, seeds of resilience were planted, and I began to find strength in the face of uncertainty. At the age of fourteen, I was encountered by a woman I will refer to as Marie, who asserted to be my long-lost biological mother. The revelation stirred a whirlwind of emotions and marked the beginning of a chapter in my life filled with questions, uncertainty, and the profound search for familial truths. Feeling torn, confused, and betrayed by the universe is completely understandable in such a complex and emotionally charged situation. The sense of being potentially manipulated into a family with questionable intentions. The moment Marie claimed to be my long-lost mother, a tidal wave of conflicting emotions crashed over me. It was as if the sands beneath my feet were shifting, and the quest for familial truths unfolded like a suspenseful novel with unpredictable twists. The arrival of Marie, accompanied by two small children that looked very close in age and one of each gender in her hands like teddy bears. The visual portrayal of Marie's story, combined with the presence of young children, tugged at my heartstrings, and contributed to a sense of connection to her tale.

Despite its initial incredibility. The subsequent arrival of Marie's (partner) Mr. Mudi came very soon after. I could recall one summer day sitting on the porch watching Marie in the distance having a phone conversation in tears yelling in panic for Mr. Mudi to join her along with two additional siblings; this time two boys older than the first set of children yet younger than I to further deepen the complexities. Discovering this revelation intertwined our fates in a complex maze of shared heritage and familial ties, leaving me to grapple with the profound implications of this newfound, forced connection, a distraction to discovering my true identity. Throughout my upbringing, the new family structure never made the opportunity to visit my birthplace, and family members seemed disinterested in making the effort to establish traditions like family reunions or galas with different members. This absence of connection to my place of origin became a poignant thread, emphasizing the emotional and physical distance that existed between my present life and the roots of my existence. Despite my desire to visit, the lack of resources, and references, and the unstable state of Congo left me feeling disconnected, as if the ties to my birthplace had been strained and distant. The challenging circumstances surrounding the country further added to the complexities of reconnecting with my roots. The absence of any tangible link to my birthplace is a hindrance to understanding the roots of my existence. The harsh reality of an unstable homeland creates a poignant thread of disconnection. When I would ask questions about my biological father, Marie would refer to him as "LaBear". She shared stories of him being drunk and physically assaulting her on their wedding night because she refused to take a sip of beer.

Later, it was discovered that she had fabricated this name, creating a fictitious identity to mislead me. The term "LaBear" (the bear) was Marie's way of referring to the children in her arms at the time of arrival. Marie symbolically and metaphorically used the act of introducing her children to me and my reaction as a child welcoming an infant and toddler "straight off the boat" with a warm greeting upon arrival in the United States as a chance to come up a name to represent that moment, so she chose "LaBear". She used this term to disassociate her act of carrying them, likening it to a couple of stuffed teddy bears, subtly luring me into an embrace. As Marie interjected life's process with the confusion of this makeshift family, I found myself entangled in a complex web of relationships. The sight of her children, akin to teddy bears, added a surreal touch to the unfolding drama, making me question the authenticity of the newfound connections. The intricate branches of my family tree unfold a generational dilemma. The revelation that "LaBear" is a fabricated persona struck me with a mix of confusion and betrayal. It made me question the motives behind such elaborate deception and wonder how many more layers of the family tree were yet to be unraveled.

Marie claimed to be the daughter of the deceased diplomat. Her presence and news of this revelation quickly created complexity and raised questions about her motives, as well as the authenticity of her familial connections. The intricate web of relationships and identities continued to unfold, creating a tapestry of uncertainty in my quest for self-discovery. Aunt Betty-Ann, ever astute, immediately cast a discerning eye on the unfolding narrative. Suspicion clouded the air as she questioned the authenticity of Marie's claims to be my biological mother. The mother named on my birth certificate claims to have given birth to me at the advanced maternal age of 48. Aunt Betty-Ann's keen intuition became a guiding compass in navigating the murky waters of a story that seemed to be woven with threads of uncertainty and potential deception.

Notably, at the time of her arrival, Marie had not adopted her husband's last name, suggesting potential nuances and complexities in her relationship dynamics and the reasons behind her choices, leaving me to grapple with the shifting identities and the veracity of the connections presented by and through her. Marie's claims of seeking asylum from the war in Congo were clouded by conflicting details, including her assertion of being the child of the deceased diplomat, a figure who had never previously acknowledged or mentioned her. Additionally, the appearance of a family structure fueled skepticism, added complexity of the history, and cast doubt on the credibility of her reason of involvement. The tangled web of Marie's asylum claim deepened as investigators uncovered discrepancies in her timeline of war or civil unrest, raising questions about the authenticity of her connection to the alleged deceased diplomat.

One afternoon while I was in Middle School in, during one of our hair styling sessions, Aunt Betty-Ann had left ten dollars on the dresser. As I got my hair straightened, I could hear curious faces peering into her bedroom, admiring the length of my hair. My enjoyment for styling and braiding hair stemmed from Aunt Betty-Ann. After she finished straightening my hair, the natural length reached the middle of my back. I expressed my gratitude with a hug, but when she asked for the ten dollars from the top of her chest, it was nowhere to be found. I quickly informed Aunt Betty-Ann that the money was missing. In shock, she began searching around her room. As her frustration mounted over the missing bill, Aunt Betty- Ann started questioning everyone in the house if they had taken money from her chest.

Marie promptly defended her boys, claiming they weren't in her bedroom while she was styling my hair. Redirecting the blame, Marie insisted Aunt Betty-Ann ask me to find the money. Despite my persistent search, the ten-dollar bill remained elusive. Marie, seizing the opportunity, instructed me to sit on the bed while she grabbed scissors, unleashing a horrifying act of cutting my freshly straightened hair in a fit of rage and jealousy. Aunt Betty-Ann was devastated, realizing Marie's motive wasn't just to serve as a supportive connection but to foster an unhealthy dependence to her and those in connection to the conspiracy. Aunt Betty's heartache echoed through tear-streaked eyes and trembling hands as she began to realize I was forcibly stripped of the confident, delightful, charming, happy kiddish personality she had nurtured prior to Marie's arrival.

Grief and anguish painted her expression, creating a haunting portrait of a mother's profound sorrow and helplessness. After the traumatic buzzcut, Aunt Betty-Ann's husband, John, discovered the ten-dollar bill had slipped behind the chest. I was forced to attend school with a buzz-cut hairstyle, wearing a hoody and in tears. For three days, I hid in the girl's bathroom stall until another student noticed my absence from shared classes. A janitor discovered me in the girl's bathroom after a student reported hearing crying from one of the stalls. A call was made for corrective action before my return to school. My path is one of not just cultural negotiation but survival and a testament to the strength cultivated through hardships and the unwavering spirit that emerged from the ashes of loss. My desire to remain with the woman who had already shown me love over the years clashed with the forced acceptance of yet another person claiming to be my mother. The aftermath of Marie's jealousy-fueled act left me grappling with the cruel reality that family ties could be severed with a pair of scissors. The pain and humiliation etched a lasting scar, a stark reminder of the fragility of trust. Amid Marie's assertions of a united family, the stark image of her wielding scissors against my hair painted a stark contrast, a bitter irony that stained the canvas of our supposed connection. In the puzzle of my identity, the pieces laid out by Marie seemed to be made of smoke, each claim dissipating into the air, leaving behind the bitter taste of irony. In claiming the diplomat as her deceased father, Marie asserted authority by pushing Aunt Betty Ann out of my life by garnering support from her brothers and sisters in this assertion of power over my life. The sudden shift in dynamics, coupled with the involvement of these newfound family members, created a tense atmosphere, and raised further questions about the true motives behind Marie's claims and actions. Family connections became ensnared in a network of uncertainty and conflict.

CHAPTER

4

Winter's Weight

I went through the throes phase of adolescence, a rebellious phase unfurled like a tempest in my life. Defying boundaries and testing limits became a daily ritual. The rhythm of conformity was replaced by the discordant notes of defiance, as I sought independence and self-discovery. Each act of rebellion carried a whispered declaration of autonomy, a fervent desire to carve out my identity amidst the chaos of teenage defiance. Despite the intricate family dynamics and unfolding mysteries, I found solace in focusing on my appearance and delving into the realm of dating at an early age. Embracing a newfound sense of independence, I embarked on a journey to skillfully navigating the intricate complexities of personal identity against the enigmatic backdrop of a family that had intricately woven itself into the fabric of my existence.

Despite the intricate challenges posed by my family situation, I showcased resilience by maintaining my grades at a passing level. The delicate balance of navigating through complex personal dynamics while achieving academic success stands as a testament to my strength and determination. However, the inconsistent support from family members became a hindrance, impeding my ability to wholeheartedly pursue an open talent. The absence of consistent familial support proved to be a formidable obstacle, limiting my capacity to fully explore and develop my innate abilities. The transition from being a solitary child in a quiet home to suddenly having four younger siblings and cousins running around marked a profound shift in our family dynamic. This change, while bringing moments of joy, also posed significant challenges, forever reshaping the landscape of my life. Amidst the liveliness, a subtle sense of loss emerged, the peace and solitude I once cherished seemed to slip away. Adjusting to the newfound presence of energetic younger siblings and cousins brought a blend of challenges and shared joys, reshaping the daily rhythm of my life.

The expanded family circle also ushered in a shift in responsibilities, introducing more chores, a necessity to share possessions, and a noticeable decrease in the individual allocation of resources. This adaptation to a more communal living arrangement brought forth the realities of shared obligations and the challenge of adjusting to the new dynamics within the family unit. During these changes, the school became my refuge from home. The educational environment provided a sanctuary, a space where I could momentarily distance myself from the complexities of my home life. In the routine and structure that school offered, I found solace and a sense of normalcy, creating a valuable escape from the challenges within the familial setting. Being part of Blair High School was a distinctive experience, as I belonged to the inaugural freshman class of '04 that entered the newly established building when its doors opened. Navigating the freshly painted hallways of Blair High marked a unique chapter in my educational journey. Embracing a carefree attitude toward fashion, race, sexuality, and culture, you effortlessly stood out as one of the regular girls at school. Your approach, shaped by your American upbringing, drew admiration from many African girls. However, within the intricate web of family dynamics, conflicting feelings arose about your true purpose in life, sparking questions about your connection to African identity and how you would contribute to the rich tapestry of African culture.

Despite your bubbly tone, lack of a strong accent, and preference for sleek jeans and crop tops over traditional African garments, I navigated the intricate balance between cultural expectations and personal expression.

The complexities of bridging these worlds became a nuanced journey, where the threads of heritage and individuality interwove in a dance of identity. My academic journey took an unexpected turn when I encountered Bascone outside the school building, initially unaware of his dropout status. This meeting proved to be a pivotal moment, setting in motion events that would significantly shape my life. Bascone, engaging with senior students posted at the entrance of the high school building, noticed me as I stepped off the school bus and signaled for me to approach. He handed me my first plug-in-the-wall house phone, assuring me it would serve as a means to reach me if needed. The phone he handed me, with its whimsical appearance more akin to a toy than a serious communication tool, became an unexpected conduit to a connection that would soon impact my life in unforeseen ways. Little did I know this seemingly innocuous encounter would unfold into a connection playing a crucial role in shaping the course of my experiences.

In the year 2000, the advanced technology of cell phones was still novel, particularly for high school freshman, amidst the evolving landscape of technology during that time. The concept of these handheld devices was just beginning to weave its way into the fabric of daily life, marking the early stages of a transformative era in communication and connectivity. Under the sway of his influence, is what began as the occasional act of skipping school transformed into a habitual ritual. His persuasive demeanor guided me down a path of truancy, turning it from sporadic to a routine that ultimately reshaped the trajectory of my high school experience.

In the initial stages, Bascone's gestures were seemingly caring. He cooked breakfast for me each morning I spent away from school, and we indulged in listening to slow jams. He presented me with specific gifts, such as a diamond ring and a designer belt with gold-plated letters spelling out M-O-S-C-H-I-N-O. However, the seemingly generous tokens later took a dark turn as he repurposed the belt to inflict harm, transforming what initially appeared as kindness into a painful reality. Over weeks, Bascone's demands escalated, pressuring me to stay with him. Despite his insistence, I held my ground, asserting that while I could see him the next day, I had to return home at some moment. This push-and-pull dynamic introduced a growing tension to our interactions, creating a palpable strain within our relationship. Ignoring Bascone's threats to attend school prompted him to take matters into his own hands. He began showing up at my house after school, seizing moments when there was no adult supervision. This intrusion created a sense of vulnerability, further encroaching on the complexities of my daily life. At that time, we resided in a two-level duplex nestled in the middle of a block-long, one-way street where homes were closely built. Parallel parking was the norm unless a resident could afford a discreetly built parking space on their small plot. In front of our house stood a thick tree that provided Bascone with a hiding spot. Anticipating my arrival from the bus stop, he would utilize a jump scare tactic, taking advantage of my slow approach to the front door. Growing increasingly paranoid about this stalkerish behavior, my concern extended to the safety of other occupants in the house. Observant neighbors on the attached duplex occasionally witnessed him lurking, intensifying the unsettling atmosphere. In the two-level duplex on a one-way street with closely built homes, the proximity meant cars parallel parked unless residents secured a discreet parking space. A thick trunked tree in front of our house became Bascone's hiding spot, enabling him to employ jump-scare tactics as I approached my front door from the bus stop. This stalkerish behavior raised concerns not just for my safety but also for others sharing the house with me. Watchful neighbors on the attached duplex occasionally observed his actions, heightening the unsettling atmosphere. Bascone's control extended to forcing me into my bedroom, locking the door, turning up the TV and subjecting me to non-consensual acts. Disturbingly, he realized I was pregnant before I did. Despite experiencing physical signs, fear of the unknown and uncertainty about my circumstances led me to keep the pregnancy out of sight and out of mind.

Facing the challenge of an advancing pregnancy added layers of complexity and emotional strain to the situation. With Marie assuming an authoritarian role, the weight of winter circumstances led to a difficult decision. Convinced by Marie, I underwent a procedure to separate me from my growing unborn fetus. During the initial diagnostic visit, a medical sonographer warned me that I had reached a stage where hesitation to perform a high-risk abortion procedure could lead to complexities and potential risks. I was taken to different clinics until one agreed to conduct a two-step procedure, requiring a return the next day for the fetus extraction. During winter break, Marie accompanied me to the scheduled appointment. As a minor, did not fill out any paperwork, underscoring the complexities and the extent of reliance on guardianship during this challenging time. After payment, I was directed to a back room and placed on an examining table with my legs in stirrups. The doctor inserted dried seaweed (Laminaria) into my cervix for dilation, instructing Marie to return with me for the second part of the procedure the following day, the expulsion of the fetus. The emotional burden of fear, shame, and regret, compounded by the physical and mental toll of the procedure, rendered this one of the most challenging and complex decisions.

Experiencing the expulsion of my first pregnancy on the basement floor, outside the clinic setting was mentally distressing and emotionally overwhelming. Unfortunately, I didn't make it back to the clinic the next day as advised, as the pain from the dilation initiated by the insertion of Laminaria was unbearable. I expelled a very tiny baby boy, the size of the palm of my hand, and he was still breathing. The fetus had male genitals, emitted a silent cry, as if his voice was on mute, a haunting detail I later understood in my nursing career, attributing to the underdeveloped lungs lacking sufficient surfactant. Marie was in profound shock as she observed the baby's resilience. She took my baby from my arms while he was still connected to the placenta and carried him upstairs. I lay on the carpet until fatigue lulled me to sleep. Upon waking the next day, I never saw my baby again. I don't know what Marie did with him, but one thing is certain, she never brought him back to me, and I never laid eyes on my baby boy again and I was denied the opportunity to grieve properly. I couldn't shake the unsettling thought that Marie might have used the underdeveloped fetus for a sinister purpose, perhaps a satanic spell.

"It's easy to be encouraged with words, yet difficult to act in the courage of the world foretold."

"Do not follow where the path may lead. Go, instead, where there is no path, and leave a trail."

"Choose blessing instead of cursing and life instead of death" (Deuteronomy 11:26)

"I was told by the voice of an angel you were worth it all. I got my mind on you like I can see it all. You know what, you don't deserve the pain, but I don't deserve to fall."

-Toussaint
May 18, 2015 (22:00)

Returning to school while grappling with the physical aftermath of my experiences was an intricate dance with adversity. The day of my return was cloaked in an unsettling ambiance, whispers echoing through the hallways like an ominous symphony. Each step felt burdened by the weight of speculation, a silent force that seemed to envelop me at every turn. Navigating through the maze of rumors became a formidable challenge, leaving me yearning for refuge. In the sanctuary of the house party on skip day, my senses were assailed by a medley of sights, sounds, and emotions. As I entered, the rhythmic thud of the bass penetrated my being, setting the pulse for the evening. The dim glow of fairy lights draped across the walls cast a soft, ephemeral ambiance, weaving an illusion of escape. I found refuge on a plush couch, sinking into its embrace as conversations hummed around me like a distant tide. The air was tinged with the heady aroma of perfume, mingling with the faint scent of spilled drinks, creating a unique olfactory symphony. Red plastic cups passed from hand to hand, leaving trails of laughter and camaraderie in their wake.

Amid the lively chatter, I observed the ebb and flow of the partygoers, their silhouettes dancing in the ambient glow. Faces blurred into a tapestry of anonymity, a comforting anonymity that momentarily shielded me from the harsh realities awaiting beyond the party's walls. Emotionally, the respite was a delicate balance between escapism and a nagging awareness of the impending challenges. The music served as a temporal cocoon, muffling the harsh whispers that had haunted me in the school corridors. Yet, even in this fleeting escape, the weight of my circumstances lingered beneath the surface, a subtle undercurrent during the revelry. As I reclined on the couch, exhaustion mingled with the rhythmic beats, my eyelids growing heavy. The party became a dreamscape, a surreal backdrop to my internal struggles. Moments of vulnerability collided with the pulsating energy, creating a poignant dichotomy.

In the midst of this sensory symphony, I found solace in the nuanced observations of those around me. Each glance, every shared smile, became a fragment of a mosaic, a fleeting connection to a world I sought refuge. The party became not just a physical space but a transient refuge, a momentary reprieve from the storm that awaited my return to reality. Seeking solace in a moment of respite, I succumbed to the soothing waves of drowsiness, the party's cacophony fading into a distant hum. In the quiet cocoon of semi-consciousness, the persistent ache in my breasts became an unwelcome companion. Seeking relief, I reached for medication in my purse, hoping to subdue the physical discomfort that had become a relentless presence. As the medication took hold, I drifted into a hazy state, where the boundary between wakefulness and dreams blurred. In this vulnerable moment, my shirt bore the weight of an intimate struggle, saturated with the evidence of my physical challenges.

The subtle, yet undeniable, yellow hue seeped through the protective layer of nipple padding, a silent testament to the private battle I waged in solitude. The room, bathed in a muted glow, remained oblivious to the silent narrative unfolding. Every drop that escaped carried a weight of vulnerability, a nuanced dance between the body's demands and the desire for respite. The discomfort, palpable yet unspoken, was a muted symphony of endurance. Unbeknownst to me, the handheld camcorder became an inadvertent spectator, capturing the essence of a personal struggle. The lens, though detached, etched a memory that transcended the physical realm, a memory not of explicit details but of a quiet, solitary resilience amid the shadows. Faced with the aftermath of the video's emergence, a surge of adrenaline tangled with fear gripped me. Denial became a reflex, a shield against the potential fallout.

When questioned about the girl in the recording, I instinctively distanced myself, in a desperate attempt to obscure my identity and protect those unwittingly entangled, especially the members of the sports team. In the hushed exchanges that followed, my internal monologue echoed with conflicting considerations. The weight of potential repercussions loomed large, the threat of disciplinary actions, public scrutiny, and the haunting specter of relentless ridicule. Each denial became a step deeper into a complex web of decisions, a labyrinthine dance between self-preservation and the looming risk of exposure. The delicate balance of maintaining the facade intensified as I navigated the intricate social dynamics. The denial, a carefully constructed veneer, shielded not just my identity but also shielded others from the harsh glare of consequences. The internal struggle, concealed beneath a composed exterior, became a silent battle of morality versus self-preservation.

As the aftermath unfolded, a sense of isolation settled in. The burden of secrets weighed heavily on my shoulders, casting shadows on relationships and trust. The camaraderie with members of the football team became strained, their unknowing involvement in the video morphing into a silent strain on our interactions. With each passing day, the internal conflict deepened, the decisions made reverberating through my conscience. The price of denial, a heavy toll on authenticity and genuine connections, added layers to the complexities of my character. In the silence that followed the denial, a palpable tension lingered, contributing to the seasoned feel as the protagonist grappled with the consequences of their choices. In the lingering aftermath of denial and the weight of secrets, I found myself standing on the precipice of uncertainty. The echo of hushed conversations and sidelong glances followed me like a shadow, a constant reminder of the decisions made, and the intricate web of consequences woven. As I gazed into the uncertain horizon, a sense of isolation settled in, punctuated by the distant whispers of speculation. The camaraderie once shared with the football team now hung in a delicate balance, tethered by threads frayed by the unspoken. The stillness around me mirrored the stillness within, a moment pregnant with the anticipation of what lay beyond. In the solitude, I found a quiet strength, a resilience forged through silent battles and concealed vulnerabilities. The uncharted territory of the future beckoned, and as I took a tentative step forward, the shadows of secrets danced at the periphery, a constant reminder that the journey was far from over. And so, with the quiet determination of one who had weathered storms in silence, I embraced the uncertainty of the next chapter, where the pen awaited, poised to script the continuation of a story veiled in whispers and untold truths.

CHAPTER

5

Shadows of a Duplex

The duplex, a forbidding structure, stood as a constant sentinel, a stark reminder of challenges and discomfort. Nestled in the heart of a block-long, one-way street, it endured the close embrace of neighboring homes. Parking, a perpetual struggle, saw cars parallel parked one after another, except for those lucky enough to secure a discreetly built parking space. A dense tree veiled the front facade, providing concealment for unwanted observers. Within the confined quarters, a persistent feeling of being watched permeated the air, intensifying the overall unpleasant atmosphere that clung to the duplex like a lingering shadow. Junior year of high school brought a silver lining as I encountered David, a remarkable young man who would become my charismatic prom date. Despite attending a different school, he seamlessly became a cherished part of my life. David, an enchanting blend of Indian and Israeli heritage, exuded a captivating charm. His magnetic presence was complemented by a warm, genuine smile, a reflection of his confident and approachable demeanor. Cultural richness emanated from him, a fusion of the vibrancy of his Indian roots and the unique allure of Israeli influences, his looks very much resembled the Prince of the Middle East, only with long hair a couple inches past his shoulders.

Beyond his physical allure, including his long, dark, shoulder-length hair, I found myself drawn to his intelligence, showcased through his knack for fixing cars at a young age, his kindness, and his infectious sense of humor. Amidst the joyous holiday festivities in the fall of 2005, an unforeseen and tense moment unfurled at the Thanksgiving table in my residence. A cousin and David, my prom date, found themselves ensnared in a physical altercation. The clash erupted just as the opening prayer concluded, intensifying as both grappled and threw punches beneath the dining room table. Charged with emotions of rage, heartbreak, frustration, and embarrassment in the aftermath of the controversial fight, David pulled me aside. He candidly explained that the complexity of my family dynamics presented a challenge for him to continue our relationship. David's original intention of proposing marriage at the Thanksgiving table was thwarted by the unfortunate turn of events, as engaging in a fight under those circumstances was deemed the highest form of disrespect.

Despite my sincere apologies, tears, and heartfelt pleas for forgiveness, David's decision remained unyielding. The aftermath of our breakup became a poignant motivator, propelling me to seriously consider applying to college as a means of distancing myself from the tumultuous situation surrounding my personal life. In June '04, I proudly graduated from Blair High. Following this pivotal milestone, I embarked on my college journey, enrolling in a local private institution in the fall of 2006. After completing two enriching years at this smaller college, I earned acceptance into the Towson University Nursing Program, marking the next significant chapter in my pursuit of undergraduate studies. David and I immortalized the enchantment of our prom night through professional photographs, capturing both shared moments and individual poses. Yet, curiously, our 'couple' photograph mysteriously vanished, leaving us without a tangible memento of that special occasion.

FIVE CARDINAL RULES FOR LIFE:

1. Achieve harmony with your history to preserve tranquillity in your current moments.

2. Others' opinions about you are not within your jurisdiction.

3. Time has the power to mend almost everything. Allow it the time it needs.

4. Your happiness is under your control; no one else governs it.

5. Refrain from measuring your life against others and abstain from passing judgment; you will lack insight into their unique journey.

- Toussaint
August 13, 2014

Leaving the duplex behind to embark on my college journey was a liberating experience, marked by the palpable sense of joy and anticipation that filled the air. As the cramped and unwelcoming atmosphere of the duplex faded away, I couldn't help but be swept up in the excitement of new beginnings. Packed with optimism, I eagerly ventured towards the prospect of higher education, bidding farewell to the constraints of that challenging environment and embracing the boundless opportunities that awaited me in my off-campus housing near Towson, Maryland College life as a nursing student unfolded as a demanding yet profoundly rewarding journey. Each day was a blend of theoretical classes, practical training, and immersive clinical rotations. The pursuit of nursing knowledge became a vivid experience, marked not only by late-night study sessions and skill labs but also by the intricate details of patient care. The bustling energy of a diverse student community and the camaraderie among future healthcare professionals fostered a supportive environment. Despite the challenges, the determination to excel in this rigorous academic and practical undertaking was fueled by a profound sense of purpose and the anticipation of contributing to healthcare.

Amid the academic rigor, the friendships forged in the crucible of nursing coursework became an integral part of my college narrative. Bonded by a shared passion for healthcare, our connections were strengthened through late-night study sessions and the unique experiences of clinical rotations. We leaned on each other for support, shared notes, and navigated the complexities of patient care together. This camaraderie extended beyond the classroom, creating a tight-knit community where we celebrated successes, comforted each other during setbacks, and formed lasting connections. These friendships not only enriched the educational experience but also provided a network of support that transcended the challenges of nursing school. As the academic journey unfolded, the surrounding city of Towson, with its suburban escape, and Baltimore, with its urban energy, provided a dynamic backdrop. Towson offered a tranquil haven, while Baltimore added a different dimension to the overall experience. The proximity allowed exploration of Baltimore's cultural offerings, from museums and theaters to the eclectic neighborhoods that defined the city's personality.

The accessibility to both suburban tranquility and urban vibrancy contributed to a well-rounded experience for those navigating student life in Towson. Baltimore Street, renowned for its lively atmosphere, hosted a variety of clubs catering to diverse tastes. From pulsating music venues with dance floors to cozy lounges, these clubs offered an array of nightlife experiences. Each establishment on Baltimore Street contributed to the city's vibrant social scene, providing a mix of entertainment, music genres, and unique atmospheres for night owls and music enthusiasts alike. Baltimore's iconic stadiums, such as Oriole Park at Camden Yards and M&T Bank Stadium, further enriched the city's culture, showcasing sporting excellence and contributing to the rich history and spirit of Baltimore's sports community.

As a Junior in college living in Towson without a car, my source of entertainment centered around the local scene. I explored the vibrant offerings of Towson and nearby areas, relying on local events, cultural experiences, and neighborhood gems for my recreational enjoyment. Living with female roommates brought a dynamic blend of camaraderie and shared experiences. Our living space became a canvas for collaboration and mutual support, fostering a sense of unity as we navigated the challenges and joys of life together.

CHAPTER

6

Love in Cyberspace

In the ever-evolving landscape of social media, my journey into online connections began with MySpace, a pioneering platform that left an indelible mark on technology, pop culture, and music. Little did I know that within this digital realm, a profound connection awaited. My future husband J.E.T. and I unfolded our story through the pixels and messages of this virtual space. Our narrative transcended the boundaries of cyberspace, manifesting in a real-life encounter that remains etched in my memory, right at the terminals of South Florida Airport. The surroundings buzzed with the energy of reunions, and as our eyes met for the first time in person, nervous smiles were exchanged, setting the stage for a journey that extended beyond the virtual. Our long-distance relationship was a tapestry woven with lengthy phone calls and frequent visits; each moment marked by the anticipation of being physically present with one another. The decision to relocate to Florida after graduation was not merely a change in geography but a step towards solidifying our connection. I could almost feel the warmth of the Sunshine State enveloping us, uplifting my energy, and radiating our lives with newfound possibilities. Becoming Mrs. Toussaint marked the beginning of a new chapter, I was pregnant by my last semester in nursing school. I took public transportation and even walked from class to class on the huge college campus and to and from clinical rotations. We sealed our commitment in the courthouse on the fall day of August

24th, 2009, and earlier that month, we immortalized our love through beautiful wedding pictures taken on the beach and at a serene pond, capturing the essence of our journey with the camera of Life.

———◆———

Happy Anniversary (Married: August 23, 2009)

"My beloved wife it is you who has by the counsel of Heaven, been ordained to me as a special gift. Please! Pardon my hubris, I love, care, and long for you Ms. I desire to fall in love with you again! Many times, over were only getting older. Let agape restore us to the right relationship with God and with each other. Close to me you're like my brother, close to me you're like my sister, close to me you're like my father, close to me you're like my mother... You are the only one my everything and for you I give everything. I pray for you all my life and I thank God, I found you. Let's start all over and change back the hands of time, let us mature in our relationship and leave the negative behind forgive me if I've let you down, pushed you around, for putting you down. You're my queen, and you deserve my crown. I hope this makes you smile and secure your heart. Soothe your emotions, you'll be seeing me in a little while. I love you just the way you are. My clarity reaches serenity, forever we'll be, I protect you still from a distance, this short of a time is only required for much will be given. It is a testing of our hearts and our faith. I wait for the day when I can brace your face once again and plant on you a kiss like a groom at the altar parting the lips of his bride".

- Toussaint
August 23, 2014

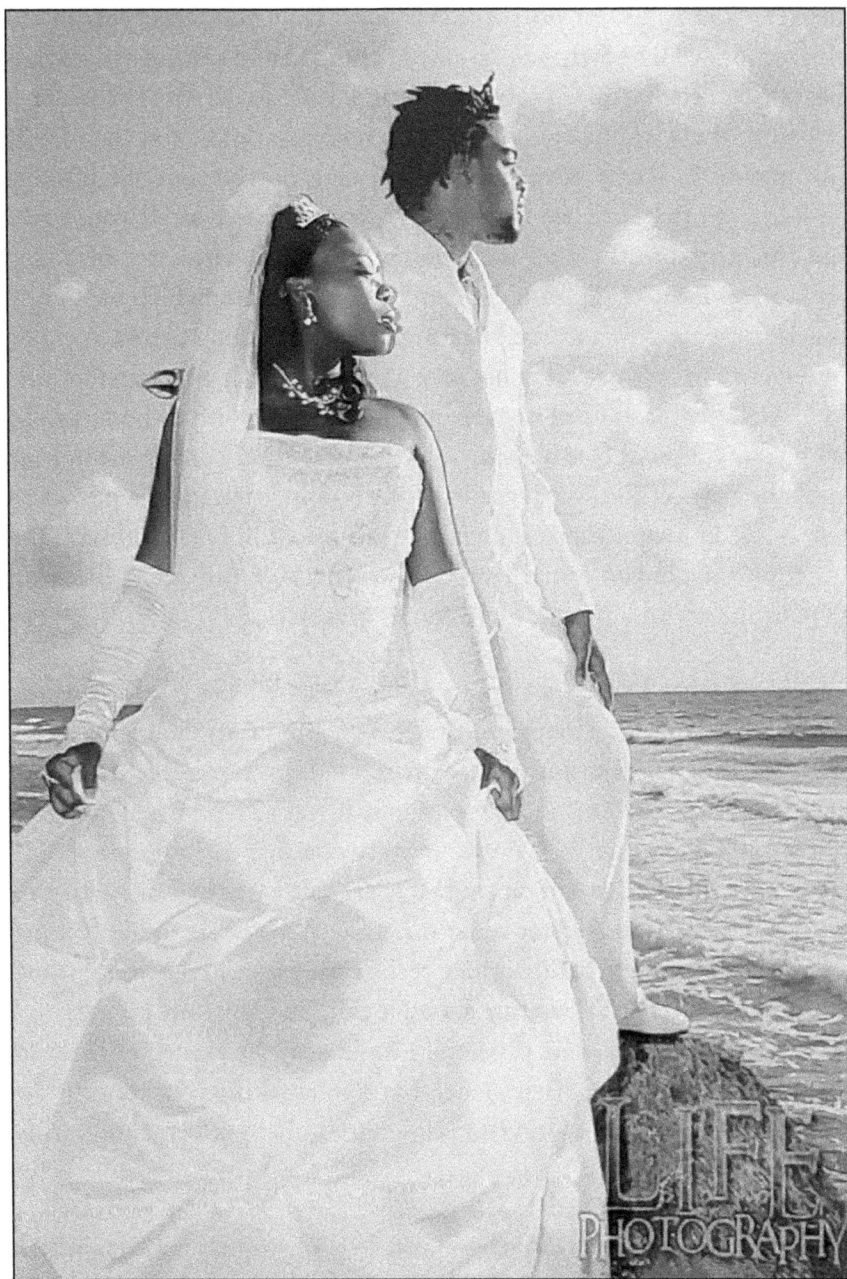

"My Queen, let me begin with three words I LOVE YOU then I move on to saying HAPPY ANNIVERSARY although there is a distance between you and I, my heart is never apart from you. Next year round this season we'll be fortunate to enjoy the mood and setting of a foreign Island, something like InterContinental Le Moana Bora Bora or a cruise to the Caribbean - Yes sounds relaxing right! You deserve it, we deserve it. Right now, I am reminiscing on the time we initially converse, to the time we first came to contact, first of all your voice has this airy, breathy, and melodic tone that resonates. So, from the jump I was intoxicated from that lengthy conversation which seemingly lasted from Sundown to Sun-up (laugh out loud). Oh, I can't forget our indulgence in cyber sex. I'm not sure about you but it was a first for me. I enjoyed every minute of it, entering into the room only to be surprised with your gorgeous face blessing me with those eyes casting me in your spell the best yet to come revealing your bosom, even more amazing as you fiddled on your nipples, cupping your breast in one hand with the other on the phone. While I sat on the other side fully erect listening to your moans and groans. Here comes greatness..."

"You'd do what I say "I want you to play with it" just by those words seem to have instantly increased the flow of your juices. Suddenly down went the camera, exposing your woman hood. I was eager to meet you, eager to please you like no man ever has. It was around May 2007. I'm not sure of the exact date however you were due to fly in seemingly cool about it. I greatly anticipated your arrival. I was infused with this yearning that has longed for you it was around five or six in the evening when you landed, my buddy prince at the time escorted me over. I stood outside of the terminal waiting for your call. Suddenly my phone rings with a low tone, I ask were you here. I could hear the excitement in your voice "Yes" you replied. That's when I saw you making your way out the elevator like Beyonce making a grand entry to her performance during the Superbowl XLVII."

"Your body is amazing! I believe you had on some leggings, which wrapped around those hips, thighs, and ass like latex. I watched you move slowly through the corridor a little confused of which way to go, your breast bounced at every turn, it was as if bells rung when we finally have come close, we hugged tightly not wanting to let go. It was beautiful. I felt the magnitude of the wind in you and my burning sensation of meeting with each other in the air. I could not wait to get home and enjoy your every bit of worth and that I did along with the mix of booze and weed for the "first timer"…"

"Anyhow, we have had our ups and our downs. In the worst cases maybe more downs then up, however every dispute, altercation, disagreements, disorderly conduct, and physical altercation, all has its significance, it brings us forward into our future and on how to be better at it, and how to be a better parent for a most wonderful child. Also how to be a better lover (husband/ wife). We've been through phases that have processed us to growth. It has been, I would say, the last six years of my life trying to live with and understand someone totally opposite of me. Coming from two diverse backgrounds but some origin has made it a secret hard to crack. Often we questioned our belonging, our faith, and our purpose to destiny, we've doubted the high power and its force of bringing us together we've left many doors open both us individually to allow demons into our temple, sanctuary and our house allowing our vessels to be filled with pollution, forget the reason we started to hate our situation, we begged to get out, which only leads us to death. We lost the consistency of prayer, love, family, value, and ethics we opposed one another in our heart, distrusting ourselves and our own capability of being righteous towards one another."

"We have allowed ourselves to be led by the blind in means of money and the vain life around it, only by desire where we taken off course. Instead of being masters above - had we fall slaves below it. I blame myself for I've allowed the emotions to rule me and when I fought against it, fired back an evil mind and my heart elevated into the cool to be honest. I feel and have felt what you've expressed either I felt that way personally or it's been planted in my mind."

"I want us to work, I want us to grow and appreciate the many gifts that heaven has to offer us. For this to occur we have to stay focused on the golden opportunity. Which is to establish our family's Legacy in history with a continuing line of fortune, the drugs pass, the club passes, the sex becomes important. What matters and what sticks, is the struggles, turmoils, and sorrows we rise above the good name we make for ourselves and our name, the business we start, the people we help, the places we've travelled, carving a trail, those marks are more superior than our being. I know and believe that your works are great, your beauty will soon come to the light of the world, your gifts and natural talents will begin to reveal themselves to you. You don't need no one to believe if you first believe in yourself. Have more care and care will do its part, all the negative needs to be eliminated from the subconscious mind, we will turn things around. You will get your career started at the same time developing the plan for nursing assistant living-will be in the works. I partnered with an individual to begin our services in a whole new fashion which will soon have its benefits. You'll take pole dancing lessons, choreography, singing lessons, and your image will be astoundingly transformed Faith of course will take her course and we will do these things in secret becoming untouched by the public and even amongst attend class of celebrities this will make us infamous. Let's stay strong and continue with the faith. Love and hope our life will soon change. Once we change our minds and be a firm believer in our own fashion and design... TO MY WOMEN FOR LIFE"

- Toussaint
February 14, 2013

<hr />

"*Flesh of My Flesh Bone of My Bones*"

"Dear Jenny,

First and foremost, I give thanks to our heavenly father, who has mercy, given us grace, and forgives us of our sins by our fellow brother lord and saviour "The Christ". It is so that we shall die and live again, that is of the redemption! Amen. We have been given the free choice of worshiping God, in doing so we inherit the "Kingdom of Heaven", and to walk the earth in power; with spiritual gifts, given to us to keep the ways for the ancient patriarchs, Matriarchs and the "lamb" of the ultimate sacrifice. We are to let die the "evil impulses" that reigns over us time after time, we ought to conduct ourselves identity, ethnicity, and ritually in the "Laws of Faith" from which is added to us in abundance, divine attributes. The need of improvement is severe in order to compel to orderly desires and then transform to a God being. I'm at awe with the idea that our created source allows us to rule the world; lawfully, bring in life, transform lives, and recreate time. We are not far from the beginning nor are we far from the end, there must be a foundation set to our existence. Where do we begin?"

"Finally, secondly thank you! for the warming photo of my lovely daughter, your reassuring letter, and the enticing letter that followed along. Naughty girls aren't ya! Just as I'm picking back up on my writing to you, it so happens an envelope is being slid under my door. Time is 15:20 on August 15, 2014. They are poems inside. Aw thank you for this as well they mean so much! I wish I could give you a bear hug and a big fat wet kiss. Anyhow, I have had Immeasurable thoughts running rampant on my mind and in my heart, enough to process ten International Business Machines Corporation Buildings. I do understand the difficulty to express yourself behind the struggle of this situation under these tough circumstances."

"Not only is it depressing; but it is also suppressing. I too even prior to my confinement, have found it difficult to express my strongest emotions without genuine anger and frustration. The burden has been carried over so long that it's like trying to pay off a twelve trillion-dollar deficit, or unearthing a war that occurred a couple millenniums ago. Will only find ourselves in more debt and continuing in war. At this very moment I recognize the problem, I understand the battle, I know the struggle. I can see why we are troubled, behold it is WAR!"

"What therefore God has joined together,
let no man put asunder.
—MARK 10:9

So they are no longer two, but one flesh.
—MATTHEW 19:6

"The evil in me versus God, like a rebelling son casting vengeance against his father, disobeying my assignment told to me, tough to me, dishonouring his unconditional love all for my own selfish reasons. I have been in and out of love with you through the ups and downs, has brought me unto the lowest point of brokenness, I've until this point because a scoffer to wonder even, acquiring nothing but death. Death is gain, to kill off the old person which inflicted me with so much pain can only be redeeming. I'm after my tikkun (spiritual healing) these days. In many ways, I've failed God, my father, my mother, you, Faith, myself, myself especially! I let the primordial realm of Tohu (chaos) get the best of me. My heart filled with unforgiveness and all superfluity that follows when in a trance by the Kelipot (demonic forces). Only in my solitary confinement can I recognize the control, the stronghold that had me fixed on my hurt, my pain, my lack, myself! This concentration only suffered me from reaching my divine purpose, trust potential and innate powers. No matter what done unto me, said unto me, I shall remain steadfast, take the beating, digest the hurt, and remain obedient. See I benefit from being here, but I'll profit once released back into the world.

My mind is in training, my flesh is being tamed, my soul is waking up, my spirit is renovating. Know this that success is not defined by what you got but by what you do with what you got. So, from the bottom of my heart, I forgive you and say that once will never be enough. Forgive me! Life's been hard these few years of my time, but I wish to make the best of it from this point on. Unleashing the greatness that lives within us, getting out of being sorry to being so thankful from dwelling on the sorrows and sadness to come up with a new way of thinking and handling our loss, celebrating life with no cause. I end this here, to be continued... I love who you are!!!"

- Toussaint
September 2, 2014 (16:00) Song: "Mary That Girl"

"I love my wife Jenny,

She is my soulmate. I see myself with her forever, I love her smile, her sense of humor, her characteristics and personality. My wife is a faithful woman, she demonstrates her loyalty to me by remaining bound to me. Jenny has this personal magnetic effect which never seems to fail in arousing my maturity. Her voice soothes me and calms me. I love to listen to her speak. Jenny my wife is my one and faithful friend in the physical, she shares all her secrets and fears to me, she expresses her true emotions, entrusting me with her heart, she will not lie to me, and I won't cheat on her. I love Jenny for who she is inside out, she is smart, intelligent, affectionate, loving, compatible, passionate. Whatever I feel, she believes. She is a wonderful mother, has great patience and puts first the benefit of our daughter. She is warming and nurturing and performs energies of healing."

"She's gifted, creative, she is a visionary with lots of power, passion, and purpose. She brings out the best in me and just the thought of her fills me up with joy. We are in harmony with one another, were understanding of one another, we are true to one another, and she'll do anything for me. She is beautiful and she believes in taking care of herself, she is photogenic and has all that it takes to be an infamous model. She's ambitious, determined to succeed. She focuses on a certain subjects and masters them; she is very intuitive. She is resourced but got demands, a magnetic energy and the substance of her being is magnetic in nature. She is virtuous, loves to cook, clean, work, study, paint, write poems, and start studies. She loves me for me no matter what and supports me in my most trying points. She sacrificed her years, time, and other desires all to be with me. She is my kind of woman and given unto me by God himself. She is worthy and describes the abundance of joy, peace, love, prosperity, promotes morality, spirituality the universe has to offer."

- Toussaint
April 3, 2015

RESPONSE: VOW By Jenny Toussaint

"I bow down to the divine in you. I bow down to the divine in us."

To My Dear Husband James E. Toussaint "Honey"

From Your Loving Wife Jenny A. Toussaint

Happy Anniversary Married on August 24, 2009

- JENNY TOUSSAINT
August 24, 2015

———◆———

"My Jenny, my little heart,

my dear thing, my devout, my love, my dear, my sweet, my life, my light, my all good, my shadow, my castle, my acre, my loins, my vineyard, my oh sun, oh my life, sun, moon, the stars, the heavens, my past, my future, my innermost being, my heart blood my internal star of my eyes, oh dearest, what should I call you? My golden child, my pearl, my precious stone, my crown, my queen, my empress. My dear darling of my life, my highest, my most precious, my baptism, my children. You are my tragic plays, you are my second, a better self, you are my virtue, you are my merit, you are my hope, my heaven, my child of God, you are my intercessor, you are my guardian, my angel, my soulmate. How I love you so.

I Love You,
Your Husband"

- Toussaint
August 24, 2015

Love·Honor·Respect

"By what Art have you become able to captivate all my faculties, to concentrate on yourself, my moral existence? It is a magic, my sweet love which will end only with me. To live for Jenny, that is the history of my life. I am trying to reach you; I am dying to be near you. Time was when I prided myself on my courage and sometimes when considering the evil which men might be able to do to me, a fate which I had expected. I fixed my eyes most steadfastly on the most unheard-of misfortunes without frowning, without being surprised. But today the idea that my

Jenny might be unwell, the idea that she might be ill and above all, the cruel, the fatal thought that she might love me less, it withers my soul, stops my blood, makes me sad, casted down, and leaves me not even a cover of furry and despair. I have often used to say to myself that man could have no power over him who dies without regrets. But, today to die without being loved by you; to die without that certainty is the torment of hell, is the life-like and striking image of absolute annihilation. I feel as if I will be stifled, my only companion, you who fate has decreased to make with me the painful journey, the day when I shall no longer possess your heart, will be that when parched nature will be without warmth and without vibration. Love thee as your eyes, but that is not enough as yourself, more than yourself, as your thoughts, your mind, your sight, your all. Sweet beloved, forgive me, I am worn out. Nature is weak for he who feels keenly, for him when you love."

"Your illness, which occupies my mind night and day. Without appetite, without sleep, without care for my friendships, for glory, for fatherland, you, and the rest of the world exists no more for me then if it were annihilated. I prize honor since you prize it, I prize victory since that gave you pleasure, without which I still have left all to throw myself at your feet. In your letter, my darling, be careful to tell me that you're convinced that I love you beyond all imagination that you are persuaded that every moment of my life is consecrated to you; that never a day pass without me thinking of you; that never has the thought of thinking of another women has entered my head."

Your Love,

-Toussaint
June 1, 2015

⸺⬥⸺

"Every choice you make is creating your future. Choose Wisely!" - Joe Tichio

"The greatest wealth is health" - Virgil

"Motivation is what gets you started. Habit is what keeps you going" - Jim Rohn

"If you love life, don't waste time, for time is what life is made up of" - Bruce Lee

"Life is 10% what happens to me and 90% how I react to it." - Charles Swindoll

"Love, I got your pictures, both sets, thank you so much! You are Beautiful... You know what? I take that back there aren't any words to justly describe you. I'm afraid if I put a name on it, going deaf may be the result. So I will just describe what you are - you are an inspiration, and a wonder to gaze upon as though your love cometh directly from the light of Heaven. I Love You"

To: My Wifey
From: Your only

-Toussaint
November 10, 2015

"The Butterfly Rose"

"A seed is planted and from the roots formed a stem that grows, into a blooming Rose".

"A worm is born in the condition of its finite state, as time progresses, nature bounds the worm to a tight space, but this is no punishment it's only to transform the little creature to its highest place".

- Toussaint
February 11, 2016

CHAPTER

7

The Miracle of Having Faith

Ja'Faith entering into the world was an inspiring and profound moment in life. The labor and delivery process unfolded with the support of a compassionate medical team, creating an atmosphere of reassurance and comfort at a Medical Center in West Boca. The laboring process was not long and gruesome but smooth, and calm, and in those moments, the sights and sounds of the delivery room merged with the emotions of wonder and excitement, forging an unbreakable connection between us. My newborn baby girl popped right into my hands in the presence of her father and the nurse on shift. The labor and delivery nurse delivered a healthy baby because a midwife or obstetric doctor wasn't available on-site at the time of delivery but did arrive shortly after the umbilical cord had been clamped by the nurse and clipped by J.ET. Every detail, from exchanged glances to the sounds of her first cries, was etched in our hearts. The bond formed during this monumental event made it the most extraordinary and joyous occasion of my life. As I held Faith in my arms for the first time, the depth of love and the beginning of a new chapter filled our hearts with indescribable joy and gratitude, creating a melody that would resonate through the years to come.

HAPPY NEW YEAR!!!

Ja- Jamaican culture, Rastafari origin name for God

Faith - faculty of raven in the wind

Chrisette - Christ-Set, because you were born in the month of the winter solstice, which typically is a month "set" aside for sorrow and unhappiness, but upon your birth was instead hailed with joy.

Toussaint - French for 'all saints'

"My Love,

I know that your mind wanders and wonders many thoughts. Maybe you are even questioning many events past and things present. Or I could be mistaken, perhaps you are perfectly fine and at peace - that's my wish for you anyways! But in life given into the nature of our human form, it can get difficult. At least for me it's been a lot difficult having to live through the guilt of being apart from my family all because I've made some bad decisions. I'm paying for it now. It's a universal law of nature called Karma; cause and effect; and it also can be stated: 'You reap what you sow'. You do good and you are rewarded with good likewise you do wrong, then bad will come upon you, eventually, in some shape or form, when you least expect it. Can one suffer even after she's done good? Of course! Having understood that although you may suffer for even after being consistent with doing good - that which you suffer will only be a testing of your faith in doing good. Moreover, on a deeper level, everything works together for good. So, see no evil, speak no evil, and hear no evil. Imagine good and beautiful things and this is what you shall see. Peace is within you. So is heaven, so there is no need to look to the sky, except for the studies of the stars and planetary movements as they relate to man/ women. The world you see is created from the mind you possess. Visualize the world you want to see daily and so shall it be."

"The power is in you, don't allow anyone to steal it from you. Be sure to take care of your spirit, mind, body, and soul. All these make up your being. Control your thoughts and you shall have control of your environment and everything and everyone in it. I miss you and pray this will be all over soon. I am making a commitment to myself to never be absent from your life in this manner except only when I return to my ancestors. I will be there for you, and although I am far away, I am here for you; I am here to stay. Sorry I am missing and have missed some of your prime years. I will make up for it. I got your pictures. Oh my God you are getting so big and blossoming more and more into a beautiful young lady. Don't allow anyone to hurt you out there. It bothers me that I am not there to offer you my protection it's pretty up-setting. But I refuse to remain upset at myself. I have enough people against me. Instead, I am on the road to redemption - being brought back alive. You are my family and I love you. I hope I get the opportunity, again to make things right and better than they've ever been and if I do not get the opportunity then my lost be your gain."

From Your Father,
P.S. HAPPY BORN DAY!!!"

"WALK BY FAITH NOT BY SIGHT"
— BIBLE

Baby girl's arrival on December 16th, 2009, marked a transformative moment where the profound depth of love became tangible and undeniable. Holding her tiny, delicate form in my arms ignited an overwhelming sense of joy, responsibility, and unconditional affection. The warmth of her presence brought a newfound purpose and completeness to my life, filling every moment with a sense of wonder and fulfillment. Witnessing her first breaths and tender movements created an unbreakable bond, and the journey of motherhood began, enveloping me in a love so pure and deep that it surpassed any experience I had ever known. My baby brought out a more artistic side of me, I found solace in silent artistic expressions, immersing myself in the world of art through painting, sketching, and photography. Navigating the challenges of new motherhood was made more bearable by the enchanting atmosphere of Florida, where our tri-family unit found comfort and support. The serene surroundings and the warmth of the community became a soothing backdrop to the trials and triumphs of early parenthood. The Floridian lifestyle added a touch of tranquility to the journey, creating a harmonious environment where the ups and downs of raising a child were met with resilience and shared joy within our tight-knit family unit. The arrival of our daughter brought an unparalleled joy that transcended the shadows of my past experiences. The tender moments of cradling her in my arms, witnessing her first smiles, and hearing the sweet melodies of her laughter became a healing balm for the wounds of past loss. As a new mother, the depth of my love for my child created a profound sense of fulfillment, casting a radiant light that dispelled the lingering darkness of previous hardships. Her presence not only marked the beginning of a new chapter but also became a source of strength, resilience, and a testament to the transformative power of love in overcoming the challenges life had presented. In her innocence, I found solace, and in her laughter, a melody that echoed the healing of my heart.

CHAPTER

8

Embracing New Beginnings: A Guide for Nurturing

Upon my arrival in Boca Raton for the winter break after completing my last semester of undergraduate studies, J.E.T. had arranged a fully furnished villa in a delightful, gated community. Nestled in the heart of Boca Raton, Florida, the villa offered a picturesque view overlooking a serene lake. The tranquil surroundings provided the perfect backdrop for a peaceful retreat. One of my favorite pastimes became taking my baby, Faith, in her stroller for strolls around the community. The gazebo by the lake became our sanctuary, a place where we could observe ducks gracefully gliding across the water. The soothing ambiance of the surroundings allowed for precious moments of tranquility, creating lasting memories against the backdrop of Florida's warm winter weather. The villa, with its thoughtful furnishings and idyllic location, became a haven where I could unwind and enjoy the simple pleasures of life. It was a place where the beauty of nature blended seamlessly with the comforts of home, providing a peaceful retreat for both me and my growing family. The transition to Boca Raton brought about a shift in my priorities.

***

Returning to Maryland with my twenty-five-day-old baby for the graduation ceremony presented its own set of challenges. J.E.T, Faith and I endured a one-day delay that led to me missing my nursing pinning ceremony. Despite the hurdles, we eventually arrived at Towson Maryland on January 10th, 2010, for graduation day. Rumors circulated in the assembly line that Marie had gone on stage to receive my nursing pin the evening prior at the pinning ceremony, causing confusion among the graduating class about the individual stepping onto the stage. While I could not relocate anything from my dorm room such as furniture or the years of coursework, study materials, and textbooks from Towson to Boca Raton to study for my nursing board exam because my off-campus basement studio apartment had been broken into and all my academic material had been taken. Regardless of being raped of my years of knowledge, laptop, textbooks, graded term papers, tests, and lecture notes, my mind was entirely devoted to embracing the role of a new mother and fostering a deep bond with my baby. It marked a significant chapter where, for the first time, I felt the genuine sense of having a family to call my own. The coursework being taken caused a major setback and even resulted in me having to complete refresher courses, but the newfound joy of motherhood took center stage.

Finding the right balance between guidance and independence is an ongoing process.

Pay attention to your child's cues, and adjust your approach, accordingly, ensuring a supportive and nurturing environment for their growth. In dedicating this time solely to my baby, I not only nurtured her growth but also cultivated a deeper connection and understanding of the profound responsibilities and joys that come with being a mother. Faith, a warm, loving, and bubbly baby, brought boundless joy to our home in Boca Raton. Her laughter, a joyful symphony, echoed through every corner of our home, filling each room with infectious happiness. From the earliest days, her eyes sparkled with curiosity, eager to explore the world around her. Her chubby cheeks and radiant smile became a source of warmth, melting away any remnants of stress or worry. As she grew, her happy demeanor remained a constant. The sun-kissed days in

Boca Raton provided the perfect backdrop for her to thrive. Whether playing in the gentle ocean breeze or giggling during afternoon strolls, Faith embodied the carefree spirit of a child surrounded by love. The vibrant colors of the Florida landscape seemed to reflect the vivid energy she brought to every moment. Having a baby brings a multitude of responsibilities that require dedication, patience, and constant attention. These responsibilities include:

1. **Feeding and Nutrition**: Ensure the baby is fed at regular intervals, whether through breastfeeding or formula and pay attention to their nutritional needs.
2. **Diapering and Hygiene**: Regularly change diapers, maintain cleanliness, and ensure the baby is comfortable and healthy.
3. **Sleeping Schedule:** Manage the baby's sleep routine and create a conducive sleep environment.
4. **Medical Care:** Schedule and attend regular pediatric check-ups and vaccinations and address any health issues promptly.
5. **Emotional Support:** Provide love, comfort, and emotional support to foster a secure attachment.

Navigating these responsibilities requires resilience, flexibility, and a supportive network to share the load and foster a nurturing environment for the baby. Embracing the profound journey of motherhood, I chose to take dedicated time away from other commitments to wholeheartedly focus on nurturing my first growing child. This intentional pause allowed me to:

1. **Prioritize Bonding**: By immersing myself in the daily routines of feeding, diapering, and comforting, I deepened the bond with my baby, creating a foundation of trust and love.
2. **Maximize Quality Time**: Every moment became an opportunity for shared smiles, laughter, and exploration. Whether strolling to the gazebo to watch ducks or snuggling during nap times, each interaction was cherished.
3. **Promote Emotional Well-being**: Taking this time off provided a space for emotional healing, allowing me to address past

losses and embrace the joy of motherhood. The supportive environment contributes to this emotional well-being.

4. **Enhance Personal Growth:** The pause offered a chance for personal reflection and growth, instilling a sense of fulfillment and purpose beyond academic and professional pursuits.

5. **Celebrate Milestones:** Witnessing each developmental milestone, from the first giggle to the first step, was a joyous celebration. These precious moments formed the fabric of our shared history.

6. **Establish a Supportive Network:** Surrounding myself with a community that understood the challenges and joys of new motherhood provided invaluable support and encouragement.

7. **Effective Communication:**
   - ✓ *Active Listening:* Pay close attention to what your child is saying. Give them your full focus and respond thoughtfully to show that you value their thoughts and feelings.
   - ✓ *Open-ended Questions:* Instead of asking yes/no questions, encourage your child to share more by asking open-ended questions. This can lead to more meaningful conversations.
   - ✓ *Empathy:* Understand and acknowledge your child's emotions. Let them know that you recognize and appreciate their feelings, creating a safe space for open communication.
   - ✓ *Consistent Check-ins:* Regularly check in with your child about their day, experiences, and any concerns they may have. Consistency builds trust and encourages them to share more openly.
   - ✓ *Create a Comfortable Environment:* Foster an atmosphere where your child feels comfortable expressing themselves without fear of judgment. This can strengthen your bond and encourage honesty.

Fostering independence is important for personal growth. Consider these tips:

1. **Encourage Decision-Making**: Allow your child to make age-appropriate choices. This could include selecting their outfits, choosing extracurricular activities, or deciding on weekend plans.
2. **Responsibility for Chores**: Assign simple chores that align with their capabilities. This teaches them accountability and the importance of contributing to the household.
3. **Homework Independence**: Provide a quiet and organized space for homework. Encourage them to manage their assignments, plan study time, and seek help when needed. This fosters a sense of responsibility for their education.
4. 4. **Problem-Solving Skills**: Teach problem-solving techniques. Guide them in identifying issues, brainstorming solutions, and making decisions. This skill set is valuable in various aspects of life.
5. **Healthy Risk-Taking**: Allow your child to take calculated risks. This might involve trying new activities, making new friends, or overcoming challenges. Support them in learning from experiences, whether positive or negative.
6. **Communication Skills**: Encourage open communication. Let them express their thoughts and feelings, and actively listen. This builds trust and helps them navigate social interactions.

Navigating the delicate balance between guidance and allowing space for individual growth in school-age children requires a nuanced approach.

Here are some recommendations:

1. **Open Communication**: Foster an environment where your child feels comfortable expressing themselves. Encourage them to share their thoughts, feelings, and experiences. Actively listen without judgment.

2. **Set Clear Expectations**: Establish clear expectations for behavior, responsibilities, and academic performance. This provides a framework for your child while allowing them to understand the boundaries.

3. **Encourage Independence**: Gradually give your child more independence and responsibility. This can include managing their schedule, completing homework, and making age-appropriate decisions. Celebrate their achievements and efforts.

4. **Provide Guidance**: Be a supportive guide rather than a director. Offer advice when needed, share your experiences, and help them navigate challenges. Avoid being overly controlling, allowing them to learn from both successes and mistakes.

5. **Respect Their Individuality**: Recognize and appreciate your child's unique qualities and interests. Support their exploration of hobbies and activities that align with their personality and aspirations.

6. **Be Flexible**: Adapt your parenting style to your child's evolving needs. As they grow, their requirements for guidance and autonomy will change. Stay flexible and responsive to these shifts.

7. **Teach Problem-Solving**: Equip your child with problem-solving skills. Encourage them to think critically, consider consequences, and develop strategies to overcome challenges. This empowers them to make informed decisions.

8. **Celebrate Achievements**: Acknowledge and celebrate your child's achievements, both big and small. This positive reinforcement encourages a healthy sense of accomplishment.

CHAPTER

9

Rediscovering Radiance

Embarking on the journey to reclaim my pre-pregnancy weight was transformative experience that blended dedication, mindful choices, and the guidance of a motivational mentor. Beyond the physical transformation, this journey became a metaphor for resilience, self-discovery, and embracing one's strength. It wasn't just about shedding pounds; it was about shedding self-doubt and reclaiming a sense of empowerment. The dedication poured into each workout, the mindful choices made at every meal, and the guidance received from my mentor shaped not only my body but also my mindset. It became a testament to the profound impact that self-care can have on a mother's overall well-being. As I embraced a healthier lifestyle, I discovered an inner strength that transcended the scale's numbers. It was a journey of self-love, teaching me that taking care of myself is not selfish but a necessity, allowing me to be the best version of both a mother and an individual. In sharing this journey, I hope that it inspires and empowers other mothers to embark on their paths of self-discovery, reminding them that prioritizing their well-being is a gift not only to themselves but to the precious lives they nurture.

1. **Mindful Diet Choices**: I embraced a balanced and nutritious diet that focused on nourishing my body rather than restricting it. Incorporating whole foods, lean proteins, and ample fruits

and vegetables played a crucial role. Portion control and mindful eating became key principles in my dietary approach.

2. **Regular Exercise Routine**: A tailored exercise routine became a cornerstone of my post-pregnancy recovery. Starting with gentle exercises and gradually progressing to more intensive workouts, I prioritized a mix of cardio and strength training. Consistency was key, and I adapted the routine to suit the demands of motherhood.

3. **Motivational Mentorship**: Having a motivational mentor provided invaluable encouragement and guidance throughout this fitness journey. Whether it was setting realistic goals, staying accountable, or navigating challenges, their support fostered a positive mindset and fueled my determination.

4. **Holistic Approach:** Recognizing that physical health is intertwined with mental and emotional well-being, I adopted a holistic approach. Incorporating stress-reducing activities like yoga and mindfulness practices contributed to a more comprehensive recovery.

5. **Setting Realistic Goals**: Instead of fixating on rapid results, I set realistic and achievable goals. Celebrating small victories along the way became a source of motivation, reinforcing my commitment to long-term health.

6. **Creating a Supportive Environment:** Surrounding myself with a supportive network, including friends and family, ensured that I had encouragement during both challenging and triumphant moments. Their positive influence created a conducive environment for success.

7. **Patience and Self-Compassion**: Recognizing that the journey to post-pregnancy weight is a gradual process, I practiced patience and self-compassion. Understanding that each body is unique, I embraced the fluctuations and changes with a kind and understanding perspective.

CHAPTER

10

Navigating the World's Challenges

During my college years away, Marie, her children, her partner Mr. Mudi, and the Diplomat's elderly wife relocated to a single-family house a zip code away from the duplex. The circumstances of the move remained unknown to me. My graduation ceremony on January 10th, 2010, marked a milestone as Jenny Shungu, now Jenny Toussaint was graduation from college a married and happy new mother. In the audience, J.E.T. held our two-week-old baby, and the world felt at our fingertips, destined for success.

***

After the ceremony, my first instinct was to retrieve my undergraduate study materials from my off-campus housing. Opening the door, tears filled my eyes as I discovered the basement room vandalized, electronics gone, textbooks and binders taken. Saddened by the room's condition, defeat washed over me. J.E.T. took my hand, assuring me we'd find a way to obtain the information for the board exam. He emphasized that the most critical part of my nursing career had been secured, expressing pride in my accomplishment. We promptly flew back to Florida that same day. The challenges of being unable to retrieve nursing study material were significant. It hindered the ability to review essential content, prepare for exams, and engage in continuous learning. This situation led to increased stress, anxiety about academic performance, and potential gaps in knowledge crucial for nursing practice. Seeking alternatives, such as online resources and collaborating with peers, became impossible after graduation, leading to lost contacts or an inability to communicate with professors. Overcoming these obstacles required resourcefulness, resilience, and a commitment to obtaining a comprehensive understanding of nursing concepts.

Navigating financial challenges led me to explore diverse employment opportunities. From hostessing at nearby restaurants in Mizner Park, Florida to eventually 'falling to the embraced lifestyle of night life entertainment roles in West Palm Beach and South Florida's most luxurious gentlemen's clubs. This unexpected journey unfolded as a pragmatic response to financial struggles, each experience, however, contributed to my growth. In this transformative phase, I adapted to the stage name "Fortune Cookie"; a persona integral to my experiences on stage and contributing to my growth and resilience. Amidst the glitz and glamour, I navigated the complexities of nightlife, discovering unexpected facets of myself in the pulsating rhythm of the music, the allure of the spotlight, and the energy of the crowd.

A
IS
W
O
R
T
H
A
Thousand
Words

In the realm of nursing, I found myself thrust into a challenging environment where the phrase "Nurses Eat Their Young" wasn't just a saying; it was a stark reality. The camaraderie I expected in a profession dedicated to care often gave way to a harsher truth. Experienced nurses undermining and belittling newcomers. It was like an initiation by fire or a trial by those who should have been mentors. The wounds weren't physical, but the emotional toll was undeniable. In the nursing world, survival meant navigating through the unwritten rules of a culture that, at times, seemed to devour its own. The struggle for acceptance, acknowledgment, and respect became a parallel journey to providing quality care. Each shift, I faced not only the demanding tasks of patient care but also the intricacies of a work culture that sometimes felt more like a battleground than a supportive community.

Contrastingly, my experiences in the gentleman's club painted a dim picture. A world where dancers, though competing for attention, didn't hesitate to share the spotlight. The concept of "getting into my money bag" wasn't a metaphor for rivalry; it was an acknowledgment of mutual success. There was an unspoken understanding that collaboration could enhance the experience for everyone. In comparing these two vastly different worlds, I realized the profound impact of workplace culture. While nursing demanded resilience and thick skin, the gentleman's club fostered an environment where success could be collective. The journey from a cutthroat nursing atmosphere to a more collaborative space mirrored not only a shift in professions but also a transformation in my understanding of workplace dynamics, highlighting the importance of support and unity, even in the most unexpected places. Embarking on a journey of self-discovery, I delved into various hobbies that became outlets for creativity and personal expression. Glamour modeling and photography allowed me to capture moments in time, freezing fragments of beauty and individuality. ZMEG, our modeling entertainment group, became a collaborative space where individuals with different artistic backgrounds could come together to express their creativity.

Painting became a canvas for my emotions, each stroke telling a story. Writing became a therapeutic escape, giving a voice to the untold chapters of my life. Styling and braiding hair transformed into an art form, intertwining culture and creativity. Each hobby became a piece of my narrative, shaping my identity beyond the challenges I had faced. In my painting endeavors, I delved into a myriad of styles and subjects, using the canvas as a cathartic outlet for my emotions. Abstract paintings captured the complexities of my experiences, with vibrant colors and bold strokes conveying the highs and lows of my journey. Landscapes painted serene scenes, reflecting my longing for tranquility amid life's tumult. Sketch work became a more detailed exploration of my thoughts. Portraits depicted the diverse individuals I encountered, each face telling a story of its own. Symbolic sketches conveyed hidden meanings, providing a visual language to express the intricacies of my emotions. Through these artistic expressions, I found solace and a means to communicate the depths of my experiences. The canvas and sketchbook became windows into my soul, allowing me to navigate and understand the profound layers of myself.

CHAPTER

11

Love Beyond Locks

Each time J.E.T. faced legal issues, it felt like I had no choice but to return to Maryland due to lack of resources, creating a cycle of uncertainty and strain on our relationship. Amidst the legal challenges J.E.T. faced, I found myself shouldering the responsibilities of a single mother. Coping with the complexities of parenthood alone. The continuous cycle of legal troubles not only tested our connection and resilience but also shaped the narrative of our union. Staying married for fourteen years to a man who has been incarcerated for a large portion of that time is a testament to strength, resilience, and commitment. Here are some insights into how I navigated this challenging journey:

1. **Unwavering Commitment**: Your enduring commitment to marriage is evident. Despite the challenges, you chose to stand by your husband and weather the storms together.
2. **Effective Communication**: Maintaining open and effective communication is crucial in any relationship, especially one faced with the complexities of incarceration. Regular communication helps bridge the physical gap and sustains emotional connection.
3. **Establishing Trust**: Building and maintaining trust is a cornerstone of any enduring relationship. Trust between you and your husband likely played a significant role in sustaining the marriage through his periods of incarceration.

4. **Setting Realistic Expectations**: Acknowledging and accepting the realities of your husband's situation and the challenges posed by his incarceration may have involved setting realistic expectations. This realistic outlook could have helped manage disappointments and frustrations.

5. **Emotional Support System:** Cultivating a strong support system, whether through friends, family, or support groups, is essential. Having a network to lean on during difficult times provides emotional sustenance.

6. **Personal Growth**: Focusing on personal growth and maintaining a sense of self is vital. By nurturing your well-being and pursuing your goals, you contribute positively to the relationship.

7. **Planning for the Future:** Planning for a shared future after his release demonstrates a forward-looking mindset. Discussing and preparing for life beyond incarceration provides a sense of purpose and direction.

8. **Adaptability**: Flexibility and adaptability are key when dealing with the challenges presented by incarceration. Being able to adapt to changing circumstances and finding creative solutions contribute to the resilience of marriage.

9. **Celebrating Milestones**: Recognizing and celebrating milestones, both big and small, creates positive moments within the marriage. These celebrations serve as reminders of the enduring bond you share.

10. **Legal Understanding**: Gaining a deep understanding of the legal system, including any potential legal avenues for your husband, may have played a role in navigating the challenges posed by incarceration.

Maintaining a long-distance relationship with a loved one who is incarcerated can be challenging, but there are strategies to help foster connection:

1. **Communication is Key**: Regular communication through letters, phone calls, and emails can strengthen bonds. Be open and honest in your communication.

2. **Set Goals**: Establish both short-term and long-term goals for the relationship. This can provide a sense of purpose and direction for the future.

3. **Visitations**: Whenever possible, plan visits to the correctional facility. Face-to-face interactions are invaluable and can provide emotional support.

4. **Support System**: Build a support network of friends and family who understand and respect your relationship. Surrounding yourself with positive influences can make the journey easier.

5. **Self-Care**: Take care of your well-being. Balancing personal and emotional needs is crucial in maintaining a healthy relationship.

6. **Education and Understanding**: Learn about the legal system, the incarcerated individual's situation, and available resources. Knowledge can empower you to navigate challenges more effectively.

7. **Counseling or Support Groups**: Seek professional counseling or join support groups tailored to individuals in similar situations. Connecting with others who share similar experiences can provide valuable insights and emotional support.

8. **Maintain Independence**: While staying connected is important, it is equally crucial to maintain your independence and pursue personal growth. Focus on your goals and aspirations.

9. **Plan for the Future**: Create plans for life after incarceration. Discuss career goals, housing arrangements, and other aspects of your future together.

10. **Patience and Understanding**: Understand that there will be difficult moments. Patience, understanding, and a positive outlook can help overcome challenges.

Remember, each relationship is unique, and it's essential to find strategies that work best for both individuals involved. Open communication and commitment are vital components of any successful long-distance relationship, especially when dealing with incarceration. The absence of my father casts a notable void in my growth and development. It was always strange for everyone who heard her claims, yet for years she had not provided me with the correct information to understand the importance of who my father was and how he contributed to society. Experiencing forced separation due to incarceration can indeed impose significant challenges on maintaining a family structure and cultivating trust. The impact of such situations often extends beyond the individual incarcerated to the entire family unit.

Here are some reflections on these challenges:

1. **Disruption of Family Structure**: Incarceration can disrupt the conventional family structure, introducing physical, emotional, and financial strains. Roles within the family may shift, and the absence of a family member can create a void that is challenging to fill.

2. **Strained Trust**: The circumstances surrounding incarceration can strain trust among family members. The legal complexities, emotional toll, and uncertainties associated with the situation may give rise to feelings of betrayal, suspicion, or fear.

3. **Communication Barriers**: Maintaining effective communication becomes more challenging with physical separation. Misunderstandings can arise due to limited opportunities for face-to-face interactions, potentially affecting trust and understanding.

4. **Emotional Impact**: The emotional toll on family members can be profound. Feelings of shame, stigma, or guilt may surface, further complicating the ability to maintain trust within the family.

5. **Financial Stress**: Incarceration often brings financial challenges, adding another layer of stress to the family dynamic. This strain can contribute to heightened emotions and potential conflicts.

6. **Children's Perspectives**: For families with children, the impact on their perspectives of trust, relationships, and family structure can be significant. Explaining the situation to children and addressing their emotional needs becomes an added challenge.

7. **Community Stigma**: Families may also face external stigma and judgment guidelines. This external pressure can exacerbate internal challenges, making it even more difficult to foster trust within the family.

8. **Reintegration Challenges**: When the incarcerated family member is released, the process of reintegrating into the family and rebuilding trust can be complex. Adjusting to changed family dynamics and navigating the aftermath of incarceration requires time and effort.

———◆———

Acknowledging these challenges is an essential step toward addressing them. Seeking support from professional resources and support groups can guide rebuilding trust, maintaining a family structure, and navigating the complexities associated with incarceration.

1. **Unwavering Commitment:** Your enduring commitment to the marriage is evident. Despite the challenges, you chose to stand by your husband and weather the storms together.

2. **Effective Communication**: Maintaining open and effective communication is crucial in any relationship, especially one faced with the complexities of incarceration. Regular communication helps bridge the physical gap and sustains emotional connection.

3. **Establishing Trust**: Building and maintaining trust is a cornerstone of any enduring relationship. Trust between you and your husband likely played a significant role in sustaining the marriage through his periods of incarceration.

4. **Setting Realistic Expectations**: Acknowledging and accepting the realities of your husband's situation and the challenges posed by his incarceration may have involved setting realistic expectations. This realistic outlook could have helped manage disappointments and frustrations.

5. **Emotional Support System**: Cultivating a strong support system, whether through friends, family, or support groups, is

essential. Having a network to lean on during difficult times provides emotional sustenance.

6. **Personal Growth:** Focusing on personal growth and maintaining a sense of self is vital. By nurturing your well-being and pursuing your goals, you contribute positively to the relationship.

7. **Planning for the Future**: Planning for a shared future after his release demonstrates a forward-looking mindset. Discussing and preparing for life beyond incarceration provides a sense of purpose and direction.

8. **Adaptability**: Flexibility and adaptability are key when dealing with the challenges presented by incarceration. Being able to adapt to changing circumstances and finding creative solutions contributes to the resilience of marriage.

9. **Celebrating Milestones**: Recognizing and celebrating milestones, both big and small, creates positive moments within the marriage. These celebrations serve as reminders of the enduring bond you share.

10. **Legal Understanding**: Gaining a deep understanding of the legal system, including any potential legal avenues for your husband, may have played a role in navigating the challenges posed by incarceration.

Despite his incarceration J.E.T. displayed a remarkably romantic soul, passionately expressing his love for his family through heartfelt shared letters of incarceration and intricate artwork. In the confines of his situation, he remained an unwaveringly devoted husband, pouring love into every detail of anything he composed. With his intellectual brilliance, infused his writings with reflections on luminaries like Marianne Williamson, Dr. Neil Anderson, Maya Angelou, and William Shakespeare. Even in the midst of incarceration, his mind soared through the realms of profound thought, intertwining their wisdom into the messages, poetry, and artwork that became the foundation of our enduring connection. We would share our most inner hurts and pains and even reference each other to songs that remind us of the moments.

CHAPTER

12

Letters of Incarceration

In the quiet echoes of prison walls, my husband's words have been a lifeline, weaving a tapestry of emotions across the pages of his letters and poems. We have been separated by the hands of time for over a decade, yet his written expressions transcend the physical distance, serving as a poignant reminder that love can endure even in the face of prolonged separation. This book is more than ink on paper; it's a chronicle of resilience, love, and the profound connection that persists despite the passage of years. As I invite you into this intimate journey, may these written letters and poetry become a testament to the strength found within the confines of adversity and the enduring devotion to the power of love.

———◆———

"Good morning,

Really quickly, the jail here at Metro West has a Chapel where they provide the inmate population with church services. Recently, however, they've just instituted a new program called the Fatherhood program, which after completing the eight-to-ten-week group sessions they allow those in attendance to receive contact visitation with their family. I am not yet enrolled. But I've put in my request already; I was thinking maybe I can expedite the process if you will google and find the contact number for both the Chaplin and Counsel or - Supervisor, Mattews - and explain to then how you ladies are from out of town and is planning to visit me next month sometime around my b-day and that you've heard about the fatherhood program and wish that I would be able to participate so that you can plan your trip here in accord with the day or week of the contact visit."

"P.S. All three letters containing whatever pictures you sent were rejected. Unfortunately. They say only if censored out with emojis would they let them through. Ugh! Uh-oh, just noticed the paper is upside down (like the world!)"

Love,

- Toussaint
June 27, 2014 (Time 6:45am)

SORRY!

"I'm sorry for making you feel as if you were hardly loved, as though I did not need you, Lord knows it kills me to be without you. I'm so sorry for my lack of affection, the holding back of my divine passionate expression for you, to hug you, I will every moment I get. Every moment I get I will stop and hold you, just to steal a kiss even while at work I will send you a text reminding you how much you are missed. I'm sorry for not listening and considering particularly your words, your wants, your needs, sorry for the arguments, the fighting, most of all the laying of a finger on your fragile frame was not man of me. Sorry you felt ugly at times, nasty, and uncared for, I should have reassured you how beautiful you are, how precious you are, and everything you mean to me. You are very important, you are much needed and appreciated for every meal you cooked, clothes you ironed, every darn mess you cleaned, work you've done, all you've given to me. I'm sorry for my negative influence that may have likely taken effect on you, exposing you to bad habits and ideas. I pray that your mind be renewed in the will of God and you by his strength may be whole. I'm sorry for being any bit of ugly towards you. I'm sorry forever calling you out of your name, for you were born an angel, made a princess, become a woman, developed into a Queen; My Queen and soon God will transform you to a Goddess. Bless you my dear! You are loved, you are heard, God see's you and he is answering you. I'm Sorry... for all there is to be sorry for... upon this.

- Toussaint
September 10, 2014 (20:30)

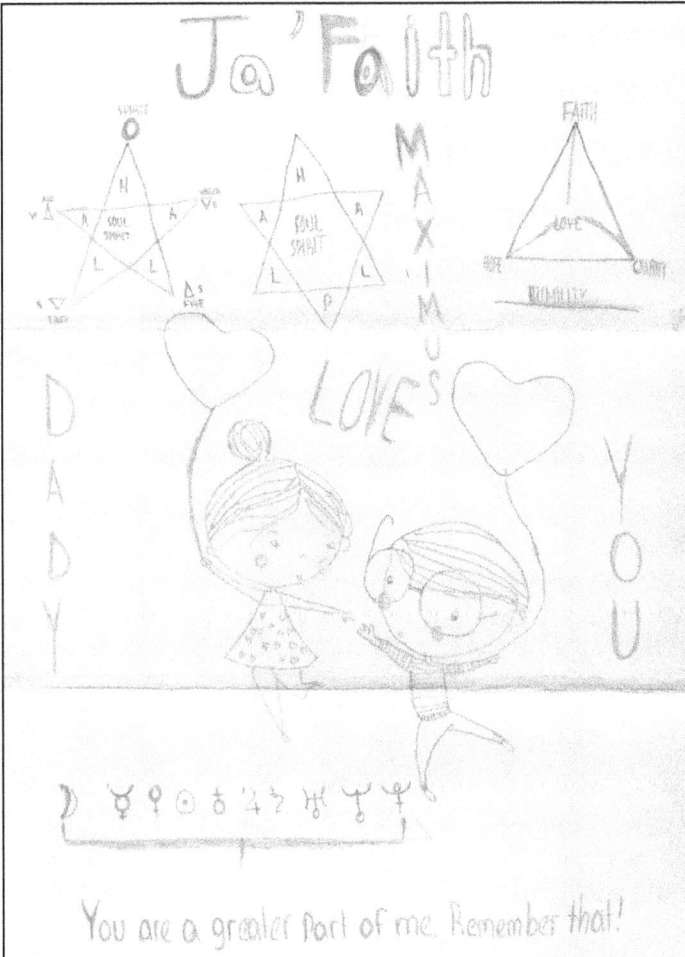

"My child you may not know me, but I know every-thing about you. I know when you sit down and when you rise, for even the very hairs on your head are numbered for you were made in my image. I knit you together in your mother's womb and brought you forth on the day you were born. You were not a mistake for all your days are written in my book. I am not distant and angry, but I am the complete expression of love. It is my desire to lavish my love on you. Simply because you are my child, and I am your father. My thoughts towards you are countless like the sand on the seashore and I rejoice over you with singing, I will never stop doing good to you for you are my treasured possession. My plan for your future has always been filled with hope because I love you with an everlasting love. Jesus came to represent that I am for you not against you, he is the exact representation of my being. I gave up everything that I loved that I might gain your love. When I come home, and I'll throw you the biggest party heaven has ever seen. I offer you more than your earthly father ever could, for I am the perfect father. I've always been a father and always will be a father, my question is will you be my child?"

'Love Dad Almighty GOD!'

- Toussaint
October 19, 2014 (22:00)

"My Dear,

What a wonderful feeling it really is to hear your voice always. Your voice is soothing to my ears as jazz is to the soul. There are day's you may grow faint, understandably, it's nature's way. Sometimes you may get the feeling of powerlessness, frankly we are powerless, but all things are possible through he who strengthens us. Receiving our power from God, He is, nonetheless, the way, the truth, and the light. By the Gospel, contemporarily known to us, it is by it I encourage you; Otherwise, you'll remain hungry and in the continuation of a voidable soul. In (Galatians 5: Verse 16), it is written that we should "Walk by the Spirit," and you will not gratify the desires of the flesh. It continues saying, "For the desires of the flesh are against the Spirit," "and the desires of the Spirit are against the flesh."

"For these are opposed to each other, to keep you from doing the things you want to do." (Galatians 5: Verse 17) (also see Romans 7: Verse 15 to 20). My love, really, I love you. I hate to be apart from you, unaware, in the numerous occasions of your departure from me, I would grow weak. Little do you know my greatest demonstration of strength was marrying you. Maybe I struggled with my adoration of you, at least grew to show it. That came out wrong?» What I am saying is, «I adore you behind tough skin». Look, you›re unfailingly beautiful! Beyond texture, you are desirable to look at, such as the moon, radiants; you are my morning star. Magical are your yes; awesome is you, like Disney on Ice, I long to gaze upon your face and dance between your voluptuous thighs, for they are like jewels, the works of a master's hand. Your breasts are like two fawns, twins of a gazelle. Your breath like the fragrance of apples and your mouth like choicest wine, let it flow to my beloved like new wine. I yearn to be rejoined with you and I will soon. In the meantime, let's continue to build on the foundation that's been prepared for us. Having good morals, strong principles and values and a core belief with faith to back it up. We shall begin to grow together in spirit, so that we are in unison. The reality of me not being there to touch you, kiss you, and make love to you, really, is all we lack."

"What is lacking and has been lacking is our intimacy with God (spirit), accessing Godly energy to releasing positive and transformative energy, granted the merits of powers beyond our physical ability we have yet to fully exercise. I once wrote, in a song a while ago, "The Body is weak, but the spirit is willing" (Galatians 5: Verse 19) can back me up on that, it says "Now the works of the flesh are evident: sexual immorality, impurity, sensuality, "idolatry, sorcery, enmity, strife, jealousy, fit of anger, rivalries, dissensions, divisions, envy, and things like that". Many, I admittedly I'm guilty of there are attributes greater than those mentioned, though not of the flesh being recognized in you."

"Verse twenty-two in Galatians five continues saying," But the fruit of the Spirit is love, joy, peace, patience, kindness, goodness, faithfulness, gentleness, self-control. My beloved it is essentially deemed upon us to make the difference in each other's live, not excluding our seeds and beyond. It's not like God to fail us, we fail us, we fall short of the glory, we stay down, we despite the power of change, and fail to notice when He is calling our name. For this time, the calling is on both parties. I learned today what the institution of marriage symbolizes. It is symbolic of our marriage to Christ, our loyalty, faithfulness to Him, which reflects our union with each other. More on that later."

"P.S. I would like for you in your spare time, to google a few people. These names are powerful women leaders in the African American community in Florida. I look on these things abroad and really believe you are with the acceptance of self, are powerful African American women. Be inspired, be innovative, be successful."

"Jennifer Carrol, she is the former Lieutenant Governor for the Florida Governor Rick Scott. She wrote a book titled 'When You Get There', by Estella Pyfrom, founder, and creator of Estella's Brilliant Bus. Antonia Williams-Gary, quote these exact words "Reaching out, reaching back, reaching down. Doctor and author, Dr. Oneeka Williams, first children's book Dr. Dee-Dee Dynamo's 'Mission to Pluto'. Dr. Roslyn Clark Artist, 13th President of Florida Memorial University. Also, these individuals can be found mentioned in the South Florida Times or the Westside Gazette. Research and see if your local area or surrounding areas distribute similar newspapers. In addition to your research, I also challenge you to embrace 'Love and Respect' by Emerson Eggerchs. Look it up, I'm curious to know what it is about, please! So, I leave you with this news my dear, Daddy loves you always!"

- Toussaint
October 29, 2014 (14:00)

"Mind for Provision"

"Jenny, it is certainly comforting to have you as my equal. Truly I am half the man with-out you. God bless you indeed, for all that you be sa blessing to me. I must give you credit for your keeping of good faith. With the learned acceptance of adversity, I by the grace of joy given to me from deep within, am proud of you. So, understand I love you, in the highest sense of the word not just a sentimental sort of thing not even an affectionate sort of thing but, thus. "I love you 99% and once I'm able to once again for all time, gently lay my hand on your flesh. In the heat of hot sex, it would then be the 00.1% apportioned. In other words, my love for you is not misery, my need for you isn't lost, my yearning for you isn't sex. Instead, my love for you is unmistakably divine, my desire for you is life, and my receiving you is for strength."

"In a passage of time, I was overcome with chaos, fear, and brokenness. Moving forward gaining much insight I am set free from the darkness that once clouded my mind. I find that I have a great peace within, in the cry of desperation I was rescued from myself and the thoughts that troubled me. Heavenly father rests my soul, for in the process of this hold have I behold the wit of life's purpose, hence in thy womb is where Kings and Rulers shall spring forth, and by my name should the be established. Bestowed upon us. Heavenly, being is the responsibility of such a dynastic ministry that we shall be conscious and harmonious in all things."

"We live not for today but for eternity so shall we endeavour today to prepare the future of our young, strengthen our genetics, thus our lineage for the latter days to come. It is relatively evident that higher education presumes higher standard of living, credibility, higher paid job opportunities, and a retirement that leaves you satisfied. Conclusively, it is these fewer perspectives that are imperative in the process of our decision making."

"My lady you've spoken of continuing your education, with shrewdness. I say, "shoot for the stars, "if you made it this far then you can make it to mars. Also, I trust all is well in your fairly new position as a maternal nurse, again congratulations! I am happy to know what you do makes you feel at ease, therefore I'm equally at ease."

- Toussaint
November 3, 2014

◆————————◆————————◆

"YOUR PLACE"

"There is a place fitting for you, tailored to your circumference, designed in style and the comfort of fine linen, only you can get in. Don't nobody wear it like you, because one can't measure out to all that women you are, nah, she can't rock it like you; you solid as a fortress, when you walk through the wind, it is with you breezing through a forest. At the sight of you I get goosebumps, like bumps in the road you're hard to get over, unless I move really slow. Not that I ever want to get over your strong hold."

"Lights, camera, action, 'Miss' you still the show, so captivating to watch; you steal the moon's glow, your static is felt from a distance, the magic of you is in effect. When you talk, I listen when you cry, I cry too. The one I'll die for; in hope I live to never forget you. Forever be with you, damn! I miss you..."

"I'm needing your soft touch, to breathe in your soft skin. I'm pleading to such a case, to spend life in your state, confined in your brace. Ruler of my heart; the picture in my mind is your face, the void in my soul is your place..."

"To The Ruler of my Heart Jenny Toussaint"

- Toussaint
November 17, 2014 (22:00)

"JAh FAITH"

"In this letter I'd like to share a story with you relating to the events occurring just before I first went to prison and saw you. We were at a vacation home, loaned to your mother and she had left for work. That morning, I awoke to look after you - my five-year-old baby girl. Sleeping in the next room, I woke you up, bathed you and got you dressed. Afterwards, I began to stretch-exercise on the floor and meditate. While laying there, you stood over me asking, "Let me see if I can lift up your head". When attempting to do so, you strained and said, "your head is heavy." Just afterward, you laid down and inquired, "See if you can pick up my head." Without any effort, I did so and remarked that your head was light. After this exercising, I took you to Grandmas and I distinctly remember turning at the door towards you. You, in turn, asked if I was coming back. I immediately remarked "yes" in a reassuring manner, then kissed you goodbye. As I was driving away, I caught you standing at the window staring at me and waving "I thought I was to return soon".

"Unfortunately, I did not return as you expected. Rather it was my first stay in prison at age 25 and would not see you again for 30 months. Look you are of foremost importance to myself and remembering these last moments with you keeps recurring in my thoughts and dreams. I miss you dearly. I was not able to provide for you as I had planned and quite naturally this still haunts me. Jah, please do not make the mistakes your father has made plenty of. Although you will undoubtedly make mistakes in life, remember you are a better version of myself. You are greater! Listen to the experience, knowledge, and wisdom of your parents, learning from their mistakes. Don't repeat them. I wish I had paid attention and listened sooner. Learning from the mistakes of others will save you the hardships that I have had to overcome. I love you so much and think of you everyday."

'Write to me, Love Dad'

- Toussaint
November 20, 2014

⸻ ◆ ⸻

"MERRY CHRISTMAS - HAPPY NEW YEARS - KEEP THE FAITH"

"Jenny,

I rather have bad times with you, than good times with someone else.

I rather be beside you in a storm, than safe and warm by myself.

I rather have tough times together, than to have it apart I rather have the one who holds My Heart..."

Yours Truly, J.E.T.

- Toussaint
December 20, 2014 (Time 22:45)

"Dr. Toussaint,

"It's surely comforting to have you as my soulmate; hence I am half the man without you. No doubt the Sovereign God be with you indeed, for all that you be but a blessing to me. I must give you, your deserving credit for being of good Faith: though, my tone, when speaking with you despite my melancholic state being inherent due to my predicament. With the grace of joy, I however afford this opportunity to say I am so proud of you. So, understand this, "Doctor", how much more you mean to me, and how much more I love! I Love You 99% and once, I am able to once - again - for all time - gently lay my hands on your, but so delicate flesh in the heart of sex, is then would the total sum of 100% be accounted for. In other words, my love for you is no misery, my need of you is not lust, and my want of you is not sex, instead my love for you is unmistakably divine, my need of you is of life, and my want of you is for nurturing strength. In closing I love the nature in which you are."

"The most wonderful of all things in life, I believe, is the discovery of another human being with whom one's relationship has a glowing depth, beauty, and joy as the years increase."

"This inner progressiveness of love between two human beings is a most marvellous thing, it cannot be found by looking for it or by passionately wishing for it.

It is a sort of Divine accident." - Sir Hugh Seymour Walpole

"P.S. I say in our case it is divine ordained."

'To be continued...'

- Toussaint
January 18, 2015 (21:30)

"All Things Are Possible to Him That Believeth" - Mark 9:23... I'm doing what I should have done years ago, which is finding out who I am and what I want. I want to have a choice. And when I make decisions through choice, and not guilt. It has to be better for me and for the people who love me."

- Louise Fletcher

I LOVE YOU...

- Toussaint
January 21, 2015

"Jenny,

"My sweet-soul lady; you already know that my heart burns with the longing to see you. If you don't know, "Now you know." With remorse I'm torn apart by the reality of the insurmountable pressure that my absence has caused you and our daughter. The tears are unprevented from rolling down my cheeks knowing the tough spot y'all are placed in, not to mention, the incurring debt was being submerged under. Yet should we settle in despondency? No! nor, should we remain in the tight grip of this crisis. Further, however, I am cognizant of you being deprived, emotionally, sexually, mentally, psychologically, and physically. Therefore, I earnestly pray that this all would go away seen, thus, I am unable to provide for you within here, support, protection, and security. There, alone crushes the very essence of my being a man, husband, and a father. There-by, our issue is evident and the one having the greatest tail out on us is me in jail."

"According to scriptures, the 'serpent' first launched his attack on the "family of God". Provided he uses the mechanism of 'Divide and Conquer'. Appearing to men/ women in many objects, shapes, and form - not failing to present his lies - appealing to our senses, hence, infiltrating the mind for the purpose of control over the body Saten wants to blind us from the truth, 'Whatever that be', consequently, setting a match to our posterity. There with my sweet soul lady... I encourage you to let your heart be merry - no matter What! And I pray that Love strengthens you, grace abounds in you, and that faith sees you through. You, my Lordess, is my Divine mate and I'm asking you to continue in the race and, be careful of nothing; but in everything by prayer and supplication with thanksgiving let your requests be made known unto God".

"(-Philippians 4:6) This is our struggle, this is our race, therefore, "Do you not know that those who run in a race all run, but one receives the prize? Run in such a way that you may obtain it. And everyone who competes for the prize is temperate in all things. Now they do it obtain a perishable crown, but we for an imperishable crown. Therefore, I run this: not with uncertainty. This I fight: not as one who beats the air". With that being said, baby we ride together - we die together', making use of all the resources and tools available to us, thus, pressing toward the goal of getting me out of jail, ASAP!"

"As a result, having a fresh start and our family back as a unit we can then with courage confidently draw up a plan to take on the new challenges-moving forward, while, simultaneously resorting to the old. Therefore, let this hope be impressed upon your subconsciousness: that "blessed is the man who endures temptation; for when he has been approved, he will receive the crown of life which the Lord has promised to those who love Him." (James 1:12) Further, "He will even deliver one who is not innocent... (Job 22:30) Look what happened for Simpson back in the day, lol; But yeah, it's hard sometimes?"

"What then shall we say to those things? God is for US, who can be against us? "He who did not spare his own son, but delivered Him up for us all, how shall He not with Him also freely give us all things?" Who shall bring a charge against us, God's elect? It is God who justifies, who is he who condemns? It is Christ who died, and furthermore is also risen. Who is even at the right hand of God, who also makes intercession for us. Who shall separate us from the love of Christ? Shall tribulation, or distress, or persecution, or famine, or nakedness, or peril, or sword?...

Yet in all things we are more than conquistadors through Him who loved us." (Roman 8: 31 - 35 and 37)

"Moreover, regarding the demand of action in my case, thus, the unproductivity, lack of performance, and idleness on Mick's behalf, evidently observe the end result of my case, so as long as he's representing me. With the preponderance of evidence, thus: his failures to file motions, explain his plan and strategy, effectively, not responding to my letters or demands, very few visits, hard to reach and just his lack of interest on my ideas and view of the case; these gives strong reasons why we've considered another attorney. If, Mick, is, what is strongly stated about him. "he's a cop-out-lawyer", then he is automatically disqualified from being an advocate for me - us.

Subsequently, as we are running this race, and we are fighting this battle - till the end, then it is only right that we have an advocate who will run and fight with us. In contrast, Regina who's a reputable trial lawyer, according to previous clients, has a close relationship with the honorable Judge, and takes effective actions in filing motions. Indeed, as it was then and somewhat as it is now, 'money' is a factor, when considering a new attorney. Additionally, the consideration of a new attorney isn't at my expense, nevertheless it's costing me indirectly. As a result, focusing on the problems only limits the mind to infinite possibilities, further, our attempt on a solution, would be to borrow.»

"In the book of proverbs chapter 22:7; it states that: "The rich rule over the poor, and the borrower is servant to the lender. As blatantly stated, this is true and far from comfort, with all, considering the fact that we are borrowers and less than lenders. Additionally, America is a nation that began as a debtor country, funded by its creditors, Great Britain, and France: thus, advancing the country into its 'Golden Age' the Industrial Revolution in the late 19th century."

"Further, America today has become debtors to China; Kingdoms Rise at the expense of another. Nevertheless, in my case it is more of a sacrifice than an investment, although it can be considered a long-term investment, it is a necessary sacrifice in order that we move forward in stimulating our own personal economy while gradually lowering our deficit. Thereby we borrow more. How do we go about this - from whom do we borrow? I don't have any credit, all this may come to mind - simply the answer is, from any entity that will approve, that is unbiased about your credit, and the agreement can reasonably be appeased. As a result, let's start with a personal loan from your bank or perhaps another bank, maybe even check the newspaper in the classified section. It has a listing of lenders under the subsection "Money to Land".

"Additionally, research what's required of you so that you are prequalified for the loan: occupation status, bank statements, pay stubs - collateral, credit and so on. Also, regarding credit, ask whether there is an alternative option other than using your credit, plus find out the terms and conditions spelled out in the agreement, namely: the interest rate, amount of principal payment - over how long of a period: and what if you default? Get a second opinion, inquire more than one entitlements, write down some thoughts and questions of your own so that you have an understanding on what route to take. Where there is a way there's a will - "if there is a shift, then there comes a break".

P.S. "Baby you are very supportive of me, and I want to pay you back, and give you what you so deserve - I will! I know this gets frustrating and can be overwhelming, perhaps you're even consumed occasionally but I need your mind sweetheart, your smart, your body in a whole perfect way right now. I need your intuition, intellect, intelligence, your emotion to steer you up and not down, and you function on my behalf. I'm sorry it's for the moment this way, but I promise I will make things right... I promise! I pray the Angels will help you and the spirit of the Goddess moves you, and the Power of the supreme force of the universe keeps you".

'Bless You My Love...'

- Toussaint
June 25, 2015

"Dear Sweet Lady,

"I make several suggestions to you regarding your personal finances. Understand that I want to see you prosper in every area of your life, especially because you deserve to and most importantly, you're the mother of my child, so keep pushing babe we're almost there, and if you grow faint don't be reluctant to pray for strength and ask the Angels of the Lord for help."

THE FOUR AGREEMENTS

1. "BE IMPECCABLE WITH YOUR WORD
Speak with integrity, say only what you mean. Avoid using the word to speak against yourself or to gossip about others. Use the power of your word in the direction of truth.

2. DON'T TAKE ANYTHING PERSONALLY
"Nothing others do is because of you. What others say and do is a projection of their own reality, their own dream. When you, are immune to the options and actions of others, you won't be the victim of needless suffering."

3. DON'T MAKE ASSUMPTIONS
"Find the courage to ask questions and to express what you really want. Communicate with others as clearly as you can to avoid

misunderstanding, sadness, and drama. With just this one agreement, you can completely transform your life."

4. ALWAYS DO YOUR BEST

"Your best is going to change from moment to moment; it will be different when you are healthy as opposed to sick. Under any circumstance, simply do your best, and you will avoid self-judgment, self-abuse, and regret."

"Congratulations on the raise you received at work, that is a milestone, along with the promotion of being a preceptor, you should be proud of yourself. Keep it up Mami, you're winning and losing is not an option."

'I Love You'

- Toussaint
August 3, 2015

"I am Happy with the decisions my wife Jenny makes. Jenny purchasing a vehicle (first time) does not affect me. It is a vehicle she already desired, so I am satisfied with her choice! I trust that the universe is good, so I trust that Jenny makes wise decisions. I rest in Jenny's choices, and I trust Yahweh that He will give her. I have joy to know that my wife Jenny is becoming self-reliant, and it makes me feel good. I love her strong will and I feel good about her making the right moves. I am happy with my wife because she is faithful and that makes me feel at ease. I feel at ease to know my wife is beginning to drive. I have confidence in her and I'm happy to know she is a very responsible driver. I am blessed to have someone who is trustworthy as she is, that brings peace to my soul. I am not worried about her, whereabouts or who she is with because we are in harmony with one another, and both share the feeling of true love."

"I have a peace of mind to feel good and confident about my wife's loyalty to me. My wife's decisions are smart because she has no ulterior motives, self ambition, nor does she make decisions based on her own self-interest. I trust that Jenny is honest and walks in her integrity."

- Toussaint
April 20, 2015

While grappling with the emotions of my husband's incarceration, I obtained the milestone of getting my Drivers License in my middle thirties. In my early 30s, I obtained the milestone of passing the road test on the first try. Motivated by the allure of cultural success stories in Atlanta, I embarked on a road trip from Maryland to Georgia. A part of me also wanted to inquire information about the whereabouts of Aunt-Betty Ann. However, fate had a different plan. In Oxford County, Granville, North Carolina, my brand-new Buick Verano met its end, colliding with imposing construction barrels. Alone and shaken after the car accident, officials arrived and immediately questioned my sobriety. Despite my requests for medical attention due to pain, bleeding, and head trauma from the airbag explosion, their focus turned to insinuation about my sobriety. At the hospital, the officer insisted on a blood draw, invoking racial stereotypes. Refusing, I felt the weight of my first encounter with racial profiling and arrest. During the doctor's examination, the situation escalated as the officer slammed me to the ground. My screams for mercy spared my life that day. Subsequently, I found myself in the Majesty office, charged with a Driving Under the Influence (DUI). A night in jail, away from my daughter, was a painful ordeal, ironically compounded by having enough money to bail myself out but needing someone to pick me up. The legal battle unfolded relentlessly over the next two years, marked by continuous court appearances and the looming shadow of a DUI charge, an experience that felt like an endless cycle with no resolution in sight. Amidst the challenging times of loneliness and depression during this separation, I found solace and purpose by immersing myself in my career, indulging in hobbies, and discovering a newfound love. This period of self-discovery and resilience became a pivotal chapter in my journey, shaping the narrative of my life in unexpected ways. In navigating the complexities of this journey, my ordeal sheds light on the profound dangers associated with driving under the influence (DUI). Beyond the legal repercussions, it serves as a poignant reminder of the emotional toll, especially for women coping with dependencies arising from stress. This experience underscores the imperative of prioritizing mental well-being and seeking healthier coping mechanisms, recognizing that the consequences extend beyond the individual to impact personal safety and the well-being of others on the road. It's a compelling call to empower women to make responsible choices.

———————◆———————

To: Jenny My Lovely Wife
From Your Husband

"Dear Jenny,

"I love you and I'm constantly thinking of you, I want you to know that you make me happy even as I am here. I thank God the Sun rises and falls on you. I thank you for being by my side during these turbulent times. I look forward to better days spent with you and it makes me feel good to know that the days will be harmonized with profitable love, pleasure, and joy. In this letter I aim to discuss the fundamental means to empowering our union. There are in every relationship a cause and effect in our case the cause is a divine unconditional love for one another to that effect we grow, were developed, consequently, living a sustainable harmonious life. Then in turn we automatically regenerate and reproduce both the feeling and expression of Love!"

"Now the question is, how can we manage such a high sense of love with the constant influx of adversity. We work them out! We exercise the power of love in solving problems. We maintain a good sense of attitude about all things, feel free to weigh in on this baby (partner) because the key is to see both sides. It's hard to make choices sometimes, I feel, if two people aren't in alignment with one another. Considering the basic, core values, belief system, and tradition. Ok maybe we can get past the tradition but if we don't have the same values and belief than our choices then become adverse to the other. In our case however, I believe we are aligned with one another more now than ever. So, considering that fact let's take advantage of the time to analyse our past, together, conflicting issues, to set preventive standards that will protect us going forward."

"Learning from experience, I realize how racial it is to be a mature responsible adult. From my observation I feel we've when occupying, once-upon-of-time, our own spare failed to establish household rules to govern us, and our child-home training is derived from this system. Just as we are a living organism it is only right for the life of us to live organized. This means having boundaries, being in our own bubble where no one can get into our sphere of influence. In today's society, we are faced with numerous problems that range from social, political, and cultural-that's called mass consciousness. There in those spheres of influence comes the tidal waves that influences us directly. Although, the pressures are great on the outside, if the foundation is laid properly then we'll be secured on the inside, while managing to stay afloat!"

"My dear, I hope that you are following my drift. The idea of the world today, as we thought we knew it, is rapidly changing; and as it is so we should not slumber nor sleep. It is imperative to have our priorities in place and all our ducks in a row. I ask how we can have a civilized discussion, without condemnation. What will help us to have a smoother day? Should we plan our meals ahead or have a standard amount for the month, so we aren't scrambling for lunch or dinner at the last minute? Do we set weekly meetings to devote time to discuss important matters, such as our troubles, struggles, plans and goals, finances, and childcare. To live a stable life is to build a structure holding firm our set of principles and ideas above our heads, while walking in the way of the foundation laid. Honey my eye is fixed on the pleasures of living a Godly life, a life in order and outside of chaos. Truly, I think about what rules or laws I have set for my daughter. How is she being disciplined? Behaviour wise, academically, creatively, spiritually, ethnically, and creatively. My incarceration has allowed me to know myself - worth, in addition to reconditioning my person. With a broader perspective all things are considered: The function of our marriage, raising children in a world that is converting towards secular ideas, and even our social functions. I mean it appears boring when one lives in a routine but, if you really think about it, our routine is the system in which we create all of life's functions. Nature laws prove to men how all things are bound by a certain set of rules and life's functions operate like an industrial machine designed to produce or manifest its idea."

"Any how if any of that makes sense as I did not prepare this letter nor create any drafts of it, I am simply saying what I've been aiming to do, is let's get our lives and family, in order to the degrees of having or creating a legacy that will surpass that of our children's children. Yes, I am thinking that far, so, with such thought we carefully, strategically make the wisest decisions today. If the ancients have done so, by passing on their wealth, their, rituals, traditions to their children unto this day, where we are now in a nation with unkempt values, teachings, principles, treasures, and order only to be carried by holidays were unfamiliar of, serving Gods while being unaware of it, and just being out of touch with who we are. How much more will our children be taken by the wall of variety if we were so easily fooled? Lite is full of blessings and I'm ready to live the life that's been promised to me–us and that's the life we customize to us! Babe Steps."

- Toussaint
April 26, 2015 (Song: Beyonce "Dance 4 U")

"HE WHO FINDS A WIFE FINDS A GOOD THING, AND OBTAINS FAVOR FROM THE LORD" -PROVERBS 18:22

"Dear Wife,

You are like a mother to me, moreover, you have been present in my life nursing me and comforting me in your bosom. Right off the back, I want to tell you how much I appreciate you; I want to tell you how much I care about you, I want to tell you how much I love you baby. I have learned so much during the course of our relationship. You have been a key part of my life, consequently, aiding me in my development, growth, and maturity as a man, father, and a husband. With the exception of our wonderful daughter, you've been remarkably a blessing to my life. Despite, the trial we both, in our respective place, face's I don't think I would have been inspired to make such the drastic changes I've made and still am making. I thank you for accepting me as I am, as God would. For I am just a sinner, but a winner. Honey I am often lonely without, especially since I've grown so accustomed to always having you around. Nevertheless, do I want to believe in this apparent reality, that I am far apart from you, it' aching my heart surely your heart grieves, and I'm prevented from providing you with the personal comfort a man is due to provide his lady and that thought alone can drive a sane man crazy. What am I to conclude now, if with you I was strongly protective of you, whereas now, my mind has run wild and I'm affected without, honestly on some occasions the adversary of my mind attempts to attack me with destructive thoughts against you. I now, realize the saying "you can't" teach an old dog new tricks", because the demons and their medium through their channels ``walks about like a roaring lion, seeking whom he may devour". (2 Peter 5) your loneliness concerns me, your needs as a woman concerns me, considering the facts that I am not there to fulfil your desires or meet your needs all concerns me. I wonder if you will faithfully without wavering endure these times".

"Don't I trust you? You may ask, strangely I do now more than a year ago. I think now I have learned to be more selfless trusting in the almighty. (Proverbs 3: 5-6) "Trust in the Lord with all your heart and lean not on your own understanding: in all ways acknowledge him, and he shall direct your paths". I've learned to let go and let God, many things and happenings are beyond my control. I now choose to have peace and I believe love outweighs everything, I choose to not worry any more, nevertheless, will I be on top of things, I just choose to not let my alter ego cause me to stumble. 'Therefore, I say to you, do not worry about your life, what you will eat; nor about the body, what you will. Put on life is more than food, and the body more than clothing". (Luke 12: 23-23) I trust that you love me deeply, and love is and always has been felt. "Love suffers long and is kind; love does not envy; love does not parade itself, is not puffed up; does not behave rudely, does not seek its own, is not provoked, thinks no evil; Does not rejoice in iniquity, but rejoices in truth." (1 Corinthians 13: 4-6) I wish I can at this very moment enjoy a gourmet dinner with you. I wish right now that I can be accompanied by you at the nearest theatre watching a horror film, but the reality is that I cannot at this moment because of the obstacle standing between us. It is inevitable that we will be reunited, and I'll be back in your arms, but will you wait until that time. I hate to hold you back from life's most joyous moments although a true companion and a rider, plus you are the type to remain true, making it just isn't you. Damn I too cannot believe this but this what comes with the life we live. Joy comes in the morning, so I hope you are able to maintain it through the nights, so I left you with a gift that will help you appreciate life. I hope you can forgive me for all the bullshit you've been through and forgive yourself in the process. You're doing great out there, and progress is still being made so far that matter where we win the war, a couple battles does not determine our outcome. The whole point of this letter is to join you in your emotions and let you know that life is not just tears in the challenging times, but joy in strength and victory, keep the faith in days like these, have peace in your heart and live".

"Happy Mother's Day Everyday"

- Toussaint
May 8, 2015

"My Queen,

I am always thinking of you, I mean always! I love you and I anticipate the glorious day that we will be reunited 'once-and-for-all'. I'm excited just at the thought alone, I even incorporated a ritual imagining being present with You and Faith every night. You would think that I've gone mad and come down with manic depression but nah, it actually gives me peace of mind. It draws good feelings and energy. Meanwhile, I am just here concentrating on how to release the power of God within me. Every day in every way I am becoming better and better. To become more fully who I am is my targeted objective; a godly Man, husband, and father, the reward of this is a harmonious Life."

"F.Y.I. I was terminated from participating in the General Educational Development Program (G.E.D program) for over two months now. One of the instructions informed me that I had been mistakenly approved for the so-called "scholarship" they had supposedly granted me. Therefore, I'm no longer at the moment active in the G.E.D. program. Obtaining the certificate of the G.E.D. is as important to me as much as it means to you, however, I'm not precluded from studying on my own terms with the material that I have in my possession. Whether in here or there even with my eventual business success. I will obtain it. Plus, in here there is a disadvantage of time as opposed to being out there in a classroom setting for two hours or more, plus, the teacher is helpful. Once restored back to my physical freedom. I intend on continuing my education, further, I plan to expand my business sense and skills by participating in various workshop seminars and even private sessions, perhaps getting an advisor or private tutor to educate me on economics, finances, business development, marketing, and sales. I definitely for all purposes desire to master the art of public speaking and writing, especially business plans."

"Since we're on the topic, to my amusement it so happens that fate led a young brother into my cell. He seems like a good kid coming from a good traditional family background. One day I heard the kid speaking and he made mention of the kind of work he does - which is a sales rep - then what really caught my interest was him stating the name of the company he worked for, "Fresh Meal Plans" formally known as "Florida Meals". He later stated he worked for Mark whom in which I know. I can recall the day me and him spoke regarding the need for the serviced meal plan, three years ago. Now, he is tapped into the North Florida region and has even expanded into the New York Market, got contracts with small private gyms, and Miami Dolphins, plus Mercedes is sponsoring the company by providing the vehicle for delivery. Bryan shared with me vital information and will continue to provide me with information pertinent to the business. Bryan also pledged that he would be willing to fly to the District of Columbia and help get the company started."

"Maintaining an industrious state of mind, I along with one of my cellmate 'Capt' have been operating and managing a store with a bakery division. With an initial start of a combined thirty items, we've been wheeling and dealing chips, pretzels, soups, cookies, coffee, envelopes, and batteries. We would do two items for three back, four for six, six for nine, and eight for twelve. We usually expect to get a return within four to five days. Although we have taken a few losses, yet we endure. Sometimes you get these sleezy slimy ugly individuals who want to think that they are smarter than God Himself and order up a tab and got moved - SMH (shaking my head)."

"Occasionally we get a cellmate who likes to think he has a hand in our belongings and steals whatever he will. It's funny because we always catch them, whether it's me or 'Capt', we are faced with this challenging situation like, 'what should we do'; kick his ass or tell the deputy, the alter is usually the best move. We eventually implemented a system to lower our risk. In addition to operating the storehouse we make cakes, every Monday, and get an average of $8 to $12 for it. The beauty is that we make the cake out of cookies."

"State cookies, before we were using our commissary cookie for personal consumption. We collect the cookies during dinner. Shaping out the bread we get for lunch and later dinner, in addition to that we added a fee to the items, leaving the borrowers the responsibility of paying us dinner cookies until they pay back. No one, unless if you in my room realizes that the cakes, we're making ours from the state cookies and not our own. Even if someone would question it, I'll iterate that they are paying for the labor. We do, however, to make it look good throw some M&M on top or some pop-tarts in between layers."

"What is a cold cake? Before I answer that, know that there are various kinds of cake one can produce in here: hot, cold, and ice. Before this unit lost its privileges of utilizing the microwave, which was recently restored to us after six months, everyone was accustomed to making hot cakes because of its simplicity. In commissary, we have the option of buying several flavors of cookies: lemon, vanilla, strawberry, chocolate, peanut butter, and jelly. Fourteen cookie cones in the Basils package. We'll take a rack of cookies soak it in some water then pour out the water and place the soaked rack of cookies in the microwave for under a minute, pulling it out and then it's ready to be eaten. The second version of this will be - simply scraping the cream from the cookies and placing the cream on top of the healed rack of cookies. Now there's a third version that follows the process of making the cold cake. I learned how to make the cold cake during the period I was erroneously released and then, consequently, transferred to another facility. I was offered a piece and was delighted, so I asked how I can make one personally."

"Obviously, around that time, I wasn't using state cookies. This is the process: first, you divide the four packs of cookies into two making it two groups of twenty-eight cookies. Then we'll scrape the cream off all fifty-six cookies and divide the cream into the cups: whipping the cream into an icing form by adding water and beating it with a spoon. With the cookies we'll divide them into two bags and crunch them up into cookie crumbs, then pour half of a cup of Wayer into both bags, massaging it like a silicone breast or stress ball (your breast is my stress ball) until the cookie crumbs form into a dough. The dough is then rolled out into a flat rectangular shape creating the cake layers in the circumference of our lunch trays."

"We use four leaves of bread as the very bottom layer placing it on the lunch tray; flattening the bread and glazing it with jelly and cream before placing one of the cookie-cake layers over it. Once the cookie-cake layers are down we'll cream up the layer and assort a chocolate fudge pop tart to it. Sometimes if we are making our famous, chocolate fudge peanut butter and vanilla cream cake, we'll make a fudge layer out of chocolate cookies placed directly on the bread layer assorting the part tart on the fudge layers, layer, later placing the vanilla layer over the fudge and pop-tart. Finally, we'll cream up the entire cake and sprinkle the crunched pack of M&M all over, and it's done, the cold cake. The ice cake being the most expensive is simply done by sticking the cold cake. The Ice cake being the most expensive is simply done by sticking the cold cake in a bag of ice and placing it in the sink of the cell."

"After five hours it is totally frozen and comes out tasting and looking like a caramel ice cream cake. Apart from tracking down guys who owe the storehouse and updating the books, the production of a cake or cakes are what my Mondays consist of. I even put my cellmates to work, one man whipping the cream the cream the other breaking down the cookies, and another molding and rolling the cake. I or 'Capt' just designed it. Our rooms be looking like a market and a cake factory at the same time, we've even developed names like "Cake Bosses" It's hilarious."

Your Husband

-Toussaint
May 28, 2015

"I Miss You"
"Without you, there's an empty place...
What is it to miss?
When you got my heart
When you are my counterpart
When you are essentially my better half...
What is it to miss?
When you are here in my heart
Look! I bear your kiss on my neck, to remind me that your lips are not far, Still, I can close my eyes and vision me next to you, as clear as day; intermingled under the blue of the sky.
Why, even with Stevie Wonder; Wonder's eyes do you shine as the morning Star does.
... sure, miss you and your beautiful smiling face

Life is a movie, and we are the stars, being viewed in 4-D in the ferment of Heaven
When the pictures enlarge, and our heavenly father is the director.
So you know we're guaranteed our award. Um, first and foremost I'd like to thank God because without Him there wouldn't be no me, there wouldn't be no you, and there wouldn't be no us (applaud)! I love you because you first loved me and I will always love you."

- Toussaint
September 11, 2015

———◆————◆————◆———

"Being apart from you is even harder than I thought it would be. I try to be logical and tell myself that it won't be forever, but that's not much comfort when I really need to touch you, kiss you, and love you. Sometimes I close my eyes and hold a picture of you in my mind and imagine all the things I'd say if I had you here. But no matter how beautiful the picture is, it will never compare to the real thing - looking into your eyes, whispering your name and kissing your lips, I miss you so much, and I can't wait for the day when I can stop holding on to a daydream and hold you in my arms again."

"To you my precious lover
From your sweetest joy!"

- Toussaint
September 12, 2015

"Hey My Love,

Just thinking of you as usual. I love you so very much - I want to give you the biggest hug ever and never let you go! Anyhow, I try to hold those images of you coming to see me this past Tuesday in my mind. Just like the image, though, it's a blur. I have had my first encounter with you in person. Damn, baby you are finer than ever. I see why I be stressing' although you're a faithful, honest, and loyal woman. I appreciate you so much and even though I may give off any indication of the opposite. It's a lie. Surely, I have been given the gift of having life, but it wasn't until I got with you, I started to live and not merely exist. Despite my current circumstances, I am so happy to have you by my side, so lucky to have you for a wife, you are such a worthy being. I admire you, I love your smile, it's so big revealing your full set of teeth, the shape of your lips, your nose, your eyes, the shape of your face, baby, you are such a work of art. May the glory be Yah!"

"For the glory that be in you, the sound of your voice, no matter the emotion: whether negative or positive - although I prefer when your positive-arouses me, it stimulates me. Still to this day from the first time holding the nine-hour extended conversations with you on the phone. You are an amazing woman talented and gifted, skilled, and creative, your aura blossoms, your soul is so magnetic. I am so drawn to you. Your eyes, my God those eyes are Angelic. it gives off my reflection. I will fight for you; I will die for you - the death of unrighteousness. Just to be right with you. You are a great fun-loving person, you shine the light of mine; your place no one can take, nor do I have any space in my heart ever to love this great."

"My soulmate you are, I truly cherish you. I said sorry once before for the hurt, pain, and damage I have knowingly and unknowingly cause, moving forward I will fight for your cause and not you. I want not to argue nor stone wall you - I may have been critical in the past - but now I'll ease off that. I will restrain from having or showing contempt against you. I won't judge you I'll just love you - build you up not tear you down, edify you nor destroy you you're so precious and fragile. I would hate for you to take my love away. I wait patiently on the day I come home to you so we can be in harmony."

"My Dear, peace be with you. I love you. 1 Corinthians 13 Love suffers long and is kind; love does not envy; love does not parade itself, is not puffed up; does not behave rudely, does not seek its own, is not provoked, thinks no evil; 6 does not rejoice in iniquity, but rejoices in the truth; bears all things, endures all things, love never fails, but whether there are prophecies, they will fail; whether there is knowledge, it will vanish away. For we know in part, and we prophesy in part. But when that which is perfect has come, then that which is in part will be done away. When I was a child, I spoke as a child, I understood as a child, I thought as a child; but when I became a man, I put away childish things, for now we see in the mirror, dimly, but then face to face. Now I know in part, but then I shall know just as I also am known. Is and now abides faith, hope, love, but the greatest of these is love".

Chapter 14:1 Pursue love, and desire spiritual gifts...

P.S "I will pursue your love and I desire our spiritual connection. What do you think about the concept of the logo for 'Capital Fresh Meal Plans'?"

- Toussaint
September 17, 2015 (Time 22:00)(Song Dedication: "Saving All My Love for You" by Whitney Houston)

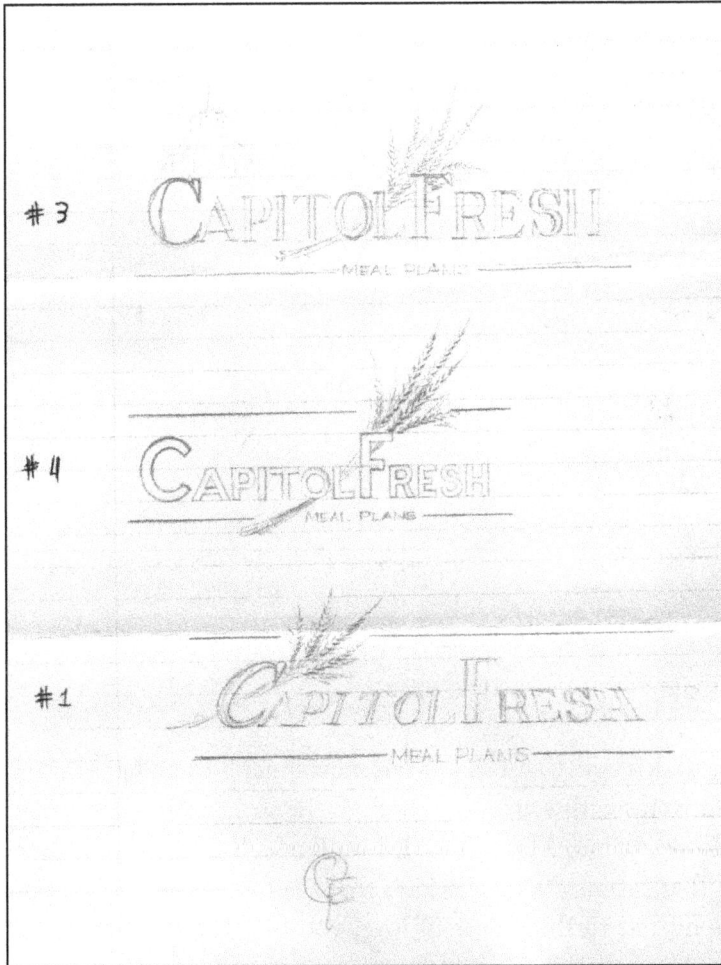

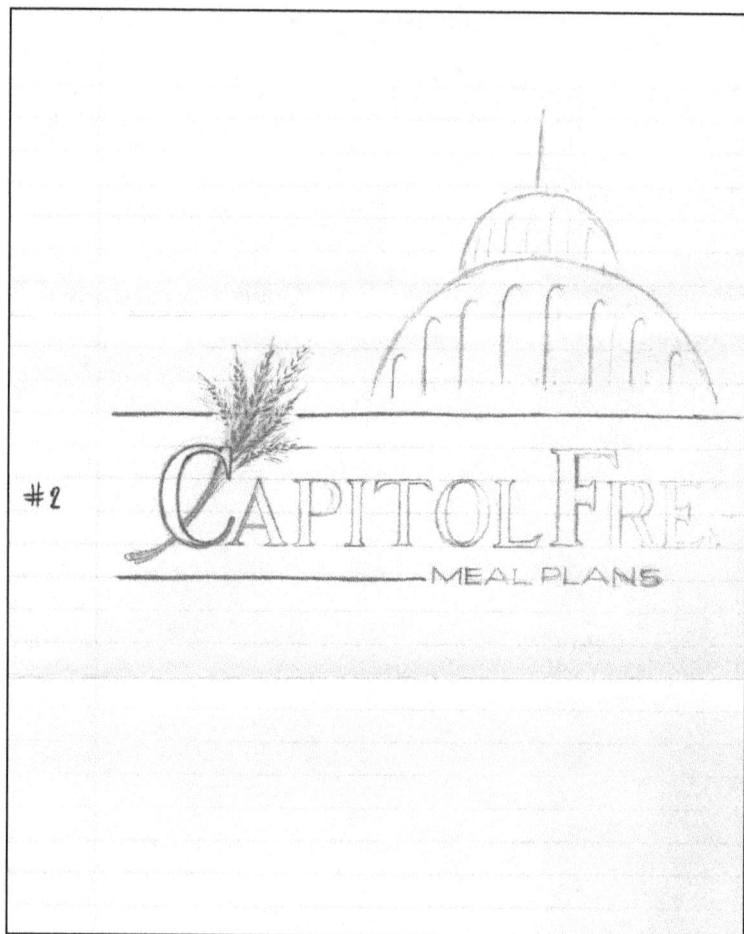

"My Lady,

Please understand that I share your most inner hurt and pain, also, I am in your world with you, going through the struggle and confusion with you. In past times Mami, sure 1, I built a wall tall and great, fortified in its foundation, None-the-less, that wall, you have collapsed, thus I surrendered to the power of love, you brought to me from up and above. Nevertheless, in our experiences of one another sharing each other's mind, body, and soul. I have shown yet still a bit of resistance. It has been predominantly the effects of past experiences going into, still further, my relationship with you. Straight up, you aren't accountable for my development my past - developed ideas and belief nor are you responsible for what many harm have been inflicted upon you growing up."

"What you are responsible for, now, moving forward is my newfound Love, my desire to improve myself as a man, my trust and knowledge of the Most High and that's just the results of meeting you but on your part, you are responsible as much as I am for nurturing that love, encouraging those improvements, and being proactive in your faith. The past is not to blame, when we are given every morning a new way to correct our ways and make changes. Therefore, on this day I choose to love you with a love so pure, on this day, I choose to correct my ways, attitude, mentality. The past is the past and I wish to not be stuck there, except we learn from it, tear down what we must and rebuild what we will."

"I forgive you baby and I carry in my heart no grudges, no hate, no strife, no resentment, against you and I try to make it like that with everyone for that matter, so forgive me if I reproach you of your sin or transgression, and I choose not to be critical of you in the aspect of the past, except it be for improvement, upbuilding, because you've cause my wall to collapse, so, it's only right now that you help me rebuild it up. I want you to talk with me baby, share with me your thoughts, ideas, troubles, and desires, share with me your anger and frustration, share with me your heart and its temptations."

"I am listening, and if you ever thought that I weren't or I gave off the notion that I wasn't, then forgive me because I want nothing more but to lay my head in your bosom and listen to your heart. Let's talk baby, let's talk babies and their process which they undergo when they are born - your reaction to patients; your relationship with your patients, how do you treat them? Do you listen, do you speak in a low soft tone, do you let them see when you're aggravated, stressed, or irritated? What goes through your head when these babies are being born, what in the divine and time are you doing there? Why are you? What's your purpose, besides the money, why are you there?"

"Let's talk 'Make-Up' baby, that MAC is no joke it's your brand all the way, but it sure gets expensive, oh well, I guess we gotta get our money right! Now, we are talking about personal finances, yeah that area could use some construction, it sure can be mind boggling trying to even put a finger on it. Don't lose hope though because I'll help you and lead you in the right direction, in seeking advice and wise counselors. On another note, we ought to teach that little child of ours everything she ain't getting from the 'public-fool system', she is a genius. I know it, I love her Mami! I desire to give you my undivided attention and not ignore you, if I evaluate myself, I must admit I have been guilty of that, now since we've been unwillingly apart from each other. I can see my shortcomings, which is cool because I'm able to recognize the areas I personally need improvement in. This is part of the breaking down and rebuilding process."

"So much more than ever do I seriously want to find balance in our lives, not to say that I have never been making desperate attempts at this equilibrium, peace, and harmony. I know we will make it, and we are making it, nothing is on pause, time has not stopped, we are proceeding through these circumstances thus learning from them, growing from them, and receiving the wisdom of life that elevates as in time. I will be with you for as long as my soul lives. Our day is coming baby where we shall travel to distinct parts of the world experiencing food, arts, and music of diverse cultures. With you I want to share life's joys, receive satisfaction and fulfilment. We share similar visions of success, a home we can call our own, in the similitude of that house we used to always pass by in the cut around the corner from my parent's house and like the house you sent me in the picture."

"We have the vision of operating our business, riding in style, living a quality upscale lifestyle, we share this vision together. We have in common the values of love, education, especially our child's education, honesty, and truth, we value being free exercising discretion, we value health, spirituality, these values we share bind us as a pair. Mami, you are so creative. Concentrate your energy on what you truly love. What could that be other then the Most High, Me and Faith. Personally, I think you have a beautiful mind full of ideas that have potential to be materialized. Right now, in your life, although there exist immediate challenges, you are in a perfect place. You must develop the courage to leap over the hurdles, go over the humps, and step out in faith - so that you can manage the obstacles before you; again, I am yours - so it is for us. Be not discouraged, Mami, be encouraged."

"What are your dreams, baby? If I took a good guess, I would say it's to own your own business or practice, but could that be all, that seems as if it is a small part of the whole dream..."

"I know that you've enjoyed taking photos of the Art of Modeling but I'm not sure if the reasoning behind that desire was wholly right, but you do shine and you are bright and no matter the field you're in you'll always be a model in it. My dreams are big - better yet they're grand; and you know what even if my dream was to make it in the Arts, Music, Acting, or anywhere in that industry, it just would not be complete without you. I am now understanding that dreams are made if we wake to it and begin to work in it."

"While writing to you at the table, I have your pictures out; the one where your hair is cut short and your rockin' the nose ring lookin' like the chocolate Monroe. Anyways, this guy - well guys, look over and ask me "is that your wife"? I answered 'yes' and then he says she's very pretty looks like a model, no kidding, just occurred after I wrote or assorted the Art of Modeling) but, yeah, she got what it takes to be a supermodel - if your attitude is adjusted to that, and you are a supermodel."

"Now look deep within yourself, truly, what is in your way right now, but a cloud of negative thoughts over-riding the many possibilities, stop and think about the times where you had an issue, such as, you had when you come from the DC/Maryland/Virginia (DMV) and your vehicle functions were acting up - you were really worked up. I guarantee if you were plugged into, I think an electrocardiogram (ECG), the equipment hospitals use to monitor the internal parts of the body, you'd notice your stress level increase, your blood pressure high etc. Nonetheless, you're no longer thinking with a sober mind but rather, as one who is drunk... thinks with madness, foolishness, you get my drift? Therefore, analyze the minor changes you need to make and do it. Confess your unhealthy habits and replace them with good ones. I encourage you to exercise for the sake of your well-being, meditate for a peace of mind, and diet (watch what you eat because your child is watching, plus to improve your quality of life and overall performance and energy."

"My beautiful lady, must another tell you how beautiful you are in order that you received validation? Do you seek validation from men? Are you so strung out on your flaws and insecurities that you fail to realize that the entire creation has flaws, are you not content with your portion of beauty? Must one flatter you with words to find means to their end? Are you looking outside for approval, do you feel the need to be accepted? Well baby by God you are beautiful and wonderfully made, thus having already been accepted, and already been approved. We not only have insecurities in the way we look but we develop social complexities in the way we communicate with others, the way we think and solve problems, and our economic status."

"So lets get past those insecurities by looking pass them and focus on the prize – pressing towards the foundation which has been already laid for us before my return home since I've been continuously praying on it, would like for us to be one minded having in perspective - our plans ideas, our goals, prioritizing them accordingly, I'm ready to take bold actions making intelligent decisions moving forward to attain all that we want for us. Our children and of course glorifying the Most High in the process. We're on a conquest baby! For social status, Economic Power, Political power, thus impacting the culture. What will we do, for happiness, we'll just simply search within. Until next time baby, Daddy Loves You."

P.S. You're the Best!

- Toussaint
September 24, 2015 (20:45) Song: "Listen to Your Heart" Roxette

———◆———

"Hey Princess-Queen,

I love you, how's that risk of yours? I'm trusting God that it heals up; Lord knows how I am going to need that hand to handle me once back in your presence! lol on a serious note what's the status with the overall process - how many more therapy sessions need you attend, what is the insurers talking about, any idea of a settlement?" Time to tell but don't be idle in staying on top of things, gotta stay on your job. Speaking of staying on your job I congratulate you on getting a raise a couple weeks back. I'm proud of you baby you are highly favored and are making significant progress - keep it up."

"On another note, if I may enquire, why haven't you shared with me the financial information I've been seeking such as the percentages of your salary that is being contributing your mutual fund account (and the properties expanding on the account), retirement Account (401K) and the other benefits health, dental, and vision. I make those reaver simply for my perusal in order that I may from within here aid you in organizing our finances. So please procrastinate not and get this information, thank you. While we're on the topic have you managed to be consistent with updating the budget tool system? I know you told me you decided to use the program Excel on the computer, was the budget tool on the website every dollar to complex?"

"With patience and perseverance baby things will run smoother. If we fail to plan than we plan to fail; and I know we both share an arousal of plans, ideas, and desires, and our own individual plans, ideas, and desires which regardless if it's yours or mines we can both have our share of it's pleasures, joy's and benefits for example I want to remove these tattoos from my face, you want in the near future to undergo surgical procedure to refigure your appearance. I'm with you baby; and you have my support, if you like it, I love it. For these reasons is why I exhort you to be financially oriented, thinking in terms of our immediate needs but more in terms of our future, our legacy, our inheritance. So, we are going to have to do a whole lot of savings, creating multiple streams of revenue to maximize our profits thus optimizing our income. You wanna look good next to me. I am about that, but I want for just as good and fat that ass is, I want for that bank account to be looking even better. I am cutting this short considering all that is written herein, and the other documents enclosed with this letter."

'I Love Your Soul the Real You!'

-Toussaint,
October 5, 2015 (21:35)

"Avoid Missteps That Make Credit Problems Worse"

"When people face out-of-control debt for the first time, it is easy to make mistakes. I have seen it over and over in my 15 years as a Florida county mediator. I've been involved in more than a thousand cases involving credit issues, and most of the time the defendants come to mediation having already nude serious mistakes, and thus are faced with poor choices. They also make poor choices in the mediations. (Unfortunately, mediators are not allowed to give advice). Fortunately, there are good guides to avoiding credit pitfalls. I recommend Robin Leonard's book "Credit Repair" (12th edition)."

"The following advice can help you avoid costly mistakes. Check your credit reports. Obtaining your credit a report is essential for repairing credit. Even if your credit is good, obtain your free annual report from any or all the national credit agencies: Experian, Equifax, and Trans-union. You can obtain it online annual creditreport.com or by phone. Look for errors; they can be corrected. You are also entitled to another free credit report within a year if you were denied credit, insurance, employment, or a government benefit. If an unfavorable action was taken related to your unemployment or insurance coverage, or if your credit account was terminated.

"Do not miss any court dates. Many who owe money simply ignore communications from debt collectors and end up being sued. If you are sued, you should appear on the date required. If you do not appear, the debt collector automatically wins, and judgement is entered against you. Once this happens, this information can appear on your credit report for up to 20 years. Also, your ways may be garnished. If you do appear, you may be able to negotiate favorable terms, or the judge may rule in your favor if the debt collector is unable to prove you owe money. Do not initiate payment after your legal responsibility has expired. Each state has its statute of limitations for debt. A creditor or debt collector has no legit right to collect a debt after the set period has expired (based on the date of your last payment). However, many debt collectors will try to collect; it is not illegal. If you make a mistake and make a payment in this situation, the statute of limitations clock begins again, and the debt collector then has a loyal right to the amount owed. Find out what the statute of limitations is in your state."

"Negotiate with creditors and debt collectors. If you have an old (but still legally binding) debt, you have bargaining power. You might offer, say 50 percent of the amount owed to be paid over 60 days. It is likely it will be accepted or that you will receive a counteroffer. You can also negotiate interest rates. If you agree to a monthly payment plan, ask that future interest charges be waived. Avoid debt-negotiation or debt settlement companies. Your fees will be too high. Negotiate terms directly with creditors and debt collectors. If you do decide to use credit counseling services, use an agency affiliated with the Consumer Credit Counseling Service (credit.org/CCCS/)."

-Toussaint,
October 5, 2015 (21:38)

"He who tills his land will have plenty of bread, but he who follows frivolity will have poverty enough" - Proverbs 28:19

"My Dear,

"I hope this letter finds you in good condition; to get directly to the point of the matter. I've grown increasingly concerned with both the well being of you and Ja's. Especially now since the issue which arises between you and your folk's this past Saturday evening (October 10, 2015). As a result, I am writing you this letter so I might give comfort to you by reminding you that you have the resources and strength within you to sort out any arising problem. Blessed be the God and Father of our Lord Yashua the Father of mercies and God of all comfort, who comforts us in all our tribulation, that we may be able to comfort those who are in any trouble, with the comfort with which we ourselves are comforted by God." (2 Corinthians 1: 3-4)

"Despite your husband's incarceration you are not alone, although it may seem that way; But know that there is a power working for us -within us. In this process of our separation, this prepares the way in the order that we may obtain Yah's promises and blessings. John 2:25 "And this is the promise that He has promised us - eternal life. For his blessing they are written in the book of Deuteronomy 28: 1-14"

✓ The kingdom of God is within you... (Luke 17:21)

✓ Do you not know that you are the temple of God and that the Spirit of God dwells in you? (1 Corinthians 3:16)

✓ For you are the temple of God - the living God as God has said:

"I will dwell in them and walk among the, I will be their God and thy shall be my people" (2 Corinthians 6:16; Leviticus 26:12)

"You're in quite the unique situation, in terms of your living condition, financial situation, and the balancing of being temporarily a 'single' devout mother and a busy hard-working professional. Hence, the obvious is assumed, your responsibilities have more than doubled, the pressure you're under seems intense, and perhaps your stress level is a bit above average. Moreover, let us hope the latter isn't the case, because you know as well as I know that stress is the number one leading cause of depression, diseases, and death. Therefore, we ought to be wise in formulating a stress prevention plan, relief programs for the pressure, and proceeding to develop a model system to manage in improving our lifestyle and the handling of our diverse responsibilities. I know - I know; it's challenging, but that's life."

"It was never said it would be easy, we learn over time great rewards are to be earned not given; (Enter by the narrow gate: for wide is the gate and broad is the way that leads to destruction and there are many who go by it. "Because narrow is the gate and difficult is the way which leads to life, and there are few who find it". (Matthew 7: 13-14) Plus, you're not in the most comfortable position, neither am I, but... you want to know the truth - the truth is that this is temporary; so, in the meantime we must learn to cope with our given circumstances and find balance therein."

"How do we attain balance? Well first, let's define what balance is: Balance is a state of equilibrium, an influence of force tending to produce equilibrium. Emotional stability, a harmonious arrangement or proportion of parts. Math, equality of symbolic quantities on each side of an account. The latter definition I like, however since we've defined balance let's illustrate how balance works, for example: Jenny has a five-year-old, Jenny works twelve hours a day for three days out of the week, therefore Jenny hires a babysitter to help with little Ja' Faith; consequently, Jenny's able to balance between work and looking after her well fair of her child. Furthermore, if however, the sitter is not duty-serving Ja, this, meeting mommy's expectation, you then get to ask yourself why. First, children are not born with a manual with the instructions on how to raise a child inscribed. Therefore, it is with time and firsthand experience we gain knowledge and understanding on raising them, hence, in our developing relationship with our children is how we can identify that they are all unique and incompatible with us, but opposites attract, anyways not to get beside the point. If you delegate certain tasks or duties to another you must set the standards in which you would like for the task and duties to be performed; you can not go assuming that everyone who has some emotional or monetary binding to serve you; do so at your best interest."

"If you do not desire to improve the conditions of your possessions no one else will. If no standard is set, then, no standard is followed again, if there is no system in place; there is dysfunction, so you lay the foundation and build on it, you need to present the guidelines your marvel on which you raise your child to the person you gave the responsibility to support her. If I hire you for a job, first, I would conduct an interview and make sure you're a suitable candidate, secondly, we'll have an orientation, so you comprehend who we are - the company, what we do, and what's required of you. Then put you through training that is where the test begins, by then you would have known our policies, rules, and standard operation; and a schedule would be given to you to follow."

"Living a well balance life means to organize and set order in your daily course of activities, and yes it's easy to expand on, but, highly technical and complex to implement, especially on your own because Daddy's not home, but it's not because Daddy doesn't love you or doesn't want to be Daddy. Daddy loves you and wants to be home. You are my counterpart and you've truly been balancing me out through these grim times. Otherwise, I would have sunken long ago. I appreciate you and I will tell you that a billion times, you've exercised great patience and strength throughout this process and I'm commanding you for that. As challenging these circumstances are, consider the greatness of life that is preparing you for. It's a test; prove yourself worthy of all the goodness that your heart and soul yearn for. Remember 'nothing worth having comes easy' and success isn't attained without having to crawl."

"You may feel pain, but those pains are really the labor pains for the birth of the things in your life! My Dear, do not become too comfortable living at your "mum's" house. It is under her rule, her regulations, and her standards that you are living in. In your current state, know therefore that it is a temporary abode but in the meantime you ought to be taking advantage of the opportunity of the space you've been allowed to occupy and gain leverage. Be grateful, have gratitude, dispose of a cheerful outlook because you got to be smooth at what you do, get past the past of your mother consequently you continue to relive these experiences and it only hinders you from moving forward. You're a grown woman, you've got plenty on your plate today that is shaping you for tomorrow. So, what she found you in countless ways be weary do not repeat learned mistakes in life. You share the misfortune of every little girl without her pops I cannot say I know how that feels, but rather I understand what is psychologically, mentally, emotionally done as a result of your past experiences."

- Toussaint
October 20, 2015

"To: My Wifey
From: Your Husband'

"Where'd I leave off... 'Oh' that's right! Ja'Faith - I was discussing how important it is important that she receives a balance of love and discipline, to guide her steps in order. Whereas now, there is a whole lot of love but a medium of discipline. Discipline isn't to be confused with harsh punishment; however, discipline is training expected to produce a specific character or pattern of behavior, this controlled behavior resulting from such training. Further, discipline is a state of order based on submission to rules and authority, moreover, punishment intended to correct or train. When you attended prep school you obtained the advantage over many of your peers, such as in the latter case of attending public school, you were disciplined at the first, academically and socially, in contrast to the latter where you weren't yet still academically advanced but socially regressive due to the change of environment".

"Is it uncommon to raise a child who has an innate goodness about them - as child; and later as a teenager in the absence of the parents' influence, having experienced more and seeing more of the world all of a sudden, changes their behavior. Why I think it's a highly common situation and most parents in America fear the course in which they're children may choose, especially with the wave of trends finding its way into the mainstream of America. We can't make the mistake of thinking we have time; the time is now. Like when gardens are fertile so is the mind, seeds must be deliberately sawn in order to provide the desired outcome of blooming roses and like fruits, nuts, oil, honey and all the earth has to offer. Through the process of time the garden is cultivated while simultaneously discounting the bad seeds planted by adversarial people, places, or things".

✓ For the children ought not to lay up for the parents, but the parents for the children... (2 Corinthians 12:14)

"In the case of our child, I'm not implying that she is some rebellious, disobedient, and defiant child. The message I am conveying is that most children regardless of their demographic aren't just born murders, thieves, and prostitutes; but given the circumstances they fall victim to a subtle system of social engineering, primary them up (the younger generation), through various forms of programming, consequently leading up to crooked paths of discord, also sorrow and pain, selfishness and degradation, ignorance and hatred, despair and unbelief, this a poisonous lifestyle. Nevertheless, Ja'Faith is a gift from God who is bright, affectionate, and empowered. However, like any gift, if you don't value it as at the first of receiving it, hence, it gets old, as a result, you lose interest in it. That happens! I felt it growing up...the loss of interest in me by my parents as I got older – perhaps, it is prevalent in the world. Therefore, regardless of my current circumstances, as long as I am alive. I will aid the little children of mine to live up to their fullest potential; this for me is purposeful". Recommendations and Procedures: In regard to our daughter, I'm asking that you: Reduce the number of hours she's allowed to watch television. During the times she is allowed to watch TV; include educational programs apart from her everyday episodes. To supplement for the hours of her not viewing the T; give her different activities like puzzles, build blocks-logos, and arts and crafts. Create a little workshop for her. Teach her to practise and exercise meditation with him, take out twenty to thirty minutes out of your day to spend in silence, also some soft music would help to stimulate the senses. Reading time, either she reads alone to herself, or someone read to her, third, she can have an audio tape player read to her".

"Additionally, I suggest you reduce the excess toys. Pick out a portion from the sum she favors most, and the rest will be donated as gifts to those less fortunate than her. Take her to a shelter where there are orphans, perhaps this can be before Christmas Eve. Further, teach Ja'Faith how to distinguish the hot from the cold water, so she's able to take a bath on her own. In terms of food, store dry foods in your room somewhere, perhaps in a large plastic container or a suitcase the container maybe ideal, to prevent insects from raiding the container makes sure once foods are open that they are immediately scaled with zip lock bags. If you find it necessary, get an economy fridge and station it in your room. (Remember when you were pregnant with Ja'Faith, and we were living at my parents' crib and how we found it extremely necessary to install the AC-portable AC Unit in the window. Also, perhaps the microwave in the kitchen is out of her reach how about buying one from a discount store at a reduced price and setting it up in a location in the house where she can reach it in addition to that you will have to of course instruct her how to operate it. Start preparing gourmet meals so all that is left is to heat it up plus prepare cold fresh gourmet meals and sandwiches, as snacks include in her diet fruit snacks, granola bars, ensure-drink etc. check out e-meals- they have some excellent ideas you share with you in terms of convenience of eating. If Ja'Faith is at home and you are working, why should you have to come home to a starving baby when you had the expectation of her being well. Teach her to fend for herself, program her to bathe, eat, and start heading for bed on schedule".

"I'm sure there is a method considering how advanced we are in technology today, place around her risk a watch program the settings in the device to alarm her at the appointed time, try having different tones for different occasions or perhaps there lies on application where the watch tasks "time to eat lunch", time to bathe". You get my drift... look into that. All of the recommendations I've mentioned are highly important and I hope you will make the effort in following suit. It's better for both you and her. I know it's not easy but don't let the enemy inside of you beat you out of being great, strong, and able".

"I Love You...
I bow down to the divine in you...
My Dear Wife..."

- Toussaint
October 30, 2015

"Hey Beautiful,

"How are you? I know you're sad I'm not around... but besides that you're better than ever and getting better by the day; I'm positive that you're able and willing to accept your fate in a positive light. Anyhow, enclosed with this letter is the summary of the budget sheet for the month of October. I hope you've been continuing in reading the book 'Total Money Over', I encourage you to do so, you have a strong mind don't get discouraged in doing good, because you are great and I don't say this in vain or to stroke your ego, I say this in observance of you, the fruit you bear."

"On a different note, I would like for you to read Jeremiah 10 lead the whole thing. It pertains to the pagan Holiday Christmas and Mick's Birthday is on the 13th of this month. I would like for you to send him a gift, if possible, nicely packaged of an Absolute 100 proof bottle of Vodka, that's his favorite. Along with that send him a coke bottle with it. Well in closing I love you."

Postcard: "Hope this isn't much to read... I love who you Truly are..."

-Toussaint,
November 5, 2015

"Fear is not your enemy. It is a compass pointing you to the areas where you need to grow" - Steve Pavlina

"You don't have to see the whole staircase, just take the first step" - Martin Luther King, Jr.

"Don't let what you cannot do interfere with what you can do" - John Wooden

"Do not wish to be anything but what you are and try to be that perfectly" - St. Francis De Sales

"If you really want something, you'll find a way. If you don't, you'll find an excuse" - J.E.T.

-Toussaint
November 7, 2015

◆

"The Fraction of You"

"My sweet, sweet, lady, my wife, my delight, I am torn apart at the thought of your being out of my sight. Could it be that I trust you not, or could it be that I love you so much it hurts, or is it fear; fear of losing you to a suitor more subtle more coming, and more charming than I? It is not you; it's me not being present with you, it's my fears of where the wrong idea can lead you - to a place the wolves could get you. I think you are unprepared, unaware, and not knowledgeable about the elements and spirits that be, but enough of what I think, look where it got me. O, I wish I were present to guide you on the uncharted path to battle the lions and beasts that jump in your way. You are me and I am around to let you go. The feeling is astronomical. I feel for us and if I let go of my better half, then I am left with a lonely dark soul. Oh, live your life, it is so much more than a bitter me awakening from the same old boring routine and living up to your dreams before you dream of me. Unpause the time and go after your desires. Be not deprived any longer. Take charge and be the woman you were called to be. Be an expert at your craft. Concentrating your energy. Whatever you do; do your best and be happy. Last, be sure to keep the faith and remain lovely. Thank you so much for being there I have never had a friend like you. You'll achieve much more if you do it for yourself but never forget charity and those you love."

Yours Truly,

-Toussaint
November 7, 2015

"No matter how many mistakes you make or how slow you progress, you are still way ahead of everyone who isn't trying" - Anthony Robbins

"I want to love you without clutching,
appreciate you without judging,
join you without invading,
invite you without demanding,
leave you without guilt,
criticize you without insulting.
If I can have the same from you,
then we can truly meet and enrich each
other" - Virginia Star

"The sexiest curve on your body is your smile. Flaunt It!"

- Toussaint
November 17, 2015

"Jenny,

What up Mami! I hope 'all is well' and I wish you peace, health, and prosperity. As for myself, I've been maintaining my inner self, keeping cool, calm, and collected. I would like to share with you some ideas pertaining to various subjects. According to the previous letter forwarded to you wholly regarding Faith, I thought of the content of programs she should view such as Educational Programs, National Geographic, Animal Planet, History, and Science. Also, there is this school I read about in the newspaper a while back I would like you to just simply look it up online and see what it's about. I hear it's supposed to be a school of Honor, Maury Elementary School. I'm not asking for you to change her school - I'm just asking that you at your discretion too look it up. How are you feeling mentally? I know life and its many responsibilities can be consuming causing fatigue, overwhelm, and stress but don't let negative thoughts predominate your mind be patient, expect salvation, and believe in the force that created our universe and its vast possibilities in which the power lays in you to manifest - you are a co-creator with the creative force that created you so continue to let your light shine. Walk in integrity with yourself, be great, be fearless, be the star that you are".

"My hope is that you are positively healthy, mind, body, and soul; therefore, the body needs different forms of Vitamin C, which is produced in the body and helps with pain and allergies. Be sure to check yours and Faith nutritional level and add more Vitamin C in your diet to minimize the risk of being sick and tired, it's a mind thing".

"In terms of saving for your upcoming procedure, I was thinking of the possibilities of your money growing on interest while it's in an account perhaps, a mutual fund, many market accounts, ETF (exchange-traded funds). I'm pretty sure that there is an account out there that you can utilize to put up that $500 a month which will compound on interest, I would recommend you call Dave Ramsey's Financial Group or a certified financial advisor and explain to than exactly what your plan is for as saving for a surgical procedure for three years setting aside $500 a month and you would want to be pointed in the right direction on how to maximize your savings instead of leaving it in the bank and depreciate".

"So those are my thoughts, I'm gone now... Be Well!"

"I Love the Real You... Your Soul!"

- Toussaint
November 17, 2015

———◆———

"What are you searching for?

Is it the answer to your many questions about yourself, life, love, destiny, and purpose?

Well, search not out of yourself for the absolute truth all lies within you... All our life we've been fooled but it is not too late for our cups to be made full of the Truth... Joy, Peace, Love, Happiness, fun, satisfaction, riches, honor, affection, fulfillment, and many more goodness of the Truth are within you. You believe that? Think it!"

- Toussaint
November 18, 2015

———◆———

"Dear Love,

I'm so happy to have heard from you; I Love you so very much I have great compassion for you and feel so very affectionate towards you. I'm excited about your love and appreciation for life which you have developed overtime through adversity and through your individual experiences at work dealing with the manifestation of creation born into your hands. It is most certainly a beautiful, magical, and wonderous.

creation, "there are two kinds of creation-linear and nonlinear, when we see linearly, we are seeing two-dimensionally, or 2D. Linear creation explains the past and predicts the future. When we see nonlinearly, we perceive our reality three-dimensionally. Because we experience life in three dimensions, or 3D, we think that everything we see is three-dimensional. The reality is most of us experience it in the 3D layered on top of the 2D, although we are not aware of it."

"What we see, track and compare is two-dimensional, and from the past. What we see, conjunctively and dream about, is contained in a world of all possibilities, making the future three-dimensional. Since we experience both as being in the present," we are seeing 3D on top of 2D," As you look at certain aspects you may see in a nonlinear 3D way. This nonlinear way is 3D, or it may be a higher dimension than 3D". For example, a painter might mix blue and green to get turquoise. If you had no experience with blue or green, only turquoise, how would you know the origin of turquoise?

Similarly, the second and third dimensions co-exist, so interwoven (like you and I are) into your reality that you cannot see them as separate and distinct dimensions". An Example of linear perception is looking in your past and tracing a line in your history that draws a direct connection between your high school, college experience, your first job, next job, first vacation etc. You can draw this line through time in a linear way, i.e., you attended one high school, not all of them, you attended one college not all that accepted you etc. If, however, you were to look at your future through the lens of time you would be looking in all directions at multiple outcomes, if not infinite possibilities".

"Imagine what life would be like if we didn't know how to use our arms or hands if they just hung limply at our sides. How limited and clumsy our daily lives would be, how much we would be missing, for no good reason at all! Yet it is even more so with our spirit. We may live, breathe, walk, and talk, but most of the time we do not use more than a fraction of our spiritual power that would make life feel infinitely more natural and more worth living. It is not that we are "bad" or wicked or anything like that. We are just spiritually clumsy; we are way out of balance because we usually see life from the view of the mouse - worrying endlessly about the terribly limited world at the tips of our whiskers. Wisdom and joy comes only from learning how to see a wider, much more wondrous world; and power comes only from the Spirit within. This is why most of us end up feeling weak, lifeless, weary to the bone; we drag ourselves around just trying to make it through each day, often pausing to I wonder whether the good times in life are worth all the effort and pain."

"Changing our vision is what this experience is about, and the change begins with a look at the two worlds we inhabit at the same time: The Outer World of Appearances, and the inner world of Spirit. From the world of appearances, life my look very different from one minute to the next; one person to the next, or one age of the world to the next; but from the "Big View" from the world of Spirit - there's only one process going on: We get born, we have good times and bad times, we experience a wide range of emotions such as desire, love, anger, and fear, we face various problems and challenges that make us feel good or bad about ourselves, we learn somethings and forever wonder about other things, and then we move on into the unknown. Life is truly just this one story, and it fits Joan of Arc as well as Adolf Hitler; primitive tribes come as well as Harvard professors. Whether we get from place to place on foot, or go-chart, or in a Ferrari; whether we carve our messages into a stone, or type them up on a computer; whether we live in causes, huts, or three-bedroom brick ranches, does it really change that basic spiritual Storyline? But here's a mystical secret: Each of us has the starring role in this Great Movie. We'll all heroes, adventurers, who have a lot of ups and downs, who may stumble and fall a million times - but we can become strong, wise, and free by the end. It's really a very beautiful story."

"The "outer" world appearance - what we usually call reality - is nothing more than a prop room. It contains everything that operates under the Law of Time. Think about it: No matter what we ever get or have, we will not be able to hold on to it for a while, but then the parts rust, the paint peels, the flesh sags, the heart stops, the Earthquakes; even the sun will eventually burn out. What time brings us; time takes away. It is all a part of the deal. But time itself is no more than a stage-prop to the "inner" world, the World of Spirit. There is a Great-Mystery going on here; a Great Natural Riddle which has lain deep in the mind of every human being ever born-including me and you. Because this mysterious spirit cannot be seen, heard, tasted, smelled, or touched, most of us let our curiosity slide as we grow up. Even though we're never satisfied in the outer world, we limit our attention to our mousy-busy-ness all our lives and try to believe that's all there is to reality. Society doesn't run too well on mysterious things, so the standard policy seems to be: if we don't understand it, it must not exist. Problem Solved. Baby, I am eager to have as many babies your body can produce and circumstance 'will' allow: In due time of course, I am looking forward to enjoying blissful moments, pleasure, happiness, peace, love, and joy with you and Ja. Indeed, lost times will and are being made up for - Exaltation soon comes, ours is rewarded and supported, and our strength is renewed. I do not know about you - maybe I do, but I am going forth even now putting all my efforts into developing as a parent and partner. Our daughter deserves us. We are setting up these pillars, putting up those walls, letting down our dome for the building of our temple, and stopping into the kingdom for Heaven is our home. I'm pretty positive that instead of us falling in Love again in which we have now it's time we rise up in love for the times of the fall is over, it's our time to rise up and above the cycles of divorces, desertion, single-parent households, poverty, government assistance, early childhood stress, juvenile delinquency, violence, and crime. We are being transformed, uplifted, and transfigured to be on the opposite end of the table, not saying we're better than everyone, it's by the grace of God these great things and happenings will occur in our lives in order that we serve the Most High with all our talent, treasures, time and possessions. We are headed straight to the top. We need not worry except we choose for the day that we shall come where we shall want for nothing."

"We will have our home, multiple streams of revenue in due process, right now let's enrich our faith, our love, find the happiness within ourselves with what we presently possess. So that we may have peace with even the things of the world later. Your letters always reach me in high spirits. I love you too, deeply love you and I am happy to know that you can feel my energy, 2,500 miles away. I too am in tune with your heart and feel the rhythm of your heart needing and wanting me close. Oh, how joyous would it be for you to wake in my arm, happy is he who finds your head resting on his chest. I am happy just at the thought of such warming, intimate, closeness. Yes, we are one and nothing can tear us apart. We will always be connected and bonded. You cannot wait for us to be reunited! Shit... I can because I have to be patient but am eager, enthusiastic about our reunion. Our dreams are coming true, we are slowly moving past those phases and I am going to love you with a pure love-unconditional Love, I am in support of you and your affairs, especially the issues of your heart. I will be by your side and behind you 'putting it in your life' lol. 'JK'-nah not really but that too, but not merely pleasure - but in confidence. I will not leave you my family on account of my foolish and unwise decisions, lest the Lord takes me on his time. I bow to the divine in us".

"On The Road to Rich's Thank the Lord..."

"Be persistent, be determined, be inspired, motivated, believe, imagine, dare to dream, dare to be bold! Take the risk, the lead of faith, the power is everything you do to be great! Regarding, monopolizing, creating streams of income, and the formation of business I have told you two ideas which are in fast growing billion-dollar industry: Diet and Fitness - Capitol Fresh Meal Plans and the Beauty Industry, namely hair. I would like to get started with both companies but realistically one is going to require undivided attention; Starting a business and operating its means to be married to it, committed, faithful and devoted to it. So, the one in which we choose we would have to marry me, you, and the business intimately together. I think it may be cheaper to start the hair selling company first, not only that it will cost less to operate, less challenging, less risky. In addition, we may witness higher profit margins. Capital FMP on the other hand would be a great service company and will be partially profitable in the long run, but it will take greater effort and more energy not to say less will be applied to the hair business. CFMP will be more challenging to start as far as cost of food rising-inflation, food poisoning, hiring a professional chart etc. It would just take more then two to three people to operate that business versus the hair where that can be operated by two of us initially. Therefore, the hair will be an ideal that will bring us to another point. The demand for hair is high, the industry is booming, the market is visible. Plus, it will open doors for wider opportunities."

"Starting of off, we will be selling directly to consumers online and off where targeted demographic are in the mmarketplace; eventually we will be able to establish several distribution enters - strategic relationship with salon owners creating contracts-called consignment to sell out of there shops, and down the line open our own salon, also I have a source for handbags - Louise V, Coach, Prada, and wholesales brand name shoes and heels. The hair business has plenty of room for growth. Not to mention selling accessories and make-up products online. Our first action plan would be to locate a manufacturer in one of the overseas countries - South Korea, Thailand, Singapore, Egypt, Mexico, Hong Kong, India, Peru, and Turkey. We must conduct a thorough research accumulating a database of names of persons and companies, contact numbers, and physical addresses as well as email addresses (wed addresses). Once that' done reach out to these companies enquire the brand, quality, and different styles of hair they sale, also enquire on the quantitative measure in which the hair is sold in addition to the minimum order sold and the cost of the select hair, quality, bond, style, color, and length."

"Finally, we would need material to package the hair such as the box and the plastic design. Find out the cost to ship the minimum order. Most importantly, because you assess each complaint you come in contact with check there 'Track Records and Road Reviews'. Learn all that you can about the industry in your spare time, don't sleep in on your off days. Treat this as a job, because it's your business although it's only an idea now, it will soon mature and become reality. Check various sources, llibrarians at the liberty to direct you to books on the industry, which may have listings of different factories overseas. Also check out AliBaba, as well as AliExpress check those websites out and see how they sell their products differently, I think AliBaba is wholesale buyers and AliExpress is discount retail buyers. I Love You, Awake from your Stupor and be Enlighted to the Infinite Possibilities you can do anything; you can grow rich, start a business, if you believe; remember as a woman and thinketh so is she... Think Rich, Think Business, Think Prosperity and speak it to existence, and act like you already have that wish you desired, imagine that..."

- Toussaint
November 21, 2015

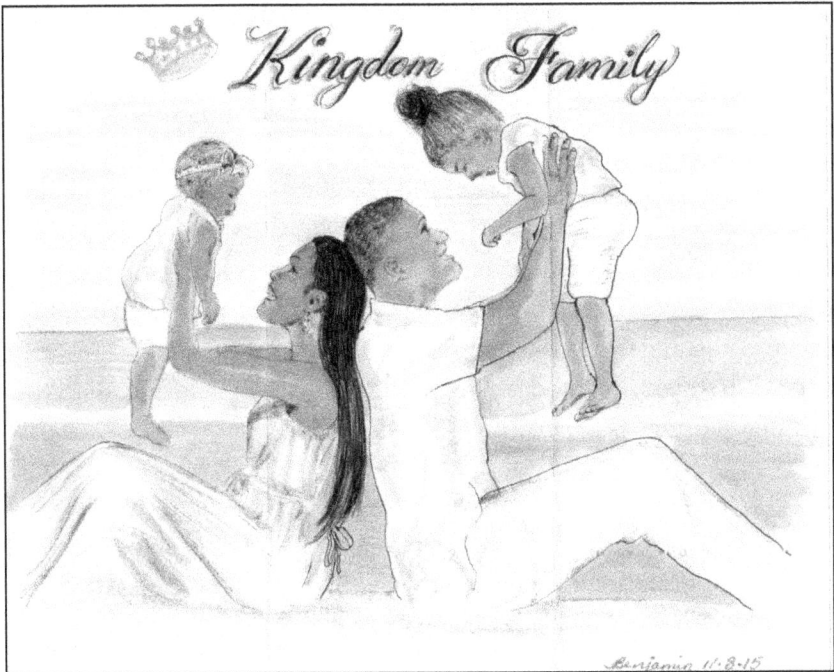

LET'S BUILD A HOUSE

"Houses and riches are an inheritance from fathers, but a prudent wife is from ABOVE" -Proverbs 19:14

"First, purchase a calling card then take the initiative to reach out to manufacturers overseas. Be mindful of the time when dealing with two different time zones. Therefore, do your homework - schedule an agreeable time to reach out to them (the Manufactures), during business hours. Also, communicate effectively with the person you'll be speaking with, be sure you speak clear and confident, projecting your voice so that you are heard and not misunderstood; plus be on point to have before you writing materials, so that you're prepared to record any useful information, e.g., the title/ name of the individual you speak with, information regarding the company's name, years of operation, any email and -or- physical addresses, website URL, the product, the cost etc. When you are speaking with a representative, pay close attention to his/ her tone and the questions to follow. More importantly, record that in which he/she is inquiring of you. By doing so you will improve your communication with the next individual from the next factory you speak with. Know promptly what to expect and what they want to hear."

"Respectfully, introduce yourself then briefly explain to the individual you are speaking with what you do, what's your plans, and exactly what's your interest. In Hollywood you have what is structured as the Producer, director, and actor or actress; God the Most High is the Producer, I am the director, and you're the actress. In this movie you are the Star so you gets to know your role and master the character you're playing; with that said the script goes a little something like this:

"I am a Self-Employed Hair Stylist operates a salon out of the garage of my home along with two other stylist' each renting out a chair from me; in addition to styling hair I also provide the hair that I dress my client, through different resources online. Although dissatisfied with the quality of the products and services received from online, nevertheless. We have managed to experience significant growth. However, we are planning to expand the business, relocating to a commercial space, hence, employing an additional stylist, to support the influx of customers occupying the shop at a time and finally to store larger quantities of hair we plan on purchasing in the near future provided we find a reliable source."

"Request specific information regarding the following:

1. The variety of hair being sold.
2. The quality of the hair and how it is processed.
3. Products life cycle (shelf life of the hair).
4. Volumes in which the hair is sold.
5. Any chart illustrating the Break down of prices for different textures, styles, and length of hair.
6. Request that you be sent different hair samples; offer to pay for shipping.
7. Do they offer any other materials, e.g., the weft, track, or piece, etc?
8. Do they have distribution centers here in the United States?

"Any additional information they may have to offer will help. And if they have any recommendations, beautiful!

Our objective is to cut out the intermediary and buy in bulk from the manufacturers. By "shopping" around making price comparisons and product evaluations we can draw the conclusion on which manufacturer to deal with. Don't think about the money on how we'll be able to acquire the goods, let's concern ourselves first with locating a potential partner and then the money will follow."

"That is our legacy... Peace & Love"

- Toussaint
December 3, 2015 (19:20)

CHAPTER

13

Chronicles of Love in Captivity

"Continuing letter from the last letter... we got pillows here, and I guess you can say the beds are a little more comfortable than the beds in the county. The problems with those beds, though, is that they look small as though they have been here for a long time. Our ancients could have possibly laid in one of these here beds coming in from the mothership. It's fucked up. Look like someone could have stabbed a hundred times on these beds. What's more astonishing to me, however, is the number of men I've encountered young and old, serving fifteen, twenty, hundred years and some, although after a hundred years you'll never see the light of day, but you got dudes with natural life sentences, moaning they'll be released from here in a black bow. A lot of these dudes have already been here for a while and others are just being transferred from other institutions. It's dangerous here, and even more dangerous at camps abroad. Could you imagine, being in one city or small community, with all the gangs, gangsters and thugs, killers, hustlers, pimps, drug lords, fraudsters (though mostly in the feds), rapists, and addicts. Oh, that's a fucked-up place to live. An Ol'G told me to avoid any problem, stay away from these G's - gays, gambling, and gangs. I'm far from the first, I don't gamble and never been one to be a follower, much less join a gang. Just the other day, I witnessed after breakfast at 4am, a dude got his skull cracked open with a lock. According to the post 'Big Shorty' was once about four hundred pounds solid muscle before he suffered from his injury to his lower back and knees; 'Big Shorty' used to knock out men out and rape them. Yeah, it truly goes down in the DM... It's a real live concrete jungle; a hostile and aggressive environment.

Oh, I almost forgot to mention, the sergeants and deputies here are quick to jump anybody and beat the living shit out of them. I stay to myself for the most part and stay out of their face, especially the women, they are the worst, they would make some shit up 'instigate it' to make sure you get jumped on. It sucks that I have to go through this and you going on without me present... yet remaining by my side. You've truly been my strength helping me through giving me something great to look forward to and I thank the Most High for that. I'm going to close the letter and start on another one related to what you have shared with me on the Real Estate tip: I admire your ambition, work, and you keeping the push forward, make the mistakes, learn from it, pick up and go hard... I love you...

P.S. El-ra-mandu may sound better of a name... what do you think? Sounds like it could be Historic or something...

- Toussaint
October 20th, 2015

—◆—

Hopewell Missionary Baptist Church/ Prison Ministry

"Each Christmas, Hopewell's Prison/ Jail Ministry and Prison Fellowship makes available a program called "Angel Tree Christmas". Wherein, Christmas gifts are purchased for children who parent are incarcerated. J.E.T. has requested that his child be included in this year's Angel Tree Christmas (Pompano Beach, Florida)".

- Toussaint
December 19, 2015

—◆—

"A New Year Brings the Opportunity of Growth and Expansion"

"Dear Beloved,

We spoke today, this Tuesday evening on January 5th, as always, I love to hear from you. FYI, I got the pictures as you know, and I thank you, they were well received. My dear, I must say, you are 'drop dead gorgeous". I gave myself a pat on the back for choosing you. I got a taste. The family is beautiful, it powerful to see you all gather together, that might explain why Grandma appears to be in tears of joy. Wow, that one picture with you by yourself, despite the blur vision of the individual coming in the door behind you; you look amazing, like some A list celebrity caught on the lenses of the paparazzi, lol. Goodness gracious, is it me or is Andy going Mike Jackson on us, what is he using... What is his secret, can I have some? Now I'm sounding like Wendy Williams, Nereah has sprouted, I remember seeing her several years back and she was no taller to my chest level, now she's damn near taller than you. And poop my hometown home girl Mondowee, blossoming into a young woman, good for her. Of course, I can't forget my little munchkin front and center shining bright like a jewel."

"I love that little lady of mine. She's a sweetheart, I anticipate holding her and squeezing her in my hands... Um, yeah, I had a moment there. Anyhow, I am excited to hear news of your involvement with the two committees you mentioned to me. I am proud of you, and like the fact that you noticed a problem and voiced your opinions of the issue thus gave your ideas of a solution. Regarding the idea of the software you have, your best is to search for a software program in your field to develop the system and implement it at work. You'll, of course, propagate the specification of the software function and have it designated accordingly. Then you can assess the system as you introduce it to the committee."

"Also, look at what other hospitals are doing, especially in your division, how are their integrities, technology with their daily operating routine. This information is publicity, online available to all, there's YouTube, trade organizations, government reports, from company's website, where you can gather invaluable information about new developments, especially, in technology, equipment/ devices, which are replacing older models, policies affecting the course of operation, and so on. It is also clever to be more involved in the Washington Adventist Corporations and not just the unit you work in. It benefits you to attend meetings, conferences, trade shows, seminars, regarding your field."

"In order that you may increase your learning in the medical and health field, inspire innovative ideas and be in a position of greater opportunities. You know if you read your daily newspaper which I think is the Washington Post - Money section and even the community, you will discover the many occurrences arising out of your industry. You'll find where it says events inside the money section, all sorts of opportunities to attend one or two of those events that will only boost your potential. Now, in regards to your slight confusion of which direction to go in terms of your career, I say do what you have a passion for, in other words, you want to take an opportunity that you might be interested in personally and professionally and that would tap into your skills and abilities. Continuing education in the future is always good. Remember, you are worthy of the abundance you desire. Change your attitude about your current circumstances and many doors will open for you. Allow the peace of mind to flow in, grace surrounds you, love you, adopt a new belief about money, reasoning, yourself and be constantly empowered my dear, this too shall pass. I Love You to Life!"

- Toussaint,
January 6, 2016

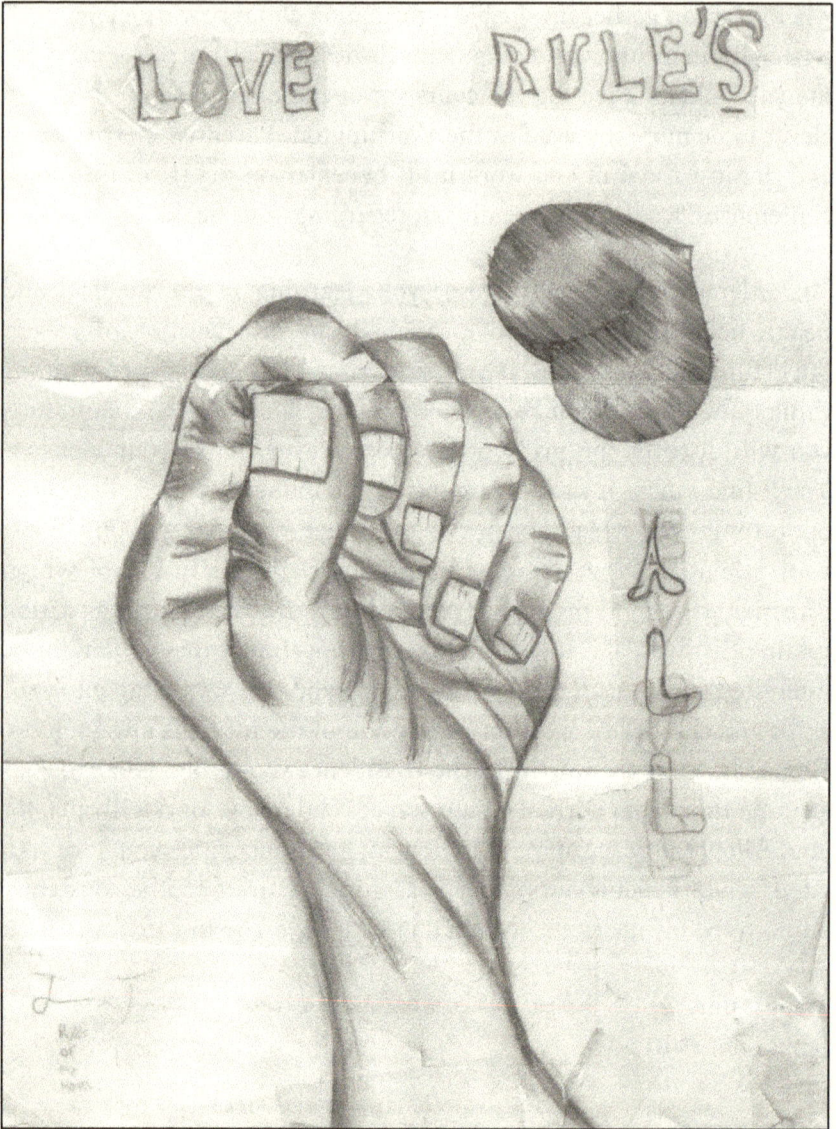

"When you have sufficiently purified your charter, controlled your senses, developed your reason, and unfold your intuition you are always ready to meet what comes and to meet it alright. You need not fear the future. Time is on your side, for you have stopped adding bad Karma to your account and every fresh year adds good karma instead. And even where you must still bear the workings of the old adverse karma, you will still remain serene because you understand with epictetus that "There is only one thing for which God has sent me into the world, and that is to perfect my nature in all sorts of virtue or strength; and there is nothing that I cannot use for that purpose. "You know that each experience which comes to you is what you most need at the time, even though it is what you like least. You need it because it is in part nothing else than your own past thinking, feeling, and coming back to confront you to enable you to see and study their results in a plain, concrete, unmistakable form. You make use of every situation to help your ultimate aims, even though it may hinder your immediate ones. Such serenity in the face of adversity must not be mistaken for supine fatalism or a lethargic acceptance of every unwanted event as God's will. For although, you will seek to understand why it has happened to you and master the lesson behind it, you will also seek to master the event itself and not be content to endure it helplessly. Thus, when all happenings become serviceable to you and when you know that your own reaction to them will be dictated by wisdom and virtue, the future can no more frighten you than the present can intimidate you. You cannot go assuming whatever happens, for you know too, whether it be triumph or joy, the experience will leave you better, wiser, and stronger than it found you, more prepared for the next one to come. The philosophic student knows that he or she is here to face, understand, and master precisely those events, conditions, and situations, which others wish to flee and evade, that to make a detour around life's obstacles and to escape meeting its problems is, in the end, unprofitable. Such a student knows that wisdom must arise out of the fullness and not out of the poverty of experience and that it is no use non-cooperatively shirking the world's struggle, for it is largely through such struggle that one can bring forth his or her own latent resources. Philosophy does not refuse to face life, however tragic or however frightful it may be, and uses such experiences to profit its own higher purpose."

'Love, Your Soulmate'

- Toussaint
January 13, 2016 (21:45)

———————◆———————

"Discovering What It Cost to Raise a Child"

"Doesn't Mark Zuckerburg know how expensive it is to raise kids? In December, the Facebook founder and his wife honored the birth of their daughter by announcing a momentous philanthropic gift. Zuckerberg and his wife, Priscilla Chan Zuckerberg, said that over the rest of their lifetimes, they would donate to charity 99 percent of their stock holdings in Facebook, now worth about $45 billion. Of course, the Silicon Valley billionaire couple is not like the rest of us income-wise. But they are like most any mom and dad when it comes to facing child-rearing bills for the first time. The expenses start with diapers, formula, childcare, baby furnishings, and other gear and seemingly doesn't end until the young one lands a full-time job. If you're lucky. That is a lot to jam into anyone is walready squeezed household budget. This raises a question that many now parents probably ponder at one time or another: How much does it cost to raise a child? $245,340, that's the amount on average a middle-income family can expect to spend over 18 years on a child born in 2013."

""The United States Department of Agriculture (USDA) is in charge of crunching those numbers, and here's the latest benchmark figure: $245,340. That is the amount an average middle-income family can expect to spend over 18 years on a child born in 2013, according to the department's "Cost of Raising a Child" report. The report showed child-raising costs, which reflect food, housing, childcare, education, and other expenses, were up 1.8 percent from 2012. Costs associated with pregnancy or expenses incurred after age 18, such as higher education, are not included. When adjusted for inflation, the report said, the cost of raising a child climb to about $305,000. Child-raising costs have risen faster than inflation since the government report was first drafted in 1960. Back then, a middle-income family could have figured on spending about $25,000 to raise a child from birth to age 18. That would amount to about $200,000 today's dollars. The next USDA report on child expenditures is due out next spring, and even the mild inflation we've been experiencing lately will ratchet up the numbers again. For middle-income families with children, housing is the single biggest expense, averaging 30 percent of the total cost. It was followed by childcare, education, and food. In addition, healthcare spending on children has gone through therefore when compared to 50 years ago. These expenses were lower in the Urban South and highest in the urban Northeast, according to the USDA. Not surprisingly, wealthier families tend to spend more on child-rearing $407, $820 more spending for households earning more than $106,820. The USDA has created a cost of raising a child calculator to help you zero in on your number. The department has other helpful child-rearing resources. Finally, here are two pieces of financial advice for new parents, the Zuckerbergs included: 'Don't try to keep up with the Jones by showing your little ones everything their hearts desire. And start socking away money in a tax-friendly account to pay for the college education that could be even more ridiculously priced eighteen years from now. I like for my woman to be sharp and on her game in all aspects of life..."

"I like for my women to run things and I just call the shots, but even then, I require her to be intuitive in making wise decisions on her own, keeping in mind the object of our legacy."

One Love,

Your One and Only SoulMate

- Toussaint
January 14, 2016 (Time 16:30)

"Progress Makes Perfect"

"Beloved,

I love you, I long to be with you, and I will be seeing you soon, very soon! In this letter, I will be sharing with you some information regarding your comfortability at work, research objectives in terms of JET EXTENSIONS, and personal information regarding my transition from here in the County to the state penitentiary. Since we are at the end of this road, I am putting forth rigorous effort to organize and set in order our plans to follow once I am set free - wait a minute, I am already free. However, in the event of me being transferred to prison, there is a visitation form that must be filled out to allow the listed individuals access to visit me at the prison. The registration for visitation form can be found online."

"At the moment I am county sentenced to three hundred sixty-four days, while at the same time serving a year on probation. This is for conditional reasons that may occur to be imperceptible to you. However, this is only up until I am called to return to court to sit in on a deposition because although I am sentenced my co-defendant may be going to trial. So, after the deposition is done, I will receive my original sentence of three years and five years probation which will be mitigated with the credited time I have in now and serving towards the five years probation. Hope I didn't lose, if I did, do not weary yourself in attempting to perceive it, but at my mark will you know to proceed with the visitation form online, for now, I am just preparing your mind. Next, once I am due to be transferred to prison, I won't know which prison they are going to be sending me, but to prevent from being sent to those four prisons in the most northern region of Florida. I'm thinking I should write classification, which are the administrators at South Florida Reception Center, a place where all inmates are taken from West Palm Beach, down to Miami and are sent to be processed before being transported to their designated facility. What I will write to them will state that my parents are not in the best condition, consequently, they won't be able to drive the distance to those facilities. Hopefully, I will be transferred to one of the private facilities that are better than the state-operated facilities and are closer to my people. In addition to that most of the state prisons don't have trade programs, ie, Automotive, Barber, and Electric."

"You can expect me to be sharing some research objectives. Do what you can, and I believe you can do the impossible. Don't be afraid to take risks in business, let go of the fear of failure, take a leap of faith, and paint a moral picture of manifesting our dreams, they are unfolding. We must perform every function in the company until we can afford to hire people better than us. Together we are building u, and the process must begin first inside then out, we have to be proven professionals ready to take on such great endeavors such master workmanship. We will get there and because we don't have the resources of the big companies, we have to be very creative in our Brand - Building Approach: Which includes, Community Events, Social Media Campaigns, brand ambassadors, and relationships with influential mixologists. Right now, we're in phase one and that phase consists of mainly research; learning everything we can about the Hair Extension Industry and our competitors, before we implement our first sale, we'll be experts at this".

Potential Brand Name Ideas for Hair Company

- CHASTITY EXTENSIONS
- CHASTE EXTENSIONS
- ROYAL EXTENSIONS
- CROWN EXTENSIONS
- ELEGANT EXTENSIONS
- ELOQUENT EXTENSIONS
- GLORY EXTENSIONS
- AURORA EXTENSIONS (goddess of dawn in Roman mythology)
- SIRIUS EXTENSIONS (A star in Canis Major, the brightest star in the sky)
- EOS EXTENSIONS (goddess of the dawn in Greek Mythology)
- GENUINE EXTENSIONS
- CROWN OF GLORY EXTENSIONS
- CROWN GLORY EXTENSIONS
- ROYAL CHASTE EXTENSIONS
- SUPREME GLORY EXTENSIONS
- HAIRDAZLE EXTENSIONS
- JET HAIR

"Sirius (the Mighty Star) a prominent object in the skies in the early part of the Solar year from January to April"

"We will organize as we go, manage as we go, and expand as we grow"

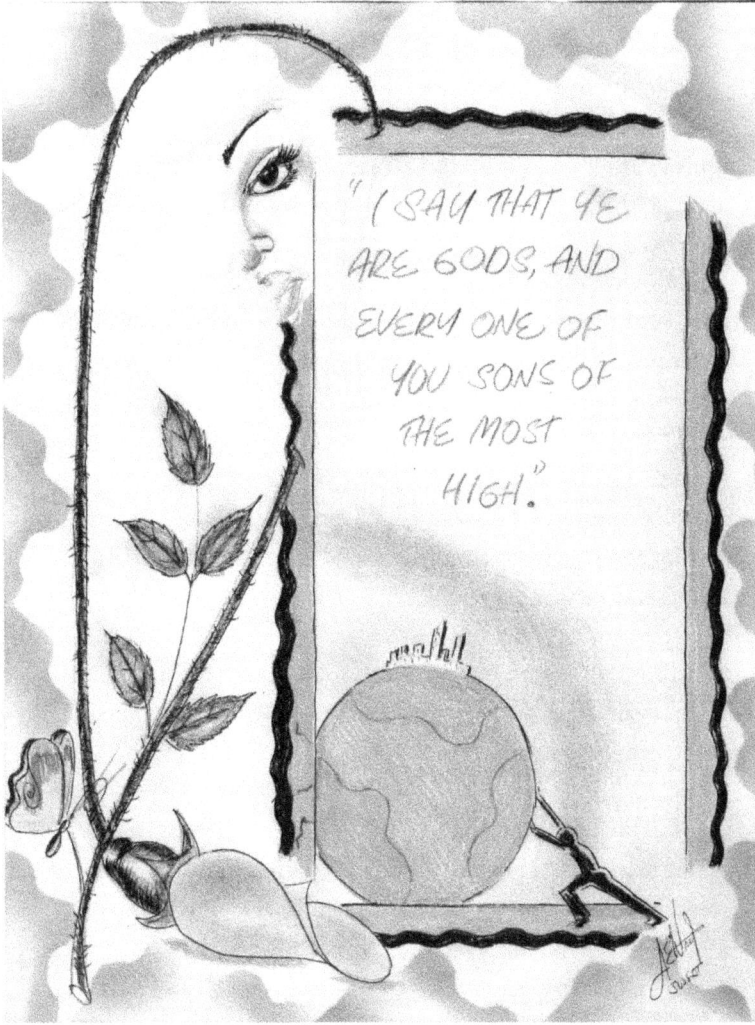

Research Objectives

✓ Make note and research premium hair options that are currently available within your local region (typically 10 - 20-mile radius)

✓ Visit luxury hair retail boutiques, beauty supply stores, free-standing booths in the Malls and or Flea Markets, etc. Describe the area of the store location.

✓ Conduct price comparisons, note styles, the different textures, length of both extensions and closures. Pay attention to the quality and style of packaging. Note the accepted payment methods.

✓ Inquire about bulk purchase prices, bundle deals, and discounts. Observe their customer service approach. Review your shopping experience.

✓ Many retailers may have websites to which they direct their customers, therefore check out their online store as well as going in personally because there can be slight distractions in prices and deals.

✓ Urban Salons in the area are any of them selling hair or any additional items other than offering the saviors of hairstyling (for example handbags, footwear, etc)".

✓ To add assets the company, invest in a salon, hair product, hair retail boutique, or even hair (hair care) export/ import company and hair manufacturing company.

✓ Target Market: Hair Salons, Nail Salons, Hair Shows, Beauty Pageants, Fashion Shows, Anything Woman's Boutique, Gentlemen's Clubs, Night Clubs, social events, colleges, sorority groups, malls, and shopping malls.

✓ Donate Free hair and luxury extensions to making units for victims of hair loss due to cancer. Create jobs and give back to the community.

- Toussaint
January 14, 2016 (22:00)

"Eskimo Feelings"

"What am I passionate about? That is a question one usually would ask when attempting to define his/her passion. To answer my own question of what I am enthusiastic about, I am glad to say I am enthusiastic about learning, and I love to read. When I was growing up, I wasn't too enthusiastic about learning; I do not know, it just never amused me, at first. With the feelings of an "inadequate mental capacity", I found myself too often discouraged from performing well in academics. Then something great occurred, after becoming accustomed to being called dumb by friends and close relatives or even an imbecile by my fourth-grade teacher, all but fueled my tank to thus be driven by a life of excellence. With this neo-ambition of mine, I knew, that only I alone could rid this hopeless expression of literacy I possessed; therefore, eager to do so I began reading as much literature as I could varying from Greek philosophers to Shakespeare, science, to mythology. As a result, more encouraged now than ever I plan on continuing my education thus acquiring useful skills and advancing my degree of knowledge, wisdom, and understanding."

- Toussaint
January 17, 2016

"What's Good in My Life"

"Life is full of mysteries, discoveries, and changes; life like any other exciting story, is bound to have painful and scary parts, boring and depressing parts, but it's a brilliant story, and it's up to us how it will turn out in the end. Therefore, with that being said, I take it upon myself to acknowledge what is genuinely good in my life. Despite being incarcerated, I've found it to be rewarding, I have made quite the discovery of myself and thus have come to terms with the low of my being. This journey of mine has led me to many truths and has brought my life and purpose into perspective. This discovery of self is great in my life because I am more clear now about my values and principles. As a result, I've learned what my purpose is ideally at least. What's great in my life is peace of mind, calmness of spirit, and control of self."

"The same power which has brought you so far will surely carry you through the next phase of your life. You must trust it and abandon anxieties, as a passenger in a railroad train should abandon her bag by putting it down on the floor and letting the train carry it. The bag represents personal attempts to plan, arrange, and mold the future in a spirit of desire and attachment. This is like insisting on bearing the bag's weight oneself. The train represents the highest self to which you should surrender that future. Live in inner peace, free from anticipations, desires, cares, and worries.

- LOVE
- BEAUTY
- HARMONY

When you can forgive God all the anguish of your past calamities and when you can forgive other men and women for the wrongs they have done you; you will come to inward peace. For this is what your ego cannot do."

- Toussaint
January 17, 2016

◆

"Sometimes I go about pitying myself and all the time I am being carried on great winds across the sky" - Ojibwa

"If you focus your attention on how bad your life is going all the things that are wrong, dumpy, unfair, sad, and hopeless - you'll eventually get fried like the ant. All that negative stuff will just get louder and louder for some of us, focusing attention on the bad stuff becomes a habit and, after a while, negativity is all we can experience."

"Focusing your attention on the good things in your life, however, turns up the volume on them too. If you can make that a habit, your life will seem better, and the world will feel like a better place to live too. Sometimes, the way we use our attention is the only thing we can control. Focusing on what's right will not fix the difficult parts of your life. But doing so will help give you a good attitude about yourself and your life. And that's the absolute best frame of mind to be in while working on your problems".

- Toussaint
January 20, 2016

"How to Make Every Minute of Your Life Meaningful"

"There's an old saying, "Time waits for no man", I once heard it quoted by the rap artist Young Jeezy in a composition. Thereby, that being the absolute truth, it is that very reason, I strive to make every minute of my life meaningful and nothing or no one is holding me back, now will they. Currently, some of the activities I'm engaged in making every minute of my life meaningful are the following: studying to take the G.E.D (general education test), "I'm going to pass", and not only is it to appease my own sense of confidence but it will be a milestone I've reached, as I aim to set the standard high in my father's house whom has no formal education. Furthermore, participating in the life skill program and adhering to the information provided by the guest speakers has been significantly meaningful, as I often pass on the useful information I received. Moreover, I've developed the habit of noting my ideas and goals, drawing out plans, and formulating strategies to achieve them, thus with that I constantly motivate my peers to do the same."

"The past five years of my life have been meaningful despite my current circumstances, which I still consider meaningful. One of the events that had been primarily meaningful was my marriage to my beautiful, strong, and intelligent wife, Jenny. In addition to that she gave birth to my sweet little munchkin' Faith, which meant that I would be a father and responsible for supporting a family of my own. Also, I made radical changes in the areas of my health where I chose to eat clean and exercise regularly, consequently influencing my wife, my friends, and others who were interested in joining the club. Charity is a virtue and it is of great value and importance to me; in retrospect, I recall times I've either lent money to my friends and relatives to pay a bill or something of that nature or I've given money to strangers to support their cause, and to non-profits such as the Make A Wish Foundation. Further, I've always kept myself available for when my help is needed whether it was, helping a friend move, assisting my father with his handy work around the house, helping my younger sister with her homework, projects, and or attending an event at her school. I would typically be the one everyone calls when they need something - anything. Realizing my purpose, I recognize in retrospect the need for improvement to make my life more meaningful. How am I going to make my future more meaningful? Well, to make my future move meaningful. I will devote more time to a desired path of service perhaps joining a non-profit organization or starting one of my own that'll be dedicated to underprivileged boys and girls, providing them with the resources that will guide them to a new mode of life. Also, I will do more in tithing 10% of my income to a foundation dedicated to the poor and suffering. Furthermore, achieving a higher level of education, being the best father and husband I can be, and creating jobs in our nation here and abroad to make the future more meaningful".

- Toussaint
February 7, 2016

"Hey,

Gorgeous, thanks for the photos, it means a lot to me; you mean a lot to me; not seeing you on a regular basis as I once. It was tough, I admit. So, to get an up-to-date picture of you, every so often, helps, it reminds me that you're still here rockin' with the man. What's amazing is how even though the pictures you sent are not sexually explicit, I get sexually aroused, Wow! You've really left your mark on me. And my God, that smile, those teeth of yours are seemingly almost perfect. I love to see you smile. My annoying cellmate seems to agree. Unfortunately, though, you'll have to meet with one of that evil dentist who's going to extract one of your precious stones, but it's all good - because we can fix it, nevertheless, you will still continue to be glorious without it. You know, I get mesmerized staring into those eyes of yours. It's like staring into the wonders of the heavens. But anyways that jacket you're rockin' in the photo is kickin' ass. Yeah, the days are ahead of us -isn't it - where I'll be home soon and we'll be reunited, aren't you excited baby? I know I am for sure... I am humbly excited. I'm anticipating this release as much as I believe to think you are, and lady... I tell you; I just can't wait to get you in my arms again. Your loyalty and fidelity mean everything to me. You'll always have my love, my utmost respect and regards for you."

Love You"

-Toussaint,
March 21, 2016 (Song Dedication: J. Cole "Love Yours")

———◆———

"My Fair Lady,

Good evening, as the Sun sets into the western hemisphere, on this good old 'Easter Day'. My thoughts... Unfailingly, how set on writing you. From the great distance we are apart, though you are near and dear to my heart, my probing... can't help but wonder where you are, the state of your condition and Ja'Faith welfare, and the engagements of your affairs. Moreover, my belief is that you are safe and sound, my hope is that you are making health choices, and my wish is that you're conserving yourself for me... faithfully. During the past two years of us being apart, you've copiously expressed your sentiments to me whether over the phone or in writing. Such... were admittingly worrisome; in fact, greatly sensitive to the dire cries of loneliness, boredom, and the protest of not having any friends, to the evidence of your emotions being repressed, sexual deprivation and the inherent strain on finances... all has been too alarming. Having drawn to my distressed mind the vulnerable position you're veritably placed in. Made me uneasy, because I perceived that you were experiencing, unbeknownst to your temporary defeat and feelings of desperation where you will naturally grow resistant towards and be disposed to a multiplicity of illusions offering you "solace".

"The battle I undertake of casting out the doubts from my mind, is a parallax one, it is not unusual for thoughts of infidelity to make my thoughts, occasion to plague my heart... It is like an incurable disease which can only be managed; but one day manages to kill you. Such wonton thoughts ought to be erased from my mind, but who am I to be deserving of such trust such loyalty. It would be my delight, but who are you to be able to endure such a plight with dignity and honor. Surely, you will be counted virtuous if innocent and if quality may heaven spare the rod for what is done, is done at odds. Yet have I have no just cause of being a jealous husband, understanding the nature of the circumstances, living with the thought of another man undoing and reshaping my doings which at thought was only fit for me? No, the hell with such thought, lost I was a conformist to some medieval or extreme lifestyle (who we have an understanding) and monogamy is ignored, and polygamy is practiced then I would in no doubt be in acceptance of my role. Do I sound a little selfish?"

"Is sharing reality carrying, perhaps there can be some spiritual bearing to this. Sense this is far from the case I am face with the hopes and expectation of your vow to uphold your duties and obligations to me as your husband and father of your child, and although weary of my circumstances preventing me from holding up my end of the bargain, I question whether I even deserve your love and fidelity".

"Where I find myself sitting isn't in the most honorable seat of government or society period. I am not here because I am a patriot and for fighting in the cause of my country and for the rights of my people. I have been taken in as a prisoner of war or political prisoner.

Instead, I am in a contemptible position, locked up as a criminal. It is shameful, and wasteful to even be in such a place for such a cause with such a child and her mother. It is embarrassing for me, and you don't deserve this neither does our child, and as much as this has set us back in my places, you need not worry of ever going through this again. I would rather let you walk than put you through such a plight. Though my cause for being here is not particularly honorable, I am sorry, and you may agree it has saved our marriage from falling apart. And I am grateful for that. I have learned much through this process of time and too have I developed much personally. With you by my side you have helped get me through from the day I realized I love you my life has changed for the better and I believe this process is a part of the better. You have helped me to mature, and you have been the spark in my life to keep me going. I thank you and appreciate your being a part of my life. All Hail the Queen Jenny"!

'Happy Easter' for what it means to you... bunnies don't lay eggs!"

- Toussaint,
March 27, 2016

◆

"NCLEX ACADEMY - An online learning center preparing you to pass the State Board and/or (GED ACADEMY)

"Instead of individuals being subject to one location (classroom setting) they will have unlimited access to the site's virtual learning center, so long as their "members" and the clock on their account haven't run out. Turn by the traditional classroom setting into a virtual learning center does away with the concerns of the classroom not having available space also, individuals can have conflicting schedules; from where they are anytime their own review course. They can study at their own pace. Like the GED TABE Test which is an assessment test design to determine what you know. You too can provide a series of testing software to monitor their progress. That will insure they've improved in areas where they're weak and ensure that they've retained the information (e.g. Entry Level Test, Practice Test, and Official Practice Test)".

ACCOUNT SIGN-IN:

Users will sign up for an account - subject to your rules, clauses, and provisions.

Users will have a limited time to get through the series of programs, lessons, and test.

"For example: based on my score from the GED Tabe Test, which lets me know where I am academically, will be used to narrow my focus in a specific area or subject where I am weak. Instead of a broad focus. The first test - the assessment test can be generally given after that based on what the user already knows. In his/her cause of the studies in the program - the lessons will adjust accordingly. The Academy Training Program will instruct and direct the individual to focus on key areas more than others. Perhaps there can be employed a virtual instructor, who stands before a group in a classroom setting, in some areas of the program that are programmed to ask questions and interact with the teacher as if in a real review session. Process of Developing the site - things to consider: the content, picture diagrams, illustrations, videos, audio, maps, figures, graphs, charts, and PowerPoints:; the framework; the layout; and you may also work some of these diagrams, charts, figures etc. to be set in motion or animated - set in motion - integrate with technology - smart phones - apps - create interactive user friendly digital index cards."

"What are some other methods other than typing up all that data, you can use to develop this site research key person that you'll eventually have to hire for work - and get their input, their feedback, their expertise, prepare a script, list-of-questions, etc. to analyze your approach. Think Critically, there are ways where you can even take photos of the frames from the NCLEX Review book and digitize them or the frames can be custom to your making. Before investing so much time into typing up the notes, plan out and strategize on the presentation of the site.

Do your research; go to the colleges; put together a team; organize; strategies; analyze, take action, and execute."

"Don't be afraid to reach out to those ideal persons whom you'll eventually need."

"P.S We shall continue our exchange of ideas and this discussion. Let us build, let us develop economically. Be determined, have the courage, have the audacity! Do not retreat, you are paving the way our daughter is counting on you, so am I, those little babies in the hospital are too, and those college graduates, who are in doubt anxious, afraid, worried, and questioning their ability to pass the test. It is all a test. THIS IS CHALLENGING, BUT IT'S YOUR TEST!"

Love

- Toussaint,
April 7, 2016 (21:15) New Moon

"Hey Princess,

I miss you... I will see you very soon. You are a great being, a special being. Never give up being who you are. I Love You"

"GOD Almighty Bless You!

From: Daddy - Your Father"

- Toussaint
April 29, 2016

To: My Wife

"Dear Love,

Today you are recognized not just as the best Mother creation has yielded; but also the Greatest woman I've long anticipated (I have ever been in love with) so I endeavor to waste no time to communicate to you with precision that which is on my mind, the derivative of my heart - for life is too short to last long; but while we're here may the everlasting God bless our union beyond the sky - in a place where we'll eventually meet again in the "gardens" of paradise. Though for a time, now, we have quartered, separate spaces, have both individually experienced lonely nights - in a cold beef, having our faces rejected; discontented with the thoughts of the days ahead. A piece of you is always with me - thoroughly reminds me of life's greatest and highest principle, out of which we were formed. This love... this love, I hunger and yearn for, with the same breath I've disdainfully ignored, like a fool I've despised the truth it imparts, the limits it implies, the roles on my heart. Disillusioned I have resisted its aid - leaving me in a crippling state, playing on my mental thus tearing me apart as I refuse to live simply. Perhaps, you can relate to this dilemma of mine; where internally I have struggled to do right, most of the time, but settled in the attempt to right my wrong. From this point on, please allow me to set things straight: I'm sorry for my shortcomings which have, consequently, produced your shortcomings. Here on this date your celebrated like a most holly day, revered in the Most Holiest way - "I honor you bae", especially your womb which has given me Faith. You are one with the Stars, I am proud of who you are and I admire your strength. You are a remarkable human being - full of energy and love".

Happy Mother's Day

From: Your Husband

- Toussaint
May 8, 2016 (22:30)

"Locked-In To Your Love"
D-BLOCK

"You're so beautiful
In every single way.
I think about you
Each and every day.
Your love is a drug
That my heart desires.
Put your hand in mine
And love me forever.
As our passion ignites
Flames of pure love.
We will unite
To form one love.
I love you!"

- Toussaint
May 8, 2016

"My Sweety,

As I kneel at my bedside given the greatest praises up above. I think back to our struggles and know that you are the 'Essence of Love'. We have faced all types of obstacles, yet we have remained firm. Because whatever adversity me and you go through there is always something to learn. Every time we are apart, I find myself thinking of only you. Let no person separate anything God blew life into. Although we are separated from one another, I will always think of you as the woman who made me better".

"Bae,

Life thought about you from the time we parted. No man can keep Us Apart".

'Forever XOXO'

- Toussaint
May 8, 2016

"My Dear Jenny,

What's good Mami, hmmm... let me see, where to begin? Oh, ok; I perceived why you might be feeling persuaded into purchasing a house. First of all, who wouldn't want a house that they can call home - a place where it is your prerogative to enjoy copiously the freedoms it offers. It is indeed every American dream, to be, a first-time homeowner ensued with the creative task of furnishing the house according to his/ her design; add fixtures to it; and fill the house with equipment, each with its own desired purpose. Besides, homeownership is a major asset, especially, when it's owned outright furthermore, if you have made an informed decision on the purchase of your home, the leverage you'd merit and the equity you'll gain as a result, will presumptuously secure all your financial future endeavors. Truly, it's an incredible feeling having found an ideal location where you've decided to settle, thereafter, setting up your belongings in their prospective places- ending the phase of buying a home."

"Perhaps your current living conditions are likely to be a leading cause to your discontentment, as a result, you're contemplating a move, which is totally understandable - I can't blame you, you must be under a lot of stress. Addition to that, my release date is fastly approaching, with the thought of Daddy arriving home soon got you going crazy. None-the-less, the thought of occupying our own space is not at all a bad idea. The question we must ask first is the time to buy now favorable for us - considering our circumstances? 'Look, I suppose, that, your intentions are good and there is a method to your madness. And you're just simply going off your intuition to make provisions for your family to live in better condition - comfortably in our own space. For that, you have my respect and I appreciate your efforts; believe you me, I sense that I live vicariously through you, so, therefore I do understand the plight of your situation."

"Moreover, the thought of us - out of necessity, abiding at your mothers, is no less of a concern for you, then it is for me. Anytime, you have a couple cohabit under one roof with either their parents or in-laws - and it is not vice versa, can incur to be problematic, especially where there's siblings involved. Let's face it, who wants their privacy restricted and potentially invaded, struggle to conserve groceries purchased because individuals are unreasonable in replacing if after it's been consumed, and not to mention the attempt to remain sane admis chaos, all this could potentially put a hamper on your personal growth and development or improve your charter - it's paradoxical."

"The transition leaving your mother's, must, however, be done with prudence, plus, I don't think it's a good idea to up and leave so suddenly. Despite the frequent discord, between you and your relatives, being there temporarily - let's say, six months to a year after my release, can serve to benefit us in the long run. This, of course, will require us: to deal wisely with the current residents of that house, compromise as well as make sacrifices until we are stabled, confident, and sufficiently able to get all our ducks in a row. By the way, I'm looking forward to being around doing what I can to help out, enjoy the presence of family, and restore family relations."

"Hey, I've learned to accept the good with the bad - sharing a 12x15 block cell with five strangers, shit, being there honestly can't be near as bad as being where I am now. If, I've learned to balance and make it here, then I can make it if anywhere; and perhaps with my presence all your worries and despair will fade away and things won't seem so bad, after all."

"Eight months from now I will be free from my captivity, therefore, I am asking baby for you to hold on for me. This is not, however, to discourage you from doing your homework and increase your knowledge of the home buying process, in fact, I strongly advise you do. Buying a home right now, frankly, just isn't a suitable time, in fact it can end up putting us in a great depression. Instead we should direct our attention and concentrate our energy in other important things that immediately Mul concern us, such as: paying off Mike, which will eventually free up our budget, paying down your existing debt (car, student-loan, credit card, etc), simultaneously, utilizing credit building programs, one like the capital one secured credit card; and yes this will take self control, discipline, determination, and commitment, to also along with the provisions above store away at least 15% of your check to an Emergency Fund Act of at minimum three to six months of your monthly expense while also saving monies for a down payment of the house which is typically a minimum of 3.5% off the purchase price with an Federal Housing Administration (FHA) loan or first and last on an apartment which might be where we should begin."

"My Dear, I strongly advise you, along with doing your own research, to get export advice in relation to buying a home, paying down your debt and building your credit. I mentioned that you would like to pay off all your debt and build your credit."

RESEARCH

✓ How to track mortgage trends

✓ Multi-Indicator Market Index: the index measures the health of housing market nationwide by analyzing home loan applications, mortgage delinquencies, affordability and employment

✓ The standard and poor's/ case-shiller index tracks prices in 20 metro areas, Nationwide

"P.S. FHA Federal Housing Administration has programs for first time home buyers to attend educational courses"

"Critical thinker, I'm no typical tiger, figure me in history; just a time as a mythical figure."

- Toussaint
May 11, 2016 (24:00)

———◆———

"A special day is up ahead of "us" and I want to be the first to wish you a Happy Birthday & HAPPY BORN DAY!"

"And remind you how beautiful you are, how much you are truly loved and how special you are to me. Oh 'I almost failed to say that you are not alone. Although, you are experiencing some delay of gratification - again I tell you - you are not alone. I imagine you are frustrated - so am I, but consider my precious Dear, the Mothers whose' husband neglected and deserted her - leaving her to raise their children on her now she grows acrimonious, distrustful of men - or the spouse who becomes widowed, bounded of her husband's untimely death or the "army wife" whose husband having been enlisted for war deployed abroad in the honor of his country, sits anticipating in anxiety and uncertainty of his return. Unlike these wives, these mothers my dear you have hope - hope that your husband is without a shadow of doubt is coming Home - Albeit, of course, it is no one more difficult for them then it is for you however as challenging it may seem, take in account what is written in James 1:2 "count it all joy when you fall into diverse temptations (or various trials), knowing that the testing of your faith produces patience.""

"My Dear, I know how you like I may have buried resentment towards those who have hurt us, if the emotion is sufficiently strong, inevitably, and up forming the basis of our thoughts, our feelings, our values - our key identity, who and what we think we are. For those young girls, who may still be fairly innocent and uncorrupted, have a notion of how men are, or at least supposed to be: were supposed to be knights in shining Armor."

"Unfortunately, these days, that picture is a bit distorted. I am distinguished from those who have hurt you, but I am however willing to make amends not just for me but for all who has hurt you, because I know your ailing man's derives from the first knight who has failed you in the onset of your conquest stages in life - your father and a list of men to follow, has deserted you, abuse you, lied and cheated you, consequently the cause of you having developed contempt and resentment towards him and if not men in general which profoundly shaped your life. My Dear Jenny, having come into this marriage having a different background than yours, carrying baggage, and problems too with an imperfect, incomplete nature crying out for all the wrong kind of love - Although, I am much mature now and have clarity of vision, nevertheless, I feel responsible for your current hurt and unresolved emotions. Therefore, I'm apologizing and am begging for your forgiveness for leaving you with the stress of raising our daughter by your lonesome, however, short the terms last for, and for fearing you unprotected and unsecure. I do deeply confess my mistakes, carelessness, regrets, failings, selfishness, and blindness that has caused you pain."

"Must our lives revolve around a love of truth that being we both have the same spiritual father and are members of the same spiritual family. And to that end, I assure you that your husband coming home to stay, to love you better, not just in word, but in dead - committed I shall prove to you I care, I'll listen, be unselfish, restraint, work hard, plan continuously, sacrifice, and shower you with endless affection and endless patience. I am your knight in shining Armor - I am your Robin Hood, your Zorro, Roy Rogers, your Lone Ranger - fighting for what is right, possessing great character and nobility - confident, unselfish, mature, wise - faithfully in word and deed to the last detail of life. With a shared standard by which to resolve our differences, all disagreements ultimately find resolution - not because one of us knuckles under the other, the submissive to the dominant, but because we both have placed God's will at the center of our lives, the center of our family. You need not be threatened by my being the ultimate and natural authority in the family, because you trust me and my judgement. Nor, however, should I be threatened by submitting to your guidance when I see you are clearly right. This is my yearning for us to share, a deep understanding of life, obtained by honestly containing our imperfections, studying up to our own lower nature (instead of running away into denial, distraction, and pleasure, facing up to each painful reality as it presents itself in marriage and in life. So let's not miss the moment-to-moment presence of the light of God shining into our lives and our relationship. Any less than that, of were failing; this is why God ordained marriage so we can find him."

"Marriage is indeed a divine institution - something created by and provided for by God. Not only for propagation of the species - but so that man and woman could discover what real love is - not just the love that brings children into the world, but the love that enables us to experience betrayal and yet not hate, the love that learns to forgive, that learns to be strong and to stand up for what's right, that learns to delay gratification - in other words, the love that moves us fully Human, despite in incarceration - I must say I have learned much, of myself, life, and I have discovered, more importantly, why I have married you; for the development of my character - a strong character, fulfillment of my highest potential, true happiness, and spiritual growth - and out of all of these I am not short of experiencing even under these circumstances apart from you. Since you have walked into my life or rather how God has taken me by the hand and led me to my hearts' desire - I've noticed a meaningful change in the care of my being. I have noticed a momentous change in the care of my being. Wonder of Wonder, for truly the Almighty is indeed a Maker of Miracles - Was it not from the sky the children of Israel is claimed to have eaten a bread known as Mona, David had his victory over Goliath, nevertheless, the greatest miracle of all - is the one I thought could not be". God has given you to me. You are a gift from God, I will regard you as such, with sufficient love, respect, and determination to make any sacrifice necessary to preserve our marriage partnership. 'You Are A Gift From God... What God Has Joined Together - Let No Man Asunder', Until Death Do "US" PART".

'Forever Love Yours'

- Toussaint
June 4, 2016

"You Are Fair"

"Behold, you are fair, my love! Behold, you are fair! You have Angel's eyes behind your veil. Your hair is like a flock of goats, going down from Mount Gilead. Your teeth are like a flock-shorn sheep, which bears twins. And none is barren among them. Your lips are like a strand of scarlet, and your mouth is lovely. Your temples behind your veil are like a piece of pomegranate. Your neck is like the tower of Day."

"I'd built an armory on which hung a thousand bucklers. All shields of mighty men, your two breasts are like two fawns. Twins of gazelle which feed among the lilies. You are fair my love, and there is no spot in you. You have ravished my heart, my sister, my spouse; you have ravished my heart with one look of your eyes, with one link of your necklace. How fair is your love, my sister, my spouse! How much better than wine is your love, my sister, and the scent of your perfumes than all spices! Your lips, o my spouse, drip as the honeycomb. Honey and milk are under your tongue; the fragrance of your garments is like the fragrance of Roses!"

- Toussaint
June 6th, 2016

"To My Baby Girl

From Your Father I Love You"

"I am with you; you have to believe!

Wait! Don't Doubt, I will never leave nor forsake you. The Faith you must keep, know that I am with you when you wake in the morning and when you lay down at night. Remember even if you don't see me, you are not alone. I am with you, your always on my heart. I am with you;

you are always in my heart. I am with you even though we are far apart. I am with you "Look! Right here, come close here I go" in the mirror. I am you; you are me, a perfect picture, do not forget to smile. I got your nose. Ha ha, I got your heart. God has us we belong to him. I am with you; you just have to pray I am with you every single day Forever!"

-Toussaint
June 6th, 2016

"L-O-V-E"

"L - OVE your love completes me and makes me whole; without you is like a body without its soul."

"I - NTIMACY I never had a friend who ly's so close, in every sense of the word, your my innermost companion."

"F - REEDOM you give me the freedom to be me, the freedom to love and be loved and this is the ultimate peace."

"E - MPOWERMENT to have you as my soulmate is the heavenly father's grace at the glance of your face empowers me every day. May the Divine Law of Love fill us both with everlasting life."

- Toussaint
June 6th, 2016

"WHOLISTIC FEMALE / MALE RELATIONSHIPS"

"The female/ male relationship is microcosmic of the culture. The relationship serves Maat and transmits and translates culture. Black female/male (woman/ man) relationships (monogamous polygyny and polygamous) are the smallest functional unit of the culture. Sex reflects the culture, and the sexual rituals and ceremonies are an outgrowth of the culture (sex, custom, and Psychopathology: A Study of South African Pagan Natives by B.J.F Laubscher; The Science of Human Regeneration by Hilton Hotema; sexual secrets by Nik Douglas and Penny Slinger)."

"The Black wholistic female/ male relationship is for the upliftment of the culture and creating a technology (children) that advances the culture. The culture (i.e. village) serves the relationship and the relationship serves the culture. It takes a village to have a marriage. In other words, it takes African centeredness to have a holistic African culture marriage. Contemporary Black folk' relationships are based upon Caucasian rituals and ceremonies, Caucasian psychology, and Caucasian group dynamics. They all have a chattel slave mentality that Negro men must love Black women as if they were white women and Negro women must love Black men as if they were white men. Caucasian-type relationships further Caucasian culture. African cultural relationships solve African problems. African female/ male relationships serve Maat. Caucasian cultural type Black relationships serve white supremacy. Consequently, relationships between Black men and women are deteriorating just like relationships between white men and women."

"In the wholistic Black women/ man relationship in Pre-Egyptian and Egyptian culture, the involvement of diet was of primary importance. The importance of foods in the maintenance of spiritual, mental, and physical health is well established (Sex, Nutrition by P. Airola). Research by Konrad Lorenz (Nobel Prize) revealed that people act like the animals they eat. Those domesticated and chemicalized animals no longer adhere to their natural mating rituals, ceremonies, and selection processes. They are forced into sexual activities based on eroticism, sensuality, mass breeding, and the animal rituals and ceremonies aspects of the mating process are discontinued or changed to meet the needs of the animal factory. In other words, they have sex but none of their animal rituals and ceremonies (culture) is attached. The animal's breeders (and slave breeders) can not afford the large amount of time that the animal naturally dedicated to the mate, selection rituals, and ceremonies. These domesticated animals become divorced from their culture and people who eat these animals duplicate their denatured cultured behavior."

"The quality of food and physical vitality have a direct and indirect effect on the quality of the woman/ man relationship. Food (nutrition) is the fuel that feeds the body. Denatured foods such as bleached white flour and white sugar are depleted of nutrients. They weaken the body's ability to defend itself and make the body an excellent host for diseases. A body thus weakened cannot be at its best. It cannot think of its best or produce superior quality sperm or eggs. A body that uses poor-quality fuel operates poorly. This lowered function and weakened vitality may not be noticed because the body has energy reserves and a resistive strain and will tolerate all types of abuse. It will tolerate drug addiction, and poor-quality foods produce a poor-quality life, even though the quantity (age) of life may be long. Foods are chemicals and chemicals (natural or synthetic) alter the health, spirit, mind, mood, and state of consciousness. The healthier people are the more able they are to serve the relationship. The relationship is the seed that the culture grows from."

"Wholistic sexual relations between Black women and men were specific. In Wholism, an orgasm was and is the subline state of the uplifted spiritual, mental, and physical being expressed with sex. A wholistic orgasm cannot be achieved without mutual spiritual and mental harmony based upon Maat. This wholistic cultural view was often expressed in the communal lifestyle of Africans. The culture uses "rites of passage" to teach the female to understand the male portion of herself. The woman has a man (not to be confused with same-gender concepts) component because she is automatically structured by male sperm. This component gives the woman the ability to communicate with and feed the emotions of the male. The acceptance and utilization of the whole society (men/ women) in sexual relations are by definition wholism."

"The man's cycle hormonal mood fluctuations and monthly sperm cycle coincide with the woman's cycle (period). These cycles are a physically dominant part of the relationship. The man's emotional and behavioral responsibility during menstruation, pregnancy, birth, and menopause is culturally defined and taught to him during his "rites of passage. The wholism of the Black relationship is based on concept (whole interrelationship) thinking. In this wholistic state, the woman/ man must use every thought, action, emotion, and sexual episode as a vehicle for reaffirming Maat. Reaffirmation of Maat dissolves the Caucasian culture's influence on sexuality and relationships. In a relationship, the couple must see a connection between their behaviors and Maat, their sexuality and Maat, and see their behaviors as African Maat sexual rituals and ceremonies. Otherwise, they will not see God and spirituality in their sexual intercourse. Without God and spirituality involved in sex; sex becomes a feel-good behavior, trust, and sex acrobatic eroticism."

"Spirituality and God involved in a Black relationship make it African-centered. In African cultures, an understanding of Maat, the unseen, invisible worlds, unmanifested, immortal, and spiritual intelligence was the only criteria for a relationship. Sexual spiritual enlightenment acquired through "rites of passage" education earned the individual's title of God or Goddess. The fundamental African belief was, that if God created man, then man would be called God just as the offspring of a chicken are called chickens. In Caucasian culture, a person whose behavior is according to the teachings of Jesus Christ is called a Christian. In African culture, a person's behavior that follows God's Maat principles is called a God of Goddess. This was not confused to mean Almighty God, The Creator, etc."

"The true essential meaning of these titles of Gods and Goddesses found in African history has been distorted by the religious bias of Caucasian writers. Spiritual growth and a Maatian life aimed towards achieving spiritual upliftment were the primary objective of all Black woman/ man relationships. Individuals in a relationship were regarded as spirits and treated as spirits. Spirit is the unified energy that moves intelligence and the world and should not be confused with ghosts or dead ancestors. In an African-centered relationship, each person was viewed as a sacred presence of God (or Creator God or One and Only God). An individual served God by serving their mate. If an argument would arise, it was resolved by one asking themselves "How is what I am saying benefiting me? How is my mate listening to me benefiting them and how is this argument benefiting God and serving Maat? Who is right and who is wrong was not the standard for resolving arguments."

"Arguments were resolved according to how they benefited Maat, the culture, God, and the ancestors. Finding out who is wrong, who is right in an argument or who is the victor, and which person is wrong or the victim does not serve Maat. Being "right" must serve and benefit the person who is wrong and benefit the village, ancestors, Maat, and God. In the "Negro Dialect" (African speech accent), Maat's logic is quite noticeable. There are words, which have many meanings. However, Maat selects the "right" meaning. The meaning most "right" for the whole sentence at the time of the sentence's usage in a conversation determines the best "right" definition. "Right" is judged by correctness, justice, harmony, balance, reciprocity, truth, propriety, and order (Maat). Relationships between Black women and men founded on correctness, justice, harmony, balance, reciprocity, truth, propriety, and order (Maat) are African-centered. The male/ female relationship is a union of God that is the balance of the spirit, mind, and body. The couple is Maat and the living will of God. Maat means the couple will not destroy their health with junk foods. Because to destroy the health means destroying the relationship. Relationship, water, air, love, children, plants, and culture were created by God and will always exist. People do not create relationships. People participate in something made by God called a relationship. Relationship is given to African peoples as another way to serve God".

- Toussaint
June 17, 2016

"Sweetie, I love you with all my heart. More than ever, now, that I understand how much you have gone through to stay with me this long. And I swear by the moon and stars I'm going to make you glad that you did."

Genuinely Yours,

- Toussaint
June 23, 2016

"My Dear,

I did the best I could with the birthday card and those written thoughts were from the care of my being. Now, perhaps, if I was freed without your knowledge of it. I would've, then arrange for a massive red velvet cake to be delivered to the staff lounge at your workplace - waiting until you get in break, and suddenly pop out of that bitch like jack-in-the-box; body all sticky with aromatic oil, while I'll be wearing nothing but some leather string underwear- ready to put this sweet lovin' in your life, lol. I love you girl, everyday when I fix my eyes on your pictures, I be hoping that the imagining I have of you can be brought to life. Although, I never really understand the feeling, but I've always known you'd be my lifetime partner - from the day I met you, in my heart I felt I couldn't let you go; what's more?"

"Later, I realized that letting you go is like, literally, letting myself go. We both individually have undergone the necessary test of time or "Divinity Test", to determine the purity of the love we share; neither would I take back any of those experience leading up to this point - no regrets only lessons learned and wisdom earned, I have no bias, no judgements, no anger towards you nor I, despite how immoral, unethical, and brutal those experiences were, because it's all a part of my journey and my journey is a part of who I am and who I am is a part of who you are. My swag is tight, baby, you have all the rights to love it, ironically, I don't even like practicing that or caring about the touch of "who got the best swag". I was just born in it, check my astrological chart. I was just born with it and like that you're born to be mine but do not think slavery and feel bound. This time I am here to free your mind, despite that, vagina is mine, I got all the rights reserved. I miss having you by my side too, your absence is truly felt times two."

"Have I shared with you my vision for us... maybe I haven't fully done so, which maybe why you are sometimes uncertain about the future, feeling empty inside, and powerless without me. But you are never without me, baby – no doubt. I see through your eyes, I move at your strength, and feed off your energy. I am the vision that has been given to me, if you fail to see then we fail to be. It will be empowering for you to not just think but feel I am always there, that way you'll never lose heart in all you do. If you're with me then you're with me to the end and our mission doesn't stop because either one of us is gone or is at a distance, we got to keep building on the foundation that's been laid for us."

"May the force be awakened in your baby, our future is in the making, we are both being positioned to be set on the mark. Planning for our future is difficult indeed, even with us both together, but difficult doesn't mean impossible, all it takes in either circumstances is clear communications on what our lifetime plans, what's our short and long term goals, here it doesn't take much for us to be creative and come up with different concepts, formulate strategies, try some techniques, find several models to follow, given our talent and skills create a program to carry out every move and our every plan. It is time to make power moves and power plays and make it count for something - in all we must get insight, knowledge, understanding. But we must have the end in mind, be prepared to put in the work - like you have been doing, sacrifice - delaying gratification, and carefully judge our emotions, during this journey into the promised land. A rule of thumb is to put our family needs over our individual needs. All that we can discuss in person we can discuss via these letters, however. Inefficient it may seem. We can begin from here outlining our future and never-future plans, as we are doing, when we are already having this discussion about our living arrangements. Are you ready, baby, to define what it is in life that we are after? Financial freedom to transform our family tree, to afford a little leisure and luxury. now made of life - you want a banging body baby then let's get it, replace that tooth, then let's do it, a dream home let's buy it, we want attain all this working pay check to pay check - we going to create multiple streams of revenue, I'll explain more on this later."

"Baby, I feel you baby, I know you want your man there with you and how much better you'll feel having me by your side and how much easier things will be for us indeed. R.I.P. to the late Marley but please "baby don't worry about a thing, cause every little thing is going to be alright - I'm coming home to support you, to love you with great intensity and velocity. At first, I thought 'fuck you good', because I knew that will get that pussy pulsating. And, yes, we would be like love virgins, because I'll be unrelenting during my performance of our sexual rituals and ceremony. A regenerative experience it will be. Albeit, I will be there to protect you, baby, please protect me too, as if I was a healer and protector of the Gods, I'll be your guide and you'll be the reason I choose to lead. Thank you dear, your prayers are felt, no need to worry I will soon be out of this hell."

"Tell my little princess that daddy loves her, and remind her that I'll be there for her, don't let a day go by without speaking of me, she must know that you love me, she must see that your committed and feel that your loyal - your her role model, never let her from now on see you sweat. Please, share your ideas with me dear, all your ideas, weather, secretly unchaste, or pure, just, and up-right, you will not be wrong - even what seems bad has a place for good. I value all your ideas, we can make them all work for something, we can refine them and manifest what's good for our course. In response to your ideas regarding the options of our "living arrangements" - see the additional letters enclosed in this envelope. And I am aware that this has been a castle experience, thank you for reminding me, but I'm not concerned with the cast of it because I gained a lot more than I lost. However, this is not to undermine all your labor and effort in supporting me through this. I am forever indebted to you, I honor you for your loyalty, I respect you for your faithfulness, and I love you for keeping it 100 with me, now turn up a notch and start keeping it 100 with your boy. Rejoice and be glad my dear for the day is near when we shall be reunited in each other's embrace, safe and secure. I assure you that I will treat you with the utmost respect you are precious to me and be not dismayed by the past. I'll touch you with all gentleness, speak to you as do the oracles do with the God, sweetheart you'll be just fine!"

"In closing, again Happy Birthday, my Goddess... Oh and to comment about 'Erick', he's a joke, he's harmless, personally, I wouldn't give him the ammunition to feel entitled or empowered. I'll kill 'em with kindness but keep an arm reach. May I feel free to say I pay attention to what he may think of me or of our name, but we won't stop the flow. Chow!"

To: Jenny A. Toussaint

From: Your Husband

-Toussaint,
June 27, 2016 (1:00am)

"My Dear,

Have you considered sitting mum down and having a discussion with her about the other house. I think it may be a considered option to choose, having the deed transferred in your name, hence assuming the responsibility for the mortgage, assuming the house isn't underwater. Controlling this asset will automatically put us in a position of equality consequently giving use the advantage of choice, to leverage the home for investment funds. Further, taking over the mortgage simply will put us ahead of paying the cost involved in buying a home. Instead, the monies that's being accumulated in savings for the purposes of a down payment on a house can be allotted to improving the house, thus increasing the value. Moreover, you will immediately be in position to continue building up your credit. Of course, as you must, ask your mom to permit you to peruse all documents pertaining to the mortgage."

"Not only would this course of action be beneficial for us but would also be equally beneficial for mum, because it's inevitable for one of her kids to inherit the house, and it's likely to be you, plus speeding up this process only sooner lifts the burden of paying two mortgages. With that being said, it may be logical to follow mum in the outset of the provisions pertaining to the improvement of the property and the arrangement of a new lease. About a week ago, I spoke with mum, she stated that it will cost her approximately $10,000 to improve the house - excluding the cost of material. I thought that to be erroneous; either I heard her wrong or she mis-understood the work order given to her because practically labor doesn't cost more than the material, and in regards to the lease, if you're planning on eventually moving into the space, say, a year or two years post-development, then mourn should arrange the lease accordingly. She can assign the lease for one to two years with the option to renovate at a 5% rate. Increase in the rent, also mum claims she has a prospective tenant who is willing to pay the monthly principal of $2,400. If we decide we are going to move-in immediately then we can disregard the idea of the lease."

"Regardless of how this turns out whether we take over the mortgage or mum continues to rent out the property, my concerns are with assuring that she doesn't get screwed. Although, I will insist that she put thing on hold and wait for me to assist her, I do understand, however, that this may be a time sensitive matter. That is why I reward you for investigating what that $10,000 entails, and with the help of an inspector evaluate whether it adds more value to repair or replace some of the items on the property. Also be sure to take hundreds if not thousands of photos of everything you see on the site and take close up photos too. These photos then become invaluable later as things you see now eventually will take on a new shape with correction, repairs, and replacements. I also urge you to take videos talking about what you're looking at while you move the camera around. Oh-note: that "mum" intends on paying for the cost of improving the house out of pocket. I asked her, 'why doesn't she apply for a home improvement loan', she replied she did not qualify, because of the second mortgage she took out of the home, as

FRAGMENTS OF IDENTITY | 177

reasonable as that sounds, I'm uncertain whether she actually applied for a home improvement loan or not; double check on that prohibition."

"An alternative to financing for the home improvement project would be for her to apply for a Home Depot -or- Lowes credit card that's specialized for those purposes. Keep in mind the credit card will only be utilized for being material excluding labor cost - this would have to be paid out of pocket in the end of us, taking over the mortgage we'll be responsible for reimbursing mum for the cash she puts out or - in the case of the credit card, taking up the debt. If mum is looking to save money on this project, then she should note that the contractors don't necessarily have to be licensed. There is usually always a labor pool of undocumented immigrants (outside of warehouse stores) - usually, seriously looking for work. Who are just as qualified for the job as any other licensed contracts - although there's a risk involve, the cost of labor is cheaper and it's a fact of life, risk is in all that we do, we just have to manage it. Of course, taking that route we must deal shrewdly with this group of laborers like any other independent contractor; we carefully screen them all and appoint a supervisor over the project. Subsequently, the materials will be provided on an as needed basis, locked, and put away in a portable storage unit placed outside of the house. I knew this may sand like much, but if were required to do more in pursuit of it would you lie down? Again, I insist mum would wait for my release; as I mentioned earlier it can be a time sensitive matter, and after spending so much on renovations mum may be pressured to immediately rent out the property to generate income. In response to the options you've listed option two - renovating the basement is a waste of money. With option one: staying in the room like I said in previous letter, I can deal with living in that space for a short time post-release; and option three, getting our own spot, we would still need to save for and carefully plan for, if the fourth option one included - the other property, is out of the question. So at this point continue to hustle, budget, slave, and pay down your debt, and wait for me to come home. In the meanwhile, have that talk with mum and continue to educate yourself on basic financing and the Homebuying process."

P.S. Research and send me information on credit privacy number (CPN), authorized user, qualifications of a small business loan guaranteed by the (SBA) Small Business Administration

Questions to ask:

1. What is the fair market value (FMV) of that home today?
2. What was the purchase price of the home?
3. What is the balance that is owed on the mortgage?
4. What is the interest rate?
5. Is it a fixed or variable loan?
6. How many years do we have left until it is paid off?
7. Was it a home equity loan or second mortgage that mum took out on this home?
8. What is the balance remaining on that loan?
9. What is the interest rate of that loan?
10. The Fair Market Value minus the mortgages plus all equity loans equals the total equity owned in that house.

To: Jenny A. Toussaint
From: Your Husband

-Toussaint,
June 27, 2016 (1:00am)

———◆———

"Jenny considered going back to graduate school during her and J.E.T's time apart and on June 14, 2016, she sent J.E.T. her "statement of intent to Coppin State University" for feedback, recommendations and suggestions.

"Your letter of intent needs to be in an essay format. Being that you are a college graduate, you're presumed to know how to write one. Rule of thumb: Take your time writing this letter; put your heart into it! Remember, you are telling a story, be aware of your audience, what story are you telling? You want to inform the reader of your interest in participating in the Master of Science program at Coppin State University. You want to convince the reader to think or act in a certain way. You will determine how you wish for them to act or respond to your letter. Your staffing information about yourself, your experience, and the knowledge you have attained from those experiences. What is outlined in the instructions you've presented me with, is what you'll be sharing. In your own words, of course."

"Revise your introduction to read like this: Education is like a child in constant development which requires a continuing upkeep of training in a long-term effort to learn, grow and adapt, as new changes bring about new challenges in the world around us. Base the remainder of your essay on the introduction statement; make it your headline. The sentence, following the introduction, makes it your topic sentence; and from there on in, the remaining three or four sentences assert the five items you'll be discussing. Make sure you word them differently from what's in the instructions. Then the body of the paragraphs in the letter needs only to break down the five items in chronological order, ditto, using your own words. Lastly, draw your letter to a conclusion summarizing the five items discussed earlier in your essay."

✓ How would you describe yourself? Use three words that would describe you (example determined, driven, industrious)

✓ Do your research about the school you would like to attend, in your case, Coppin State University and its medical program.

✓ What is their mission statement, vision, goals, and values? Now spit it back at them in your own words, of course.

✓ Who were the founders, who are the current members sitting on the board?

✓ Who is the dean and who is the professor(s) that will be teaching the medical program. Also, think in terms of the founders, it is likely that they had you in mind.

✓ Describe how choosing nursing as your career has been advantageous for you. Examples: Maybe it has offered you the fulfilment of your dream or it has been a major achievement for me.

✓ I've been driven and motivated to enhance my level of education in order so I may serve a higher-purpose

The points mentioned are some simple word plays and ideas you may consider, if not arbitrary that you do. I recommend the essay be taken to local colleges and that you seek out an English professor to review your letter and ask that he/ she share any advice, opinions, and critique. Particularly, with the structure your sentences and grammar.

- Toussaint
July 17, 2016

———◆———

"My best advice to you would be to check out the SBA's Office of Women's Business Ownership (OWBO) and take advantage of the services they provide for free or at a moderate price, these services include: business training, and counseling and are geared specifically to women, especially those who are socially and economically disadvantaged. Additionally, they provide training in Finance, management, marketing, and the Internet, as well as access to all of the Small Business Association Programs."

"True learning takes energy, passion, and a burning desire - anger is a big part of that formula for passion are anger and love combined".

"The single most powerful asset we all have is our mind. If it is trained well, it can create enormous wealth seemingly instantaneously."

Love You, Mean It

- Toussaint
August 11, 2016 (Time 4 am)

"My Love, Just for You"

"Hey! Baby Girl, how are you? Time is ticking... Daddy will be home soon. Given the report from your Mommy, she tells me you have been doing well in school, at home, and especially with how you've been coping with the circumstances of not having your daddy present with you, although it is only for the time being. I must admit that I am proud of you: for your show of strength and the progress you are continuing to make, school, and personally (academically, and mentally). You are an incredibly special person, an intelligent being, God created you with a purpose; you are unique. Discover your gifts and talents and use them to help yourself and others. You have a beautiful mind never let ugly in there. My precious daughter, you mean so much to me I am even sorry that this is how it has to be for now, at least. But I do assure you that when Daddy gets home it will be you and me again, just like old times... remember, but even better this time. Let us work more closely together, harder, to build something that will last forever".

- Toussaint
August 24, 2016

"Loyalty Ova Royalty"

"It's been an interesting seven years of us getting to know each other and I have since fallen so deep for you, yet still feel strangely unfamiliar with you. You got me, baby, got me wanting to go deeper... so deep I'm able to penetrate your soul without making sexual contact. I want to explore your mind with mine. And move you without saying a word. I hope our relationship immensely grows with the formidable ability to sustain the damage of life's dark dividing forces we will inevitably be confronted with. Stay down for me baby and we're going to stay up like celestial bodies in orbit above the sky. You are to me one in a million and I'm going to keep on loving you a million times more. I pray the next seven years of our lives together we are able to go above and beyond the current peak of our relationship; and be able to grow significantly, reach our goals, execute our plans proficiently manage every level of our lives effectively and fulfil the mission of our dreams. Until then lets continue to be proactive in building up the interior and structure of the fortress of our soul and hold on to each other tightly without ever letting go. Again, I Love the shit out of you woman!"

"Happy Freaking Anniversary

Anniversary Day August 24, 2009"

'Just For You'

- Toussaint
August 24, 2016

———◆———

"To: The Queen of My Heart

From: Your Lord and King"

"Dear Love,

I was delighted to hear from you earlier - at the sound of your voice baby, I melted at once. Man was your voice like music to my soul, sweet to my ear. In rhythm with my heart, I hardly could've missed a beat to hear you speak. Well, we are ending the night soon, we're currently on lockdown. The new shift just came on and they're conducting head court... I started this letter on Saturday, it's now Monday afternoon. There is a possibility that I might leave this week to go to my permanent camp. I'm not exactly sure where they may send me, but I hope it's in the Central Florida region. It is likely that I'll be going to what's called a re-entry program. We'll see. Either way I know you'll come to visit me wherever they send me. On a different note, ask Mick if he's read my letter and if so, how is he going to solve the issue with my gaintime.

Perhaps getting in contact with Tallahassee would be a place to start. You've been working hard, huh, damn, baby I really do appreciate you and all you have done, are doing, and will do. I can't make up for time we've spent apart but I will sure as hell try. Last week I had my property shipped to my parent's house, it was obviously cheaper to do so. It took seventy stamps just to send my belongings to their house imagine to Maryland. Do tell my father to be sure my package remains sealed as it was delivered, please. Man, did it hurt me to miss the event at Faiths' School. She probably felt bad about herself. That occurrence messed up the parenting plan of the power elites to attack the family unit in definitely working. I halo that. It is a vicious cycle that I want out of. With that being said, there is one more thing I would like to share with you out of the Essence Magazine. Then I would like to discuss more with you on the topics of real estate and our future in it, later..."

"TRANSITION" \tran-'zi-shon\verb

1. TO POWERFULLY EMBRACE CHANGE

"To everything there is a season, and a time to every purpose under heaven, says the Good Book. While new beginnings bring a fresh start, the switch from one season to another can be an intense experience. "Change can be sudden, on your wedding day, in the morning you're single and in the evening you're married. One day you are pregnant and the next you are a mom" an emotional journey and a thriving sensation. "Transition is a process, it's our mental and emotional response to change." Every autumn we get a front-row seat to how native adjusts when leaves change colors and fall away as trees conserve water and energy for the upcoming cold months. "Sometimes when we're going through transition, there is resistance to what's new" Scot. If you don't bend, you're going to break". This month we invite you to stay centered. Remember, the only thing constant is change."

RIDE THE TIDE: FIND YOUR PEACE IN
THE MIDST OF LIFE'S WAVES

'ACKNOWLEDGE THE 'EXPERIENCE' - Whether you are leaving behind a relationship or a job, or just regretting a missed opportunity, there is always a new season to address the shift you have to make. "If you don't grieve, you're not healing properly". Once you process the pain of loss, focus on what you do want". "Thought and Talk"... 'Enlarge EVERYTHING".

'OWN YOUR 'RESPONSE': When you are dealing with things you did not necessarily want to happen, ask yourself three questions: What can I control? What do I value? How will I respond? "Take complete ownership" the solution lies with you, whether it is an adjustment to your situation or an adjustment in your attitude".

'STAY IN THE 'PRESENT': Ships do not sink because they're in water. They sink when water gets inside. Do not allow your externals to change the internal self and who they were as a person. In times of Hux, stay grounded in your greatness. This, too, shall pass.

'PLUG INTO YOUR 'PEOPLE': "Though you may be in a situation you've never experienced before; you are not the first person this has happened to." Do not isolate yourself when you are going through transition. Go get your future! Connect with others who have walked through the valley and come out on the other side. Check out new podcast!"

P.S "Baby, I don't share with you this type of stuff to persuade you or convince you or manipulate you in any kind of way. I'm not tryna get in your panties MOM - I'm in there... I'm not tryna get in your head because I'm there too needless to say, I got your heart baby. As it says in the good book baby, 'Iron sharpens Iron' and I'm willing to do whatever it takes to make sure you're sharp and stay sharp. I love you".

'The One and Only'

- Toussaint
September 1, 2016

"My Dear,

The conditions are horrible here, there is no AC here so you cannot even imagine how hot it is. The process we went through or rather I went through was humiliating and demoralizing. I felt as if I were a slave coming in from Africa, and going through the normal routine procedures one would go through before being auctioned off. Anyway, I have thirty days to mail out my belongings, they are currently in 'property' before they discard everything. It's a decent amount of things and may weigh a couple of pounds. Therefore, I will need you to mail me as soon as possible at least a book of stamps or more to be on the safe side. Secondly, I can't call you unless you send me a bill - an original bill and the contact of your telephone service provider. And it can't be with Metro, Cricket, or any of the month-to-month plans. The phone bill has to be with a major provider like Sprint, AT&T, and Verizon. There is an option to put it on the house phone landline, in this case, I would need the full name, address, phone number, original bill, and copy of the contract on which the phone is under. Again, you have to be added to a phone list for me to contact you. As far as visitation goes you can't come and visit me here unless I become what they call a 'permanent'. In that case, you'd be able to come see me. Since I have such little time left chances that they will allow me to remain here instead of being transformed to what they call a Main Camp. This place where I am now is just a reception center transitional routine and processing."

"By Monday or Tuesday, I should find out whether I would become a permanent and remain here. So, I'll let you know. Still, nevertheless, I believe I'm to send the forms out to you and my people, and once the forms are filled, mail them back to me so that I may turn them into classification. Perhaps we can simulate the process and you can contact the Classification people here and request the form and any additional information concerning me. Now, here I have nothing except for what they provide me with and that is the uniform I wear, one pair of socks, one undershirt, and some Crox. I have no shoes, no deodorant, soap, or any of the materials needed to survive in here, even this pen is borrowed. That text I had sent to you the other day cost me the rest of the stamped envelopes. Those books of stamps I was inquiring about and wanting you to purchase, let us hold off on those. I know you just spent a decent amount of money renovating the room for our comfort, we still have at least two or three more payments to make to Mike, and Faith's birthday celebration and Christmas is coming. I need for you to at least deposit money on my books".

"You and my Father as of love have been making alternate payments. So, figure out who is making the final payment to Mike. For Christmas and Faith's Birthday, plan ahead of exact details and create a budget. This will be over soon be over and we will work together to boost our financial position and the quality of our life, for sure. I'm so sorry it's like this now. It is so trusting, I know, but it won't be like this forever. I'll make sure of it plus God's plan for us is Great and High. I thank you so much, don't be worried about the money, at least not over me and making sure I'm good. The plans I have when I get home are promising. It ain't easy and in this life except trouble, but we gone be alright. I love you so much, I'm on my way home baby!"

"P.S: What definitely priority though is me getting those stamps before they toss my shit out..."

- Toussaint
September 14, 2016 (Time 23:00)

⸻

"Dear Honey,

It is heartbreaking to know that you had to endure such traumatic events to get into the Reception Center. I wish I could take away all of these horrible experiences, once you get home, I will do my best to help you forget and move past it. Be strong and try to sustain these times because the future looks bright. We have a lot to look forward to. And your right we are in this together. The night you were transferred I tossed and turned all night, as soft as our bed is I could not sleep. But I do understand and all I'd like is for you to please make it back home safely. Your daughter misses you so much and she believes you will be home after her birthday. The website states your release, but I talked to Mike about the gain-time and he said one month off for every month in (he said it on paper). Please write him and ask for more details. Hopefully, your case will be resolved on your next court date. I have you on my heart and on my mind always. I hope all your money gets posted to your account. I understand it is challenging but never lose focus on your goals and keep ya head on ya swivel. I GOT YOU BABY!"

- Jenny Toussaint

September 19, 2016

◆————◆————◆

"To: The One I Love
From: The One Who Loves You Most»

"Hey Baby,

Sounds like you're pretty motivated about this real-estate game - I like, I like... Now, all we have to do is get diligent in getting properly trained and educated to effectively develop the necessary entrepreneurial mindset for success. As my longtime companion I have learned that we have much in common. We share the same Dreams on the same mission, and both are destined for greatness. Therefore, I know our all-time goal, which is without the details, to attain a lifetime of wealth and personal fulfillment. And Real Estate can take us on the fast track there. That is why one of my goals, as soon as I'd jump to go take that cause that is one that would become just an agent. Because I eventually want to know the Whole Real Estate dialogue, but I'm going to start with what the sellers (agent) knows. Hence, of course I'm down with the plan of sticking it out at "mums" for a couple years until we are able to get ourselves in good financial standing. So you can expect for my pride to be to the side, like I told you before living at "mum's or anywhere for that matter can't be as bad as living under these current conditions, plus I understand what matters to me the most and that's having you-and-my-baby-by my side. "United we stand divided we fall, "Our Union Makes the Force". So, you say, you have completed the room... I look forward to seeing the result of your creativity and enjoy the feelings of the rehabilitating atmosphere you're responsible for creating."

"I have more to write to you, I just can't seem to buy enough time to get them out at the same time.

So expect more..."

"At least you're in a lot better condition than I am in. And I ain't hate in either, better me than you. Honestly, being here has its nuances, although this isn't where I'll remain, but it is like my living conditions just went from bad to worse, literally. Though, I prefer to be here than the county jail, doesn't make being here any less of a living hell. First of all, the county was prevented from absorbing the 'sun' period. Was confined 24/7 in a small space, although we were given the option to participate in rec(recreation) or not. There was only but so much you could've done on that little patio they called a rec yard anyways. Plus, not more than thirty people could fit in there comfortably. So you figure tryna have eighty four dudes, hollering, 'rec' tryna squeeze in there'. Where I'm at now, there's three scheduled rec's a day, the first and second ones are mandatory. So, you have hundreds of dudes out in this large field about the size of a football field, toasting for a couple hours under the blazing hot Sun. My complexion went from Drake to Omar Chestnut - IMFAO, but I ain't mad at the Sun, I appreciate its purpose, plus I've been able to work out a lot more and a lot harder, especially, following this routine this Haitian dude got me on. Apart from that, unlike the County Jail where we're in the AC 24/7, here there is no such thing as AC, the only place cool air exist is in the building where all the people like the Nurses, Classification Officers, administrator are. Other than that, we have a small window in our cell, and we sit and hope to get a draft in. You would think I'm reliving a past back in Africa Dwelling in the mud house."

"Far as the food is concerned it's just as disgusting as the County jail except that they serve three hot meals a day, they mix up the menu more, and on Tuesday they prepare real baked chicken. Some days, I'd pass up and resort to eating whatever it is I bought from the commissary. Oh, and thanks to you. The commissary line is a hassle itself. It is not easy to spend your own money. It is different here from the county, where your money has to be in on a certain day and your groceries are delivered in the following week. Here we are allowed to hit the window (commissary) any time so long as we have money on our card. We only get a hundred dollar limit a week. Each dorm has it's assigned day when it goes to the window, but not everyone makes it, either, time runs out, inventory runs out, or it starts to thunder. It's always something."

'I love you very much'

- Toussaint
September 25, 2016

———◆———

"To: The Love of My Life
From: The Love of Your Life»

"Real Estate is definitely a venture I am seriously towards getting involved in. While we are there living with mum, we can build up our reserves, improve our credit, paydown our debt and prepare to make investments that count. We would have to lay out a clear plan, be patient, communicate effectively, persevere through the challenging times, and devour our plans. It's great that you're beginning to speak with realtors and lenders, get familiar with these individuals, learn what they expect and what you expect. Remember, like our sales motto "they're only going to sell you on a product they carry". Yes, I agree with the real estate agent you've talked to about purchasing a multi-family unit. It is an investment property that generates cash flow from the collections on rent and would pay itself along with all other expenses. We choose to live in one of the units which is termed as owner-occupied, and received more favorable terms and a low to no down payment on the mortgage we will be required to stay in the unit for at least a year before moving out, thus renting the unit we just were living in. We can repeat that process three to four times but not definitely."

"The lenders would eventually catch on to our mechanism. In addition to the occupied - owner we will still be able to qualify for the renovation loan. Ask the lender about how this process would work - the owner-occupied mortgage financing. Nevertheless, do not accept the lender's prequalifying standards at face value. No simple qualifying formula can tell you "how much mortgage you can afford", or more important, "how much property you should buy". Plugging your credit and finances into a prequalification or preapproval computer program pushes aside the real questions you need to answer:

1. What are your goals to build wealth?
2. How do your budget constraints differ (positively or negatively) from those assumptions embedded in the prequalification program?
3. Are your current spending; saving, and investing habits consistent with your life priorities?
4. How long do you plan to own the property?
5. What steps can you take to improve your qualifying ratio?
6. What steps can you take to improve your credit record or credit score?
7. What percentage of your wealth do you want to hold in real estate investments?
8. What types of real estate financing (other than those loan programs offered by the lender you're talking with) might best promote your goals for cost savings or wealth building?
9. What type of real estate financing (other than those loan programs offered by the lender you're talking with) might best enhance your affordability?
10. What type of property (fixer, foreclosure, duplex, fourplex, multi unit apartment building, single-family house, condo, etc) might best fit into your financial goals?

"As I mentioned earlier, loan representatives want you to buy what they are selling. The majority of loan representatives lack the time, the intellectual acumen, and the practical knowledge necessary to guide you to your best investment and borrowing decisions. Where we stand versus where we want to go. Most loan representatives start explaining (and measure) where you financially understand. We must look into our personal future. Most lenders emphasize your ability and willingness to pay your mortgage as evidenced by their approval formula. You need not accept their view. You must decide for yourself, should I buy more (or less) property then the standard underwriting formula suggests? And correspondingly, should I borrow more (or less) then their lender's guidelines recommend? You can make your qualifying ratios look better, in addition to credit, the lender's underwriting program will likely incorporate two qualifying ratios:

(1) the housing cost (front) ratio, and

(2) the total debt (book) ratio. These ratios often apply regardless of whether you apply for owner-occupied financing or investor financing. Some specialist conduct a first review and then, if desirable, suggest ways that you can improve your financial profile. The Federal Housing Administration (FHA) (section 203K) allows owner-occupant investors to acquire and improve a random property with a low - or - no - down - payment loan.

"For example, Robert Arrowood of California Financial Corporation reports that up-to-date, direct endorsement (DE) firms like his "close 203K loans in four to six weeks instead of four to six months". Be advised that The Federal Housing Administration (FHA) sets loan limits for each location around the country. In high priced cities such as Los Angeles, San Diego, Washington D.C., and Boston, The Federal Housing Administration (FHA) maximum loan currently tops out (for single-family houses, condominiums, and townhomes) at $362,790. In the lowest priced areas of the country, the maximum The Federal Housing Administration (FHA) loan comes in at $200,160 because The Federal Housing Administration (FHA) limits vary; HUD.gov should have the current FHA insurance limits for the area and type of property we have in mind. The loan figures would obviously be different because we plan on housing in multi-unit properties or small apartment companies. As long we live in one of the units, we'd still get a low-down payment. Also, if we buy let's say a two-to-four-unit property, we won't have to qualify for the loan using just your monthly earnings. The rent that you collect from the property also will count. Since I'm running out of time right now. I'm just going to send this letter out. In the following letter, I'm going to be sharing with you the other advantages of the FHA loan program... I Love You".

Truly,

- Toussaint
September 27, 2016 (Time 9:13am)

To: The Woman of My Dreams
From: The One Who Dreams of You

"My Love,

I was just sitting here perusing this Essence magazine and thought of you when I came across several articles. They're very inspiring and empowering, and I'd like to share them with you, my love. Before I did that for as long as I've been hearing about it. I am interested in attending the Essence Festival one of these days in the near future, so long as God's willing. I think I am just going to go ahead and write that down on my 'Bucket List'. They have all sorts of interesting activities going on such as: Money and Power Showcase, Music and Entertainment, Beauty and Style Expo, Lifestyle and Wellness Experiences, Essence Eats - where celebrity chefs prepare their specialty dishes, and arts, crafts, and culture. This year the event will take place in Durban South Africa between November 8 - 13. Supposedly a lot of influential voices will be present, last year I seen that Oprah gave a keynote speech at one of the events. Sounds like it will be an empowering experience indeed, also, a great opportunity for networking."

"Anyways, I definitely want us to get out and explore more and get involved in this Black Excellence - Black Power Movement that is taking place here in America and across the Globe. Hey, random thought and question, say we're doing pretty well for ourselves a couple years from now - we own several income producing properties or products, have a stake in several cash flow positive businesses in different industries and a well diverse mutual fund account, not to mention an Individual Retirement Account (IRA); Faith's a little older, we'll be planning for our next child and your at the height of your career, which you can technically retire from because you'll have multiple streams of revenue coming in. Would you ever consider moving to another country and settling there? If so, what country would you consider moving to?"

"I look forward to what your answer will be. Moving on now, let me proceed to share some inspiring messages I came across in the Essence Magazine..."

"A dream is more than a notion or fantasy. It is the masterpiece of your intention, and you must not only dream big but also remain steadfast to achieve it." - Essence Magazine"

"Correspondingly, out of a book I've been reading in relation to Real Estate, it reads a little something like this, "what's realistic? It is a goal with a deadline. To start now, act now to reset your priorities.""

A PRAYER FOR DREAMERS - REMEMBER GOD'S PROMISES AND ROCK

To thee with whom all things are possible, we give thanks. We thank you for the divine assignment that you have placed in each of us, and we ask your guidance on the journey to completion. Help us to trust, thee without measure cast out any doubts and apprehensions and fill our spirits with assurance, fortitude, and gladness. Help us keep our eyes on the finish line and never on the sidelines lest we be thrown off course. Great us transformational thinking and strength to leap every hurdle. Embolden us to stand on our promises by Faith and to trust that we are purposed for success by your divine order for such a time as this. Amen!

REALIZE YOUR VALUE

Knowing who you are and whose you are, sets the tone for everything, as research tells us that we act in harmony with our perception of ourselves. Honor your destination: One of a kind, divine-inspired, unprecedented. Not only were you created for greatness, but you were also validated by the highest source there is.

BE FEARLESS

Allow your faith to silence all angst. Avoid being disempowered by the opinions of others, daunted by what it takes to meet your goal or so limited that you settle for less when you should be reaching for more. The Creator didn't give you a 'spirit of fear'. He gave you power and purpose and the ability used them.

TREASURE YOUR VISION SPACE

Your mind is your leadership territory from which you ideate and execute. Guard and respect it. Manage who and what has the power to influence you. Like the wise man bearing the gifts, you are bearing a dream that must be realized. Opportunity favors the prepared mind; therefore, keep focused on your future.

PACKAGE YOUR PURPOSE

Even the Word says, "faith without works is dead." Don't just dare to dream; visualize how it will manifest, glean the purpose, do the work and know how it will serve others. Power to your dream! I Love You..."

Forever Yours,

- Toussaint
October 3, 2016

"What's up Baby,

As you are already informed of my being transferred, I figure I'll take this opportunity to explain to you the process of visitation, provide you with the form and amongst other things first, let me say, that, I Love You... I appreciate you being who you are and the role you're playing in my life, as my Lover and Friend. With that being said, I look forward to seeing you, therefore, let's talk about visitation. If I'm not mistaken, visitation is on Sunday and to be certain I'd check for time details. I have to double check or you can check the institution's website. The visitation form is enclosed with this letter as you'll realize. Fill it out completely leaving not an area blank. If you don't know the answer to a question, simply fill in with N/A (non-applicable). When you are ready to mail the form back in, you will address it to the classification officer assigned to me. You'll notice the information on the top right corner of the form. If, we agree and decide to allow Ja'Faith to visit me then it wouldn't be required to fill out a form for her. As you probably know we get contact visits here so, that means I will be on my worst behavior when I finally get your pretty ass in my embrace... lol!"

"On a different note, there are those seasoned care packs that you can order online on my behalf. The first day to order was Monday, October 3rd and the last day to order is Friday November 4th. There are two separate orders that you can complete online. The items in those care packs are items that we aren't able to order directly from here. There is a hundred-dollar limit for each pack. I will on a separate paper list the items at my choosing and the quality of each of those items for you to order for me. Also, I almost failed to mention. I sent my father the visitation forms as well check and see if he received it and be sure he comprehends well what to do with it."

P.S. "I'll send you a list of the items in the following letter".

'I Love You... You're The Best'

Sincerely Yours,
- Toussaint
October 6, 2016 (16:00)

"Colonics"

"Happy People...
live minimally, tell the truth,
never make excuses, take time to listen,
don't hold grudges,
speak well of others, choose friends wisely, establish personal control,
dream big,
see problems as challenges,
nurture social relationships, avoid social comparisons,
treat everyone with kindness,
exercise,
don't sweat the small stuff,
accept what can not be changed,
meditate,
avoid seeking approval from others,
express gratitude for what they already have, eat well,
wake up at the same time every morning,
and get absorbed in the "Now".

- Toussaint
November 4, 2016

"Mediterranean Diet: A Meal Plan That Can Save Your Life"

"The Mediterranean diet is based on the traditional foods that people used to eat in countries like Italy and Greece back in the year 1960."

"Researchers noted that these people were exceptionally healthy compared to Americans and had a low risk of many killer diseases."

"Numerous studies have now shown that the Mediterranean diet can cause weight loss and help prevent heart attacks, strokes, type 2 diabetes and premature death."

✓ Be physically active; enjoy meals with others

✓ **DAILY SERVING:** fruits, vegetables, bread, pasta, rice, other grains, potatoes, olive oil, beans, nuts, legumes, seeds, herbs, and spices

✓ Often, at least two times per week: fish and seafood

✓ Moderate portions, daily to weekly: poultry, eggs, cheese, and yogurt

✓ Less Often: red meats and sweets, sugar- sweetened beverages, added sugars, processed meat, refined grains, refined oils, and other highly processed foods.

AVOID These Unhealthy Foods on A Mediterranean Diet: You should avoid these unhealthy foods and ingredients!

✓ *Added sugar*: soda, candies, ice cream, table sugar and many others.

✓ *Refined grains*: white bread, pasta made with refined wheat, etc.

✓ *Trans fats*: found in margarine and various processed foods.

✓ *Refined Oils:* soybean oil, canola oil, cottonseed oil and others.

✓ *Processed meat:* processed sausage, hot dogs, etc.

✓ *Highly processed foods:* everything labelled "low-fat" or "diet" or looks like it was made a factory.

You _MUST_ read the ingredients list if you want to avoid these unhealthy ingredients.

EAT These Healthy Foods on A Mediterranean Diet:

✓ *Vegetables*: tomatoes, broccoli, kale, spinach, onions, cauliflower, carrots, brussels sprout, cucumbers, etc.

✓ *Fruits:* apples, bananas, oranges, pears, strawberries, grapes, dates, figs, melons, peaches, etc.

✓ *Nuts and Seeds:* almonds, walnuts, macadamia nuts, hazelnuts, cashews, sunflower seeds, pumpkin seeds, and more.

✓ *Legumes:* beans, peas, lentils, pulses, peanuts, chickpeas, etc.

✓ *Tubers:* potatoes, sweet potatoes, turnips, yams, etc.

✓ *Whole Grains:* whole oats, brown rice, barley, corn, buckwheat, whole wheat, whole grain bread and pasta.

✓ *Fish and Seafood:* salmon, sardines, trout, tuna, mackerel, shrimp, oysters, clams, crab, mussels, etc.

✓ *Poultry:* chicken, duck, turkey and more.

✓ *Egg:* Chicken, quail, and duck eggs.

✓ *Dairy:* Cheese, yogurt, Greek yogurt, etc.

✓ *Herbs and Spices:* garlic, basil, mint, rosemary, sage, nutmeg, cinnamon, pepper, etc.

✓ *Healthy Fats:* extra virgin olive oil, olives, avocados, and avocado oil.

A Mediterranean Diet Meal Plan

There is no one "right" way to do this diet. There are many countries around the Mediterranean Sea and they didn't all eat the same things

This article describes the diet that was typically prescribed in the studies that showed it to be an effective way of eating.

Consider all of this as a general guideline, not something written in stone. The plan can be adjusted to individual needs and preferences.

- Toussaint
November 4, 2016

———◆———

Natural Juice Recipes

Mean Green Ingredients:

1 cucumber
4 celery stalks
2 apples
6 - 8 leaves Kale (Tuscan cabbage)
1/2 lemon
1 inch/ 2.5cm piece of fresh ginger

Low Sugar Green Juice Ingredients:

1/2 green apple
3 kale (Tuscan cabbage) leaves
8 stems and leaves of mint
3 limes, peeled
1 1/2 cucumbers
2 handfuls of spinach

Ease Your Joints Juice Ingredients:

4 slices fresh pineapple
1 large handful of cherries
1 large carrot
2 inch/ 5cm piece of fresh ginger
4 small pieces of turmeric root

Morning Green Glory Ingredients:

4 - 5 large kale leaves
1 large handful of spinach
3 romaine leaves
1 cucumber
3 celery stalks
1 green apple
1 lemon, peeled (you can leave the peel on but it will taste very bitter)

Warrior Princess Ingredients:

1/2 wedges of regular-sized red cabbage
1/2 small watermelon
2 oranges
1/2 fennel bulb

- Toussaint
November 4, 2016

What is Protein?

Proteins are part of every cell, tissue, and organ in our bodies. These body proteins are constantly being broken down and replaced. The protein in the foods we eat is digested into amino acids that are later used to replace these proteins in our bodies.

Protein is found in the following foods:

- ✓ Legumes (dry beans and peas)
- ✓ Tofu
- ✓ Eggs
- ✓ Nuts and seeds
- ✓ Milk and milk products
- ✓ Grains, some vegetables, and some fruits
- ✓ Meats, poultry, and fish

How much protein do I need?

Maybe you've wondered how much protein you need each day. In general, it's recommended that 10 - 35% of your daily calories come from protein.

Protein Amounts

✓ *Soy:* Soybeans are the No. 1 source of vegetable protein, and are a complete protein, meaning they contain all the essential amino acids. Each cup of cooked soybeans offers 29 grams of protein. Soy products such as tofu have less protein, coming in with 11 grams in every 4-ounce serving.

✓ *Beans:* Beans pack a punch of protein. White beans and lentils contain about 19 grams of protein per cup, while kidney, lima, black-eyed, navy, and pinto beans contain about 14 grams per cup.

✓ *Broccoli:* Beans are another vegetable that contains an abundant amount of protein. Its protein is 34 percent of its dry matter, offering 4.6 grams of protein per cup of cooked broccoli. Cauliflower, a cousin of broccoli, is not too far behind at 27 percent, or about 3 grams per cup.

✓ *Spinach:* Known for its excellent nutrient profile, spinach is also a reliable source of protein. Cooked spinach contains 5.3 grams of protein per cup, while frozen or canned, drained spinach contains slightly more at 6 grams per cup.

"Top Sources of Veggie Protein"

Where do you get your protein?

1. *Spinach* (49% protein)
2. **Kale** (45% protein)
3. **Broccoli** (45% protein)
4. **Cauliflower** (40% protein)

5. **Mushrooms** (38% protein)
6. **Parsley** (34% protein)
7. **Cucumbers** (24% protein)
8. **Green Pepper** (22% protein)
9. **Cabbage** (22% protein)
10. **Tomatoes** (18% protein)

Protein in <u>Meat</u>:

✓ **Beef** (25.8% protein)
✓ **Chicken** (23% protein)
✓ **Eggs** (12% protein)

- Toussaint
November 4, 2016

HEALTH RECOMMENDATIONS

Healthy Weight Gain versus Body Fat Gain:

✓ Many thin and skinny women set out to gain any weight and gaining body fat is fine with them. However, there is a major problem with this approach in putting on weight. If the weights you gain comes primarily from increased body fat, you have no control of where those extra fats will be going to on your body.

✓ Your extra ugly fat could end up unevenly distributed in all the wrong places like your tummy, love handles, butt, thighs and so on.

✓ Therefore, your best way to improve your physique in the way you want is to go after lean muscle weight gains. In this way, not only will you put on weight, but you will also gain healthy weight and is able to dictate where the extra pounds are going to be. In other words, you can sculpt your body the way you want it to shape.

✓ It is better to have a more planned approach to weight gain. The best way to gain healthy weight is through diet and exercise. We want you to gain weight in a healthy manner and not pig out on junk foods.

✓ Can lifting heavy weights make you muscular? No. Women simply don't naturally possess enough of the male hormone, testosterone that will allow them to become huge muscular hulks! Hence weight training will NOT make you a bodybuilder unless you try so hard to be muscular.

TWENTY PROVEN TIPS FOR HEALTHY WEIGHT GAIN

Have you ever been told that you are skinny or just underweight? You are a skinny girl who eats everything and never gains weight? Are you looking to put on some healthy weight?

Remember you are fortunate elite of women who must have fast enough a metabolism to find putting on weight hard as 90% of the rest of womankind is likely to have the exact opposite problem and find that they put on weight too easily, thus finding they must work incredibly hard to then burn it off again.

However, being too thin as skinny fashion models is disgusting. Not flabby, but healthy women with curvaceous hips or larger breasts like the classic hourglass figure, makes men salivate. Meanwhile if you cannot put on any weight, it can actually be quite dangerous and being underweight can pose various health risks that are no laughing matter (no matter how well you fit into your dress). Hence, with so much information out there aimed at losing weight, how do you go about doing the opposite to everyone else and actually gaining some?

1. Increase your caloric intakes by about 500 to 1000 Calories per day. Extra 500 Calories/ day will help you gain up to one pound in one week.

2. Eat frequently - Eat your three main meals (breakfast lunch, dinner) spaced about five hours apart. In addition, eat two or three snacks a day in between meals.

3. Snacks should be high in calories such as milk shakes, yogurt, and high carbohydrates food bananas.

4. Eat more complex carbohydrates like whole-grain breads, pasta, and brown rice etc.

5. Never skip your breakfast. Include one egg and fruit juice for your breakfast.

6. Eat bigger than normal portions for your regular meals.

7. Eat food with higher calories, moderate fats, higher protein, higher fiber, higher nutrition.

8. Choose high-quality protein sources such as eggs, meat, fish, milk, seeds, protein, to build new muscle.

9. Since most of the calories for weight gain comes from carbohydrates and fats, do not replace them with protein.

10. Eat starchy vegetables (potatoes, peas, cauliflower pumpkin, sweet potatoes).

11. Consume nuts, calories dense ripe fruits like bananas, dried fruits like dates as snacks between meals.

12. Eat the right kinds of fats, avoid trans fats. Add healthy unsaturated fats in moderation such as olive and canola oil, nuts, seeds, peanut butter, avocados to your diet.

13. Do not drink water before meals. After meals, wait about ten minutes before drinking water.

14. Beverages can help you gain weight too. If it is possible, drink shakes, milk, juice, etc. instead of tea, coffee and diet sodas.

15. Avoid alcoholic beverages. It's High calorie with minimum nutrition.

16. Do thirty minutes of resistance training. Weight training helps to convert the extra calories into muscle, hence adding some extra ponds to your body.

17. Do some compound movements like body-weight squat, push-ups, row, or deadlift.

18. Aim to lift a heavy enough weight that you're fatiguing within the 8 - 12 rep range, completing a total of 2 - 4 sets for each exercise.

19. Do NOT engage in aerobic exercises (running stationary bicycling), aerobic exercise helps you lose body fat (weight loss). You may lose more weight than gain weight.

20. Keep track, if possible, keep a food journal to track your weight gain progress. Keep a record of daily calorie consumption. Weigh yourself at the end of each week to see your development. Keep doing this each week until you start seeing noticeable progress.

Concisely, you must increase your intake of good calories and encourage the risk of cellular growth through weight training. One thing is for sure, you must eat! What you eat is the key to putting on the pounds and keeping it there so those new sexy curves stick.

1. Healthy eating is effective. You can lose as much as 20 pounds after several weeks of following a good healthy diet. You need not also starve yourself or take medication.

2. Healthy eating is your all-in-one pharmacy on a plate. This is because you can effectively fight and prevent diseases if you eat healthy foods. It is a known fact that most diseases today are caused by an unhealthy

diet. Whether it is because the quantity of fat and calories leads to obesity, the lack of nutrients needed for a strong and healthy immune system, or the amount of chemicals and trans fats that are included in processed foods, unhealthy eating can lead to major health problems.

3. Healthy eating can increase your energy levels. You can become more productive and socially active if you will only stick to healthy foods. Whole foods are best because they are unrefined and processed. The more processed a food is, the less nutrients it will have.

4. Healthy eating can make you look younger and fresher. You need not seek the fountain of youth anymore. All you have to do is to eat healthy to keep a younger-looking skin. Healthy foods promote good cell growth and can eliminate harmful free radicals and toxins in your body. Because of this, your skin will regain its natural glow and suppleness. Along with eating healthy, drink healthy too. The benefit of green tea can help you look and feel younger, as can just staying well hydrated with water.

- Toussaint
November 4, 2016

"Namaste or Prayer"

"Put both palms of your hands together pointing palms up toward the sky. The gesture Namaste represents the belief that there is Divine spark within each of us that is located in the heart chakra. The gesture is an acknowledgment of the soul in one by the soul in another. "Name" means bow "as" means I, and "te" means you. Therefore, Namaste literally means "bow me you" or "I bow to you."

P.S. 'MAIN CHAKRA CENTERS'

- *SPIRITUALITY* (Crown Chakra Sahasrara)
- *INTUITION* (Brown Chakra Ajna)
- *COMMUNICATION* (Throat Chakra Vishuddha)
- *LOVE* (Heart Chakra Anahata)
- *POWER* (Navel Chakra Manipura)
- *SEXUALITY* (Sacral Chakra Svadhisthana)
- *SURVIVAL* (Root Chakra Muladhara)"

- Toussaint
November 11, 2016

‹—————◆—————›

To: The Most Amazing Women in My Life
From: The One Who Feels You're Amazing

"My Love,

It›s Saturday afternoon and I›m thinking of you as usual. I attempted to call once, earlier knowing you were likely to be resting. Of course, I'll be calling you back a little later when I feel you've been fully rejuvenated. I'm deciding to rest my muscles myself after a long week of exercising. I'll get back to it tomorrow. I aim to get into the best shape of my life while here - that freakin' county rotted me. It's all good because, "when you train hard, you fight hard, you die hard". Moving on in a previous letter I began sharing with you some information I gathered from reading a book by Gary W. Eldred, "The Beginner's Guide to Real Estate Investing," about some of the other benefits and advantages the FHA (federal housing administration) provided beginning investors. Before I share with you that information, I'd like to say that I am really eager to make a difference in my life, in yours and Faith's, my parents and anyone who I am able to help along the way. With so much odd against me I pray to really break away from this system that manages to pull many men in and crush them. I think it's safe to say that I'm determined to beat the odds of even returning to such a place, to ever have to so desperately want and need. Hence, I'm compelled to sell drugs. I just won't allow myself to be so limited to the options of making money. I know I'm my own Boss, and my own leader. Therefore, in past times I found it difficult for me to adjust my attitude and work for somebody, but today decidedly, I won't necessarily work to earn. I will work to learn, whilst minding my own business. That's why I ask you about, if there were any network marketing company in that region that has a good Marketing and Sales - training program. Because if I'm to be anyone's boss and/ or leader then I need to acquire the skills and culminate the experience needed to be a prominent example. Also, I heard about this Toastmaster Communication Training program. I'm interested in joining. I must be a skilled communicator if I plan on being a Great Leader. So, while we're engage directly in Real Estate, we'll be getting the OJT (on the job training) of Managing and Marketing the properties we plan on controlling, simultaneously, developing our knowledge and sharpening our skills, by attending relative-courses, programs, seminars and workshops to be the entrepreneurs we were born to be."

"I intend on learning the basics of accounting as well. Like how to analyze financial statements, know the story that the numbers are telling and the difference between the ratios - income/ expenses, asset/ liability etc. I will spend the rest of my years learning to live a fulfilled, satisfactory, fun, prosperous, healthy, and healthy life. Now, about those FHA (federal housing administration) Advantages. They are as follows: Besides low (or no) down payments, FHA (federal housing administration) OFFERS borrowers other advantages:

1.   You can roll many of your closing expenses and mortgage insurance premiums into your loan. This cuts out of pocket cash you'll need a closing.

2.   You may choose from either fixed-rate or adjustable-rate FHA (federal housing administration) plans. FHA (federal housing administration) adjustable-rate mortgages gives you lower annual caps and lower lifetime caps than nongovernment (NOG) programs).

3.   FHA (federal housing administration) authorized banks and other lenders to use higher qualifying ratios and easier underwriting guidelines. After you shape up your finances, FHA (federal housing administration) will do all it can to approve your loan.

4.   If interest rates drop (and if you've paid on time for the previous 12 months), you can "streamline" refinance your FHA loan at

the current lower interest rates without a property appraisal and without having to requalify.

5. If you can persuade parents or other close relatives to give you the down payment, you won't need to come up with any closing-table cash from your own pocket. (Undoubtedly, many gifted down payments are really loans in disguise).

6. Unlike most non-government loans, FHA (federal housing administration) mortgages are assumable. Someone who later agrees to buy your property need not apply for a new mortgage. When mortgage interest rates are high, an assumable low-rate FHA (federal housing administration) mortgage will give your property a great sales advantage. I Love You Always!!!"

Your One and Only,

- Toussaint
December 2, 2016 (Time 12:30)

"Jaja

"Hi, my Love, How are you feeling today? Daddy misses you very much. You are always on my mind. I decided to write to you since this is my only channel of communication with you. Also, I hope to inspire you to write too by writing to you. It's not hard at all. You just need either a stamped envelope like the one this letter was enclosed to or a blank envelope and place a stamp on there in the top right corner of the envelope. Once you have that all set, the next thing you'll need which you'll find on the envelope I sent to you, is my name, arrest #, and address. You'll write my information in the center of the envelope and yours - name and address opposite of the stamp on the left-hand corner. Hope that makes sense. I love you very much! Respect your Mommy no matter what. Be thankful for everything and in everything be thankful! No matter what you do; do it your best! Say hello to your Mommy for me and tell her I Love her. I wish you the best. Peace, prosperity, happiness, and success. Never let my absence is an excuse on why you fail to be Great. You're great no matter what. Always guard your mind and protect your heart from everyone. Show love but keep your heart, never give it up to no one, only you can love yourself best."

'I Love You,

- Toussaint September 4, 2018 (17:30)
(Song dedication: forgive-me; myself and I)

"Culprit Of a Broken Heart"

"If I died today, I would fade away into timelessness and formlessness, patiently waiting for the return to the sense of belonging. That way my forever with you won't be thwart by death nor time. Jenny, I love you, in the most imperfect way, I perfectly do, and I will continue to, no matter what! Now, in contrast to me loving you my actions appeared differently informed. Not to make any excuses or offer up a lame explanation, however, I am compelled to pour out my consciousness to you in hopes to provide you a sense of relief. Imagining your long suffering, your pain and confusion it will be selfish of me to remain mute in this situation."

"My Dear, if I may, I admit I've been wrong in many ways. Perhaps I should've listened to you, perhaps I should've stayed. "How could I?" unsettled by the thought of having to permanently relocate under the condition that I'd be, even if it for a time, solely dependent upon you for my well-fair and material need, especially, while living under your mother's roof. Please have no thought to what I am writing here, just yet hear me out first. Due to my shortsightedness, ignorance, and base desires. I thought being in Florida would've been a better idea for me to get my shit together. Since it is familiar territory - bad idea. Nevertheless, having had that physical altercation New Year's Day didn't help either."

"Baby, at this present moment, you are not to be blamed for anything that has led to my current circumstances and condition. I brought it all upon myself - have the Law of cause and effect. I was thinking all wrong soon after my release thus my ignoble thoughts manifested, equated to my actions, a character and personality with which you were unfamiliar. I was overtaken by every form of evil-I was not myself. Anyways I am not tryna make this all long and drawn out. I've hurt you, lied and cheated you. It's messed up. I wish things could be different right now, but this is just what I deserve, this is the consequence of my actions and the effects of my thoughts. Fuck if it's a hard pill to swallow, but I must in order for me to grow."

"As for my case, I don't know where it is going. I do wish and pray it'll end soon. Although, I missed the opportunity of being the ideal man I knew I could be for both you and Faith, I pray it's not too late. But even then, I don't want you to feel like you're in some kind of shell because of my absence. You don't need me to be complete and feel fulfilled. You just need to look within you and know that in the essence of your being you are already complete and whole. Live on my dear, in strength and Love. You have accomplished and achieve your purpose and attain the objects of your desires if you will put your mind to it."

"All I'm asking is for you to not completely shut me out. I want to hear from you, I want to hear from Faith. I would like some pictures of you two. I am deeply grieved by the situation, but I must forgive myself and I pray that you can forgive me by living up to your fullest potential. I'm all alone and I feel now What it's truly like to be apart from you not just physically but now even emotionally and mentally. If you choose to never speak to me again, I can also understand, there's no pressure on you. Live Your Life, Bye for now."

- Toussaint
September 14, 2018

"Hi Faith,

My little goddess, I miss you SOOO much. It aches my heart to continue to be apart from you. I think about you every single day. I pray for you day and night. I encourage you to be strong, loving and kind. Although it's unnatural for a young child to be raised without both its parents, I pray you do not make that an excuse to be anything other than good, positive and yourself. Learn to control your anger - which is your emotions; think before you act and think of what to say before you say it. Know this you are NOT WHAT HAPPENS TO YOU; YOU ARE NOT YOUR MIND - YOUR MIND IS AN INSTRUMENT GIVEN TO YOU - USE IF IT'S POWERFUL - DON'T LET IT USE YOU."

"Mommy told me you are doing very well, in school, I expect that you are, keep up the good work. I AM PROUD OF YOU. You're a great person, a beautiful soul. You are very smart, wise, and intelligent. I believe in you. You don't need anybody to tell you that all you have to do is look in the mirror of your heart and you can easily see what I see. You are Love, I could not love you more than you already are. Focus your energy - Never give up, you can do whatever you put your mind to. You have the ability to do all things and be anybody you are willing to be. Say this every morning when you wake and every night before you sleep: "I CAN BE WHAT I WILL BE"

'Chew until next time Love "HONEY" Muah!'

-Toussaint,
October 21, 2018

"We Can Make It If We Try" - Will Smith

"My Dear,

Do you know about a site called go fundme? I have little knowledge about it myself, except that it's a platform where an individual, group or business can use to raise capital to fund for they're cause. The reason I am bringing this up is because I am thinking of creative ways to fund for my lawyer fees, and I thought of the GoFundMe site. What I was thinking more specifically, with all the tails of prison reform, is to produce a GoFund me project with Faithful Stars starring in the production. If done right, we would not only raise an excess of the requested amount, but the GoFundMe page may potentially gain national attention, hence pushing the issue of REFORM in our Criminal Justice System. To do this effectively and ensure our success like any old Blockbuster movie or a NY TIMES Bestseller we need a complete storyline or storyboard. The Theme being "A 9-year-old girl turns to GoFundMe to Raise $50,000 to pay for her father's legal fees and pushes the issue for Criminal Justice Reform". We can revise that, but it should definitely be along these lines. Although, it's a genuine issue, the means in which we utilize to attain our funding is going to take strategy; and getting others to join us on our cause is the goal. So, to begin I ask that you would go and review the GoFundMe site and similar crowdfunding sites to check out how it works. Secondly, create an account on the behalf of Faith. Then once I've received a report from you on how it works. I will be, in the meantime, writing several scripts for Ja'Faith to familiarize herself with and perform on camera (iPhone)."

"The picture we will paint is this happy nuclear family who has had the leading man in their life ejected from them. To show this, producing a slideshow of whatever photographs we have as a unit, just me and you; and me and Ja'Faith will be a necessary tool. This is the Protocol to my Idea. I will elaborate more when I know and hear from you that you are on board. Whatever surplus there is in what we raise can be allocated to your business expenditures. Also, I think that whatever contribution a person or business corporation makes is tax deductible, so that's on incentive for many who deal mostly in cash or earn too much to want to contribute. Hope you got my drift babe. I am remorseful I really would like to come home and be the best man, husband, and father I know I am and can be. I know I've failed you both and now I owe my life to you both. And I am willing to lay down my life for you but not like this."

LOVE TRULY,

-Toussaint,
November 24, 2018 (2:40am)

"PEACE EDUCATION PROGRAM"

"I may have lost my Liberty but I still have humanity and in this will I prosper". -J.E.T. <eye3i>

"Dignity begins when you realize what you're all about.

The Grand illusion looks incredibly real, the decision to remain content at any given day or any given time lies with no one but with you. Regardless of the environment. Regardless of the circumstances the decision can still be yours."

"From nowhere breath comes and brings the gift of life to you"

We measure with what we do not have because we have no clue about what we have!!!"

"Find out what you have because what you have is unparalleled."

"Don't be confused by your circumstances. All that you thought you have lost is still coming."

"The Farmer and the Buried Treasure 'Elbow room' - room to grow and be free."

"We are the ones that come up with the systems lost at your humanity".

"We want to make a difference"!

"Do not forget yourself our liberty is gone but our humanity can not be taken from us"!

"Where one road ends another begins, if you get to the end of the road, turn around and that's where the road begins".

"Then disappears then comes again and brings the gift of life again and again and again one breathe at a time not two, not three, not five, one at a time that's your beat that's your rhythm".

- Toussaint
December 30, 2018

<hr>

"Ja'Faith Chrisette Toussaint Favorite Bedtime Story
By Daddy (J.E.T.<eye3i>) James Edward Toussaint

"Once

Upon A Time, there was this Bird called Blue.

(Blue represent the Blues) This bird was a crazy egotistical bird because he felt that he was the fastest bird in captivity. (Represent pride and Ego) While all the other birds flew south for the winter, blue kicked back relaxing but the next day, a cold front came sooner than he expected. So, blue had to clear it before preparing or packing. As Blue Flew South, it started to rain harder and harder. Blue wings got heavier and heavier from the rain. The wind begins to blow harder and harder, preventing blue from flying straight. Then the rain became snow preventing blue from seeing, eventually his wings froze and he plummeted downward to a farm. (Storm represent trails and tribulation) (farm represents a place or situation you don't want to be (example: prison) Blue thought he was going to die, regretting the fact that he should have left with the rest of the pack. (when you give up on). As he cried in quiet, a horse approached him asking, "What's with all the ruckus?" Blue replies by begging for help. "Please Mr. Horse, could you help me by taking me somewhere warm?" I'm about to freeze to death". The horse grunted and then shitted on Blue. ("we all have found ourselves in a shitty situation") Blue replies, "O my God, what's next." But at that moment he realizes that the horseshit was hot enough to keep him warm. (Be careful what you ask for) So, the next day, he was chirping and singing because he lived to see another day. Now, all the noise he was making caught the attention of a cat. (Another form of bragging or boasting) The cat dug Blue out of the shit. Blue was grateful and thanked the cat for his help. The cat said, "No problem," then informed Blue that it was a pond down the hill where he could clean up. The cat escorted Blue to the pond and when Blue was done, he thanked the cat once more before he left to fly south. The cat responded by saying, "No thank you because I was mighty hungry this morning and ate the bird."

"The Moral of the Story is, "everybody who shit on you, ain't your enemy and everybody who takes shit from you, ain't your friend".

- Toussaint
(Course: Peace Education Program Workshop Seven Dignity: Create your own illustrated article series)
December 30, 2018

———◆———

"My Betrothed,

If I can put into chronological order the trajectory of my divergence, then let it be said that I first, admittingly, was ultimately divided against myself and my own moral principles, before leaving you. It's so hard to explain without the certainty that you'll have an open mind to pick up what I'm putting down. It's a complicated matter and to ration the reason in simple logical terms in a letter will do no justice. I am deeply grieved by my actions and am paying for every a bit of it. What's even more deplorable is the fact that you and Faith, presumably, have to suffer too. Moving on, your feelings, betrayed, indignant, and broken heart.

Furthermore, your self-concept changes, you lose confidence, and your self-esteem is lowered. Subsequently, your judgement ain't clear, your hour living in fear and your anxiety intensified, - what now - boredom and loneliness becomes a vice. A troubled mind makes for a troubled life, and here you are too caught up in living a double life. No real hope there except for in the light of falsehood. My deepest sympathy goes out to you because I understand what you are going through. But I want to remind you that I was weak too, for a time I couldn't see clearly, let alone see you. Your soul is still there if you will only save yourself then chances are you'd be provided the strength and the guide to save those for whom you age. I might of fucked up but ultimately there is a supreme order above us for whom we ought to pay our tribute to. Two wrongs don't make no right and as for me I am spending this time to right my wrong. Love yourself better and then you can altogether love me. You must learn to let up off the burdens of the past and remain in the present."

"Yesterday I don't remember you and the future doesn't know you. You aren't your past life situations; your emotions are like the clouds they're meant to pass you by, but we've been conditioned to hold on to our traumas, pain, and losses, consequently hindering our progress of evolution and ability to see things for what they truly are. We run around justifying our behaviors, weakness, and excuses by what we feel and are going through. At what point does one having gone through the crucible of the world will he/she be refined for greater use and higher purposes... Look, I love you too!!! I wish I had you close so I can show you how much I really do. We have had some supernatural phenomenon in our life together which supersedes our sinful nature in the lower worlds. Why have we not ever discussed in depth, what occurred in our life back in 08-09. Is it that you forgot or am I just crazy - cause you don't know. We are different, special and unlike many we've come across. We have a higher purpose and neither one of us is serving it. Instead, we by force of circumstances have and are becoming conformed to the ways of the worldly consumers. Easily swayed, hypnotized, and mesmerized. What occurred here in regard to my arrest was not God's plans but the result of my mind by the sure Law of Cause and Effect.

And now having come to my senses and aligning myself with the moving forces of the universe all things are working itself out for good. Now if there be a host of terrestrial, extraterrestrial, and celestial beings who are defending my cause then I lay aside hoping it is so, if not, then all I have is my own consciousness to offer me comfort and consolation."

'Peace & Love'

- Toussaint
December 31, 2018

"Jenny,

When you get a call and it's my father's number it just may be me calling you off a three-way, so please pick up the phone whenever possible. I need to communicate with you, it's just hard under these circumstances, especially with the unresolved conflict between us. Not only that, but I also have the concept in my mind that you aren't open to communication and that somebody may be in my wifey's head. Enough to get me in my feelings now! But forget my feelings, this shit is not a game."

"I shouldn't be doing no time for the charges they say I allegedly committed. Fuck No! Perhaps you shouldn't be out there starring in your role alone as a single mother. It is what it is and I'm refusing to just lay down and throw my life away. Jenny I'm broken, I have nothing left of my pride but my ambition and love. Does me needing you now more than ever pushes you away? Is it really circumstances or is it emotion - is it attitude?"

"For me, for you, for Faith I want for you to maximize your potential. I need you to come up. If you will harken on to my words and hear me out, we still have a fighting chance. OSIRIS died and ISIS came and pieced the fourteen parts of his decapitated body together. The only part missing was his penis. She along with her sister surgically replaced his manhood with a Golden Shaft and they later gave birth to Horus, the Sun God. OSIRIS was killed by his evil twin Set. ISIS being the 'Mother of God,' nature, love, and fertility was endowed with the power to perform such a Divine Act. Yes, I am comparing you to ISIS a Goddess of antiquity, in my eyes, you are that; I've made you that! You're my saving Grace and I need you."

- Toussaint
January 8, 2019

"Princess,

"How are you, my Love? I imagine wonderful things for you. I'm working on having a portrait of you drawn. You should like it. Daddy's always thinking of you. Sometimes I feel just thinking of you isn't enough; and honestly, it's not, I prefer to be there for you but there are obstacles in my way. I'm fighting to get back to you baby. It's like Daddy's at war. I pray my falling short doesn't hurt you too bad, and the unseen forces of nature protect you forms of darkness. Keep your head up my love and don't allow anyone or anything to steal your peace and love away. Dad"

- Toussaint
January 10, 2019

"Jenny,

I am hurting and afraid. Having no end in sight, yes, is terrifying. What's more, is the evidence of my lack of support; not that I deserve it or am even worthy of it. Jenny, I feel helpless and hopeless. My pride has been robbed of me and my ago abandoned me. I no longer know who I am. What have I done, my life is ruined and my future seemingly dim. All I've ever truly wanted in this life of sin is the abundance of joy, peace of mind and contentment gained from health, wealth and true love that I could enjoy with a family of my own."

"O'how, I wish I had not taken that initial deal from my last case, yes, I got out, but they've kept me away from my family in order to do their dirty work so that they can closely monitor me. I've not known how to tell you, but it's always been my intentions to keep you and Ja'Faith out of harm's way. Still am unable to explain in detail the real reason why I've not been the same. Now here I am, tricked again, deeper into the hands of the law. Stripped away of my liberty and barely do I feel I have any bit of humanity left. The result, insanity. If even I can buy my way out as an option, I'm at a loss, for, I have no resources. I have plans, I have ideas, but I lack the opportunity or a vehicle to express my plans and ideas through. Love Again, Until We Meet... In the End..."

'Still Wishing to Be Yours'

- Toussaint
January 10, 2019

———◆———

"Dearest Jenny,

"It is very important for me to express to you how much you really mean to me. I wish I could do this in person while holding you in my arms and gazing into your eyes. But since we are physically separated by miles of emptiness, this expression must come in the form of letters such as this. My Dear, I know it is difficult for you, as it is for me, to be separated for so long. Life seems to be full of trials of this type which test our inner strength, and more importantly, our devotion and love for one another. After all, it is said that "True Love" is boundless and immeasurable and overcomes all forms of adversity. In truth, if it is genuine, it will grow stronger with each assault upon its existence. "Jenny, our love has been assaulted many times, and I am convinced that it is true because the longer I am away from you, the greater is my yearning to be with you again. You are my enchanted Queen, and I am your devoted consort. I cherish any thought of you, prize any memory of you which rises from the depths of my mind and live for the day when our physical separation will no longer be."

"Until that moment arises, I send to you across the miles, my tender love, my warm embrace and my most passionate kiss."

'Love Always'

- Toussaint
January 10, 2019

"FAITH BELIEVE IN YOURSELF - I LOVE YOU"

Always, Dad

- Toussaint
February 5, 2019

"Jenny,

How are you? I was watching the Grammys last night and I thought of you. It was like music therapy for me, considering my access to choose music is limited, I sat there daydreaming of mine and your presence there merely as a quest. Time is passing us by and that sucks but I am actively putting in the effort to face myself so that I may be more proficient at taking on the outside world. Besides that, I hope you'll one day truly find the courage to forgive me, forgive your father and all of those you hold an unyielding resentment towards, so that the unbearable weight of unforgiveness can finally relieve you of its burden. Moreover, I pray you master up the strength to especially forgive yourself."

"P.S. Do you recall the name of that hospital I was admitted to in Baltimore back in 2009? If so, can you forward the name to me please or call my state paid attorney and provide him with the information, say it's the hospital I was admitted in at that time for mental health issues. That's all you need to tell them no-more-no-less, if you decide to call. Either way your assistance is appreciated. Thank you for everything."

Respectfully,

-Toussaint
February 6, 2019

———◆———

"Are you using your brain today or is it using you?"

"It's Not Your Fault I am where I am right now. Don't or try not to be angry with yourself, your Mommy and me, especially. I did not abandon you nor have I forgotten about you. I Love You very much although I can't be there with you. I really would like to know what you are feeling inside and wish to discuss those feelings with you. I am prepared to answer any and all the questions you have honestly, and all you have to do is write them down or ask Mommy and she'll write them down and I'll respond. Please try it."

*'If Ever You Fail and Don't Succeed - Get Back
Up and Try Again - Try Again.'*

P.S. Failing and then being encouraged to pick yourself up and go to the next challenge with the lessons learned from that failure are the life experiences that promises high achievement. Always Dad".

- Toussaint
February 6, 2019

———◆———

"You Can Do It!!!
LOVE YOU UNCONDITIONALLY
4EVA,Honey"

-Toussaint
February 6, 2019

◆

"Know Thyself"

"Princess,

Daddy loves you and misses you much. Although I make the best of each day, times are difficult for me. Mainly, because we are physically apart, and I couldn't reach out and touch you if I wanted to. So therefore, we must, working together, be creative and proactive by utilizing our only channel of communication (mail correspondence) to further develop and maintain our bond."

"Look, if I must be honest with you, Daddy is in time-out (jail) and it's no one's fault that I am here but my own. I deeply regret my poor choices and decisions and my being here is more the consequence of those series of actions. In other words, this is payment for inaccurate thinking (wrong thinking), ungoverned speech (wrong speaking), and misdeeds. Ultimately, I am here - not for the crime they say I committed, but for my dissolving commitment to you! My family".

"Although we grow in size and accumulate knowledge through experience over time, were never quite there. In life we never fully know anything, believe everything is subject to change and the only thing that remains constant is change itself, except for the immutable laws of the universe humankind identifies and attempts to align itself with what is called the Law of God. The point I am trying to make here is that although in essence, I am perfect. I make mistakes! Mistakes that can and have evidently cost me my freedom liberty, options of time and opportunity, and most importantly invaluable personal relationships to be cherished."

"My hope in being vulnerable and honest with you, particularly, in respect to me making mistakes is so that you can learn from them and not make the mistake your father has made. You are the new generation and the latest model. You are destined for greatness and no one or nothing can stop you!"

"Faith, study yourself and know yourself and study your environment and those around you. You should also express yourself. The best expression in life is self-expression. You should keep a diary. Every day of your life you should express not only how you feel but what you are learning from each experience".

"Keep your spirit strong. Never allow the forces of my absence to break your spirit. What "I mean by "your spirit" is your inner essence - not only what you think about, but your soul, your vibration, how you see the world, and your aspirations."

"P.S. I know you are probably wondering when is "my Daddy" coming home? Honestly baby, I don't know. I pray soon."

Love Dad

- Toussaint
February 11, 2019

———————◆———————

"Courage isn't having the strength to go on - it is going on when you don't have the strength" - Napoleon Bonaparte

"Hey,

Ya Jenny, I remember asking you a while back if you had ten dollars, would you give it to me - and you replied "Yes", then I went on to say to just put the ten bucks on the phone for as long as I've been knowing you it's not been easy for you to express your truth, how you feel and your reasoning. I guess you can say the same about me too. However,

I am evolving and have become more emotionally mature. Since I've learned to come to terms with my past. Oh, I didn't tell you, I've been for the past couple of months participating in counseling and therapy. I go to like those more difficult group sessions a day, such as anger management, domestic violence, substance abuse, stress management, and behavior therapy".

"Honestly, in my personal opinion, it's been helping me a lot along with the experience of being here particularly, but the counseling allows me to not only express my subjective views of things but to see things objectively as it's perceived by others. So, I say all that, to say, that all my life I've lived with many fears, doubt, anger, and resentment. I suffer from anxiety and from my past traumas which I've learned is exhibited in some of my anti-social behaviors. With the understanding and clarity of things especially of the self-knowledge I am constantly gaining. I am training or reprogramming my mind to be better sorted for the great challenge of being sent back out into the world naked".

"I'm a survivor and am not going to give up no matter those who have given up on me. I've always been ambitious and driven. I've always had a plan for achieving something worthwhile. The ideas I've had and have had all been great! The only problem had been the thoroughness of the plan. The plan must be detailed, realistic, and measurable. It's common sense that has not come so easily. Anyways, what I'm getting at is I got plans still greater plans - detailed plans that I'm currently working hard on and won't stop until I see it through. But my primary plan is to give that little girl the life she deserves! And moving forward, I declare, all that I do, will be in part, for her."

"For you baby, I got you. I want to help you. I owe it to you. And I will show you better than I can tell you regardless of the status of our relationship. You're my sister, we are friends and have been lovers for a while now. There may be a strain in our relationship at this time but I'm hoping the good can outweigh the bad and we can truly make amends reconcile and bond again, no matter what or who. I say it like that because I'm still unsure of where we stand. No, I don't know when I'm getting out of here, and won't keep my hopes up. So, I have it set in my mind to be content either way and not react but to respond appropriately in any case. I just hope that we can be adults and improve our communication to be more effective. That way we both know what to expect. Without assuming expectations. In other words, I can understand and respect your decision while reserving my opinions".

"Look I will be contacting you soon. I have a guy here who says he is willing to put up the funds and hire me a five-star attorney. I'll have to pay him back of course, but the key is getting me out and the payback will be handsome. Anyway, we had a small talk about it, and he asked that I make him a proposal and he likely will want some kind of collateral. I'm tryna put something together. I must think creatively. I Love You. TTYL"

"P.S. What's the address to the townhouse in Baltimore again?"

- Toussaint
February 12, 2019

"Your time is limited, so don't waste it liking someone else's life" - Steve Jobs (Apple)

"Hey Ja'Faith,

Daddy is sitting here attending a group session, while the counselor is reading off an Article by Erik Erikson's Stages of Psychosocial Development, and you came to mind. I got the feeling that you gave up the attempt to source out used merchandise (shoes, clothes, electronics, etc) to sell them via apps such as OfferUp or LetGo and Online on Ebay. Then you were successfully able to save up money and partner up with Mommy to purchase and activate your own mobile phone. What happened - what challenges were you confronted with something that discouraged you from proceeding with the project? You were really driven on the bleu of selling used merchandise and the accomplishment of obtaining that phone must have been eating for you as well. It just sucks that you no longer have service on the phone to make a phone call and that you've given up the efforts of earning yourself some money."

"Look I know what it is like to have an idea - typically without a plan, and when you go to execute your unwritten plan to bring your thoughts into fruition, you're those all of a sudden faced with some obstacles, barrier, or challenge of some sort that pressures you to either give up or get creative, think outside the box and overcome whatever you may feel as though is in the way, hence, coming up with a solution. When you start searching and don't finish it this can oftentimes cause one to feel like a failure. This behavior pattern then becomes a habit. Failure is then the result of the majority of your attempts and effort at selling problems in your personal affair as well as Business in general. I want you to know and understand that failure, poverty, and sickness is a mindset. In the Caring is a success! I want you to start while you are young to practice and develop a winning attitude by completing what you start no matter what. "If you aim for the mean, you may hit the stars and that's for". Ja'Faith I know you are in the developing stage of life where you are trying to find yourself, your strengths and weaknesses; and we've not given you any consistent platform where you can explore your talent like acting, music, dance, sports, etc but it's not too late you can do whatever your desire all your need is to believe and just do it!"

'I Love You So Much'

Dad,

P.S. "Tell your lovely Mother I said Hi and thank you for being such a loving, caring, and resilient parent and human being."

- Toussaint
February 20, 2019

"My Dear,

"Forgive me if it sounded, as if I was combatively, over talking to you on the phone tonight. Not only do I feel rushed and a sense of anxiety due to the limitation of time we have to speak on the phone but the complexities of my explanation of the collecting data concept was a factor. Maybe I didn't hear everything that you said and for that reason I'll practice being a better listener. I know that you are passionate about your idea of, the NCLEXNOTESNOW Online Review Course; I'm excited for you also. I want you to understand that my intention isn't to take away from the creative side of the business but to add value with new and useful information."

"You have something great on the Horizon and my perspective will help to crystallize things for you. I am looking at this from a marketing point of view; I am looking at the scope of this project and seeing it's potential for being a platform which is to search and gather information concerning medical professionals and nursing students like to understand certain behaviors and their mental processes. Analyzing this information will not only help you to improve your criteria, but can the information be significantly used in conjunction with dang business with other business. Also, you may in the process come up with your own license proven memory/ learning model that maximizes student retention."

"You can even in the future form a Strategic alliance with different agencies in placing employees/ nurses with their local hospital and get a commission. Baby there's way more to speak on, girl I do love you. I know I fucked up, but everybody fucks up, I will make it up to you, if, you let me. We must work together, it's more than about some emotions, sex, and carnal love bae. This is bigger than both of us. Send me pictures, divide them in different envelopes, sooner than later, that is. Remodel that house, it's your business too. Treat it like your own, take care of it. Get out of your feelings, it's logical reasoning and rational baby. It doesn't care if you're frustrated, stressed, or broke. It's shit going to be there for you to take care of. Get on your job! Fuck if I'm not there. Prioritize, get a routine going. Schedule your activity. Network amongst the right professionals, seminars, small business, Administration Conventions etc. Come from up under that rock and stop hiding. Go handle your business".

Love,

- Toussaint
March 28, 2019

"Success Requires No Explanations, Failure Permits No Alibis"

"Jenny,

You want to be a businesswoman, my advice to you is, don't be afraid or intimidated by the initial learning curve. Two P's you can attribute to your success. They are 'Patience and Passion'. When learning to run your own business, there are so many things to learn. It will be frustrating: You'll want to quit. But you must find the patience to continue. Where does that patience come from? **PASSION**. Your Passion will drive you to come back and ultimately acquire the knowledge you need to get the job done. Patience and Passion are two very powerful traits that can overcome many other weaknesses".

"P.S. I want you to be a Success".

- Toussaint
April 1, 2019 (2:00 am)

"Jenny,

My sister, my lover, my heroine. I get excited when I hear your voice especially, when you're gracing me with the reports of Your progress.

Hearing that you are back in the gym is refreshing. I encourage you to begin now and at once to stay on top of your health and remain constant with your exercise routine: get Faith in the habit as well, that mind of hers is very fertile. The time is pivotal where we must arouse our mind and body to have and strength and energy enough that we may outline a plan of action, creating for ourselves (our tribe) more desirable circumstances and conditions. We have no choice, but to both begin with where we are and work with what we got. But we must work smarter not harder and by smarter, I mean transcending our current mental limitations, using our intelligence and strategic thinking."

"We are all we got. We ought to think of our progenitors; Faith, she is because we have taught her, shown her, and passed on to her what guide does she have from us, that she will follow in keeping with the traditions, customs, and values laid at your feet. In the United States, neither can we expect anything to be handed to us. Anything we as a race of people ever gained here, politically, socially, and economically has always been at the expense of our leaders, ladies, our children. Today we are still paying for our rebellion and resistance against the powers that be. Now we must be wise, knowledgeable, intelligent, peaceful in our economic quest. Let us, however, in our plans direct our attention not so much to what is good and moral, but as to what is necessary and useful."

'Love You'

-Toussaint,
April 18, 2019

<hr />

"IN-IT-TO-WIN-IT"

"My Dear,

After speaking with you earlier today left me feeling disturbed and my thoughts racing for some mystical solution. To shine the light on the fact, we are Indeed facing a STATE OF EMERGENCY... I am deeply grieved by what you spoke to me on the phone and the sound of your voice. The hurt, the pain, the agony; the frustration, sorrow, and distress all resonated with me. I can relate. Sometimes I too can feel powerless, hopeless, and neglected. Powerless against, the established rule and system of things in our society, hopeless - without the means and resources to live and pursue a stable, secure, and well-balanced life: Neglect by the same life principle that formed all things by which we live, has brought us forth only to suffer."

"Don't take what I mentioned above literally, although there is conviction in what I say, however, as I begin to learn and understand more and more the external world around me -the world of effects, and this inner world within me. I recognize that the power lies in me us - each individual can cause what it is we desire to experience and see around us to be manifested. Yes, our ancestors for the most part, were brought in to those Americas as slaves, Yes the inequalities of "Minorities" in comparison to Whites are quite apparent all across the board - Socially, Economically and Politically; and no doubt there is a stinging injustice everywhere in our country and the Criminal Justice System or the "Prison Industrial Complex" is an organ in the body of every state on the Institution of Modern Day Slavery. Once you're in it takes great pains and effort to get out and remain out. Cool fine, shine the light on the facts America, has become subjects dependent on survival. I can still see the light! If an individual wishes to think and act a certain way, he/she/they/them must think and act in a certain way. Choose wisely the thoughts you entertain. Forget that inferior thinking and complex, think superior, fuck limitations. Move and know that you have an unlimited source of supply of everything you need."

"Begin to adopt an attitude of gratitude no matter what your energy is, contagious and if you're thinking at a low frequency then you can expect little to come back to you. Change up your routine/ exercise, limit, how many hours you sleep a day - and use the time that you're up for high productivity. Educate yourself, become money conscious, health conscious. Develop the faculties you need to run and operate a successful business. When you register an entity, it has no emotions; it works to serve two purposes - one, to generate profits and - two, solve a problem. If you will go through great pains in laboring and improving the system, function, and the way professionals operate - to be more efficient, how much more will you go at length in taking care of the affairs of your life. Yeah, baby it's hard, it's challenging, it's tough, you have no formal education in all this real-life stuff. That way there's something called self-education. The power, wisdom, knowledge within us. You have the potential, and you have the capacity, rise up in strength and have you some audacity. If you're going to do what's necessary, then manage your affairs like a business, you have many functions, divisions, departments, roles, duties, tasks. You are an Administrator as much as you are a paralegal in your legal department. You are Marketing Director as much as you are Human Resources. Until you can either creatively or afford to have some help you must be what it takes to run shit. Resilience, Persistence, Faith are prerequisites on this journey. Throw on your Wonder Woman Cape because you are worthy. No time to fall weak. No time to give up. Do more, be more. Stay away from toxins that only serve to kill your motivation."

'I Love You...

Forever Yours'

"FUCK IT - WE CAME THIS FAR"

- Toussaint
April 23, 2019 (Time 2:40am)

"Family Sticks Together Through the Hard Times"

"My Dear,

I know it's hard, but you got to keep your head up. We although knowing and feeling the oppression of the society were living in, we at the day

I still have a choice - to remain victims or become victors. I think we both can agree that being victorious is the preferred choice. We can sit here and look at everything that is apparently wrong or missing in both our lives, but what would be casting judgement, condemnation, and criticism upon our own head. That is simply counter productive. "Where attention goes, energy flows." And if you are to give any attention to your seemingly excessive woes, then at least give an inspecting eye to your problems with the mind to constructively solve them. Assess the various areas of your life and work your ASS off in improving them."

"Like you're considered a single mother and businesswoman, which requires Multitasking. Your work life balance, you'll have to figure it out by trial and error". Babe in you is the Will power - strength and the wherewithal to achieving order, balance, and tranquillity in your life. Don't get easily worked up about things and whatever difficulties come up, will eventually pass. You got to stay continually active but most importantly disciplined."

P.S. I am honestly good about stress management...- I NEED YOU

MARKETING STRATEGIES

Here a compiled a list of general ideas and creative ways of Marketing, Promoting, and advertising on and offline:

✓ First, developing beautiful, timeless, and effective content is important and necessary to fill the channels of your marketing chemicals and platforms. **Online Campaign: SOCIAL MEDIA (FACEBOOK; FACEBOOK Ads, Instagram, Instagram TV; Paid Post; Endorsements, Twitter, YouTube Channel; VLOG; YOUTUBE Ads,** Integrate all your digital marketing efforts with your website, sponsorships, etc. Advertise on complimentary websites for example post on non-competitive sites that offer a product or service to your target market.

✓ **SEARCH ENGINE OPTIMIZATION (SEO) - BLOG; EMAIL BLASTING; FORUMS!**

OFFLINE: CAMPAIGN
'Gorilla Marketing'

✓ Develop **create marketing tools**, pens, brochure, organizing material.

✓ **Promote** at local colleges, bulletin boards, hospitals (those used mainly for clinical rotations)

✓ **FORM** Strategic Alliances Retailers that sell products to your targeted demo

✓ **LEAD GENERATION** (sales/qualified data)

✓ Robo Calling/ Cold Calling

✓ Ads Publications Trade Magazines, LifeStyle, Radio Stations, TV

MORE...

QUESTION: Did the web developer encrypt the site? SSL Certificate to ensure the validity of the site. It's supposed to set the standard of security and secured Data.

✓ CUT YOUR STUDY TIME IN HALF

✓ Improve your success rate

✓ "NCLEXNOTESNOW ACHIEVE YOUR DREAMS"

✓ GUARANTEED TO PASS OR YOUR MONEY BACK

✓ NCLEXNOTESNOW WERE THERE WHEN YOU ARE TESTED

✓ PROVEN METHODS FOR MEMORY RETENTION

✓ STUDY AT YOUR PACE

"Those are different ideas of a mix of slogans as well as general context. You want to appeal to your targeted audiences' deepest needs, desires, and struggles. At least make them believe so."

Question:

✓ What is your vision for this brand/ and or business?

✓ What is your mission?

✓ What problem are you solving and how have you planned to solve it?

✓ Pre-Registration Assessment Test Requirement?

✓ Suggested Content Add-ons for Hosted site content on a virtual classroom/ online setting: modules, videos, tutorials, accommodate all aspects of learning (visual learners, text learners, and auditory learners)

✓ 'Giving it a micro-mix will be a good touch'

Fruit of thought! Just to get your juices flowing...

La Familia,

- Toussaint
April 24, 2019 (Time 2:45am)

———————◆———————

"Hey Babe,

I'm back; just had an incident where a fellow inmate or student, as I like to refer to them, lost his balance on the walker and fell on his way to the restroom. I helped him up and then was asked to wheel him down to the clinic. In this letter, I am going to share with you some ideas that are trending in social media".

"Social media allows for working your own personal profile or with Brand Ambassadors, Marketing Specialist, and starring in your own videos."

✓ What are some ways to improve your SM Marketing Strategy?

✓ What are some digital marketing channels other than social media?

✓ Observe people's behavior online to understand your audience

✓ Appropriate messages for those audiences and create engaging content.

✓ How do you engage your targeted audience in a conversation?

✓ Be present and interact with users within the site and application; go beyond using them to get visibility and traffic.

✓ Engage in one-on-one or group interactions, in addition to broadcasting.

✓ Be mindful about scaling marketing efforts by doing things like replying to every request and jumping into comments and posts.

✓ Personal Interactions - as a Brand, approach social engagements with a sincere desire to build professional relationships. If you can figure out creative ways of letting your audience know that they matter to your brand, they'll consequently help you grow your brand.

✓ Get your audience to promote your Brand by becoming an invaluable resource for them.

✓ When engaging with influencers one-on-one, know who to speak to, when, and how to speak to them.

✓ Also, as a strategy, shift more of your social media efforts into finding and nurturing strategic partnerships via relationship building.

✓ Use social media as a promotional channel, you'll get the highest return on time spent using social media to be social with non-competitive influencers, business owners, thought leaders, etc. This will lead to many opportunities for joint projects, client referrals, shared content ventures, and sharing of data for studies.

✓ Video Strategy (both live stream and upload)
Live Videos - partner with influencers and develop content that has more of a real human touch, that is not necessarily a costly production. With 'Reel' Videos (Instagram) and interactive uploads you can craft short videos that can run as ads without seeming out of tune with interactive shows on Facebook.

✓ Make smartphone-quality videos: videos made on a smartphone are the type of content customers look for and it doesn't decrease your brand equality, it makes the brand more approachable and trustworthy.

✓ Video Remarketing, many remarketing capabilities, when someone watches videos. Examine video capabilities and analytic data to continue to improve and provide us with even more granular targeting based off video advertisement.

VIDEO TIPS

✓ Set goals for the video

✓ Utilize software like Storyboard Creator

✓ Create a thirty to sixty-second video that you can use on Facebook, Instagram, and LinkedIn, and even TikTok

✓ For 'Stories' create fifteen-second micro-segment videos of the longer ones to utilize in 'Stories'. Repurpose the content in the video where and when you can.

✓ Put your best foot forward in the first ten seconds because no matter how interesting, useful, entertaining, or informative your video is, some viewers' attention spans tend to drop off at ten to fifteen marks.

✓ Look into the Facebook Messenger and Chat Bots (Market via Messenger). Chat Blasting is an effective way to reach and build audience engagement.

✓ Facebook Messenger Marketing is email blasting, except it's done via Messenger. My recommendations for optimizing this strategy would be to build a Facebook Messenger ChatBot, grow your Facebook Messenger Contacts, and start strategically delivering content via Messenger.

✓ Community and Socialization: use social media as more than just a broadcast medium but a promotional channel to drive traffic and brand awareness. People want more than artificial attempts of engagement so offer authentic communication that helps connect and create meaningful relationships.

✓ Build niche or subculture communities such as Facebook Groups. Facebook groups are a hot spot for audience engagement and a place to focus social media efforts. People crave a sense of belonging with their respective tribes and want to participate in meaningful groups. Invest in managing niche groups to foster deeper relationships with our communities.

✓ Paid Promotion Budget: Create content that naturally creates engagement rather than begging for it. Invite followers to a conversation not a sales pitch. Emphasize privacy protection.

✓ By implementing the right Monitoring and Tracking tools, you'll be able to manage all your social conversations and provide real-time customer service.

✓ Tell authentic stories and share moments that matter, don't rely solely on static updates. Instead share more behind-the-scenes, raw, and intimate stories. 'Stories' creates a more transparent and meaningful relationship between the user and the brand. Share 'Stories' that matter to the people, not the brand. This will require a knack of improved storytelling.

✓ Take your web content and create one-minute videos on those same topics, posting those videos to Facebook, LinkedIn, and other channels.

✓ Track and monitor the percentage of how much reach the one-minute video has.

✓ Take your best-performing posts from social media and convert them to an article.

✓ You can repurpose Facebook Live Videos into podcasts, articles, tweets, and other derivative content. Content that works for your audience on one channel or platform is also likely to work on other platforms even if those audience members aren't the same.

✓ Work with Influencers and Micro-Influencers

✓ Influencer Marketing; Create Campaigns; There are seasoned influencers and nano influencers (ordinary digital citizens with 1,000 to 5,000 followers). You can also look for influencer agencies and micro-influencer marketing. Search for agencies compatible with your brand and your budget.

✓ Leverage: LinkedIn has a lot of informative business content sharing and connection nurturing networks. LinkedIn gives users the ability to join groups, post videos, and link business services).

✓ Create a mobile-friendly website. A website experience that is easily accessed for mobile trends on every aspect of digital marketing, including social media from social posts and engagements.

"P.S. It's now 8:00 am and I'm getting tired. I hope much of this information is useful for you, and that you'll be able to apply them strategically. I'll elaborate more in my next letter with respect to raising capital and generating an income. I LOVE YOU TO THE DEATH OF ME!"

One Love,

- Toussaint
April 24, 2019 (5:35 am)

'Had To Get-It Out'

"My Dear,

What you are experiencing right now, sucks. Poverty sucks, living at your mother's house at 33, married, with a child sucks! Your husband being incarcerated for the second time in a row in less than a year and a half sucks. You can easily give up on everything and even me right now, but you must push on, this is testing our commitment to achieving a better life together. We didn't marry for money or power because neither one of us had it, but deep down inside we knew that our future could come. However, it's a process and we will get past the shit, although painful and it seems that there's been more downs than ups. Wos will, 'no doubt', transcend them, thus delivering strength in characteristic taking shape within us today. "Money does not make us rich, knowledge does".

"Real life financial education consists of a long-term process of classes, seminars, study, reading, successes, failures, good times, hard times, crooks, con-men, liars, cheats, mentors, bad partners, and great partners."

"My Dear, the nursing review website is your first real business venture that you've decided to take on. Building a business is a process. I know that a part of you is anxious to jump right in and make a lot of money.

Sorry to burst your bubble, but it rarely ever works like that. You got to start and dream big. Expect to make mistakes but make small mistakes, learn, and keep dreaming big. Remember you want to school for nursing students not for business, nor financing. Therefore, my challenge yourself to go beyond what's comfortable for you and develop the discipline to achieve the goals you set, and we set as a couple".

✓ Business Goals
✓ Fitness Goals
✓ Fun Goals
✓ Asset Goals

"Turn that property you purchased on Scott Street into positive cashflow real-estate. Our main goal is financial freedom; the reason I or you are in any of this mess right now. Invest time in increasing your knowledge in real estate investing. Analyze remaining income after expenses and debt. As a couple, we should be setting our financial goals together. Second, study together in order to achieve the goals we set. Attending seminars, reading books, meeting with real experts, and working with coaches so that we get what we want in life, essentially. Work with coaches, whether a fitness coach, business coach, or investment coach because sometimes we need that kick in the butt to keep us moving forward. The purpose of education is to equip a person with the power to take information and process it into knowledge. If a person does not have financial education, they cannot process information and do not know the difference between an asset or a liability, capital gains or cash flow, fundamental investing, or technical investing. Why the rich pay less in taxes, or why debt makes some people rich and most people poor. They do not know a promising investment from a bad investment, or good financial advice from bad financial advice. Work hard, pay taxes, live below your means, buy a house, get out of debt, and die poor. As the bible states, "my people are destroyed for a lack of knowledge" (Hosea 4:6). Invest in your financial education. Invest your time before you invest your money."

"My dear visit the United States Business Administration to see what information you can get from there. They can help you with the planning of your business, launching it, managing it, and growing it. They have a blooming connection with local assistance from mentors and coaches. I urge you to look into it and begin your journey in educating yourself properly."

Note: "For that property in Baltimore, maybe you could do small renovations to rent the property or 'as is'. Renovations must be done in stages, which will go against the rent. For example, if it cost $7,000 to bring the property up to live-in condition, and rental rates were $1,000 a month, $12,000 a year then we'd only ask for $500/ month to rent the row house out for the year. All this can be defined in the terms and conditions of the lease agreement. If the tenant is a licensed contractor, even better, if not then I am sure there are ways to pull a permit for jobs that need to be done. Food for thought. More on this later."

- Toussaint
May 2, 2019 (6:00 am)

"My child you may not know me, but I know every-thing about you. I know when you sit down and when you rise, for even the very hairs on your head are numbered for you were made in my image. I knit you together in your mother's womb and brought you forth on the day you were born. You were not a mistake for all your days are written in my book. I am not distant and angry, but I am the complete expression of love. It is my desire to lavish my love on you. Simply because you are my child, and I am your father. My thoughts towards you are countless like the sand on the seashore and I rejoice over you with singing, I will never stop doing good to you for you are my treasured possession. My plan for your future has always been filled with hope because I love you with an everlasting love. Jesus came to represent that I am for you not against you, he is the exact representation of my being. I gave up everything that I loved that I might gain your love. When I come home, and I'll throw you the biggest party heaven has ever seen. I offer you more than your earthly father ever could, for I am the perfect father. I've always been a father and always will be a father, my question is will you be my child?"

'Love Dad Almighty GOD!'

- Toussaint
May 11, 2019

"My Dear,

Where must we begin? How do we begin in opening a dialogue of a much needed conversation. A conversation consisting of a wide range of topics pertaining to: Love and Marriage, Parenting, Business etc."

"Consider these are general topics and are not an exclusion of the smaller details of our relations to one another that makes up the whole. There are plenty of points that need to be outlined collectively, with careful analysis and addressed by the two of us. Some topics can be sensitive to the point it arouses such emotions as - fear, jealousy, hatred, revenge, anger, and superstition. But we, in exemplification of emotional maturity must endeavor to set aside our selfish negative emotion if we wish to find peace and harmony within ourselves and mutuality between one another, especially, if we are to constructively begin healing and restoring our union."

"Which issues are at the moment, the most pressing? My need of an attorney, the conversation of a liability into an asset (the Baltimore Property), Strategic planning for successfully building a business, Faith enrolling in an advance school, and the proper use of your available source of income. I have my ideas and opinions but to be totally honest with you, ever since I come out from doing my first bid, I've felt excluded from much of what's been going on to the point where decisions weren't being made correspondingly. I felt inferior, I felt small and as though I lost control of things, I sought whereby I imposed my dominance as a man, elsewhere, to no avail. This isn't entirely your fault; I lacked the skills at the time on how to effectively communicate my actions with my thoughts. Much harm could've been prevented".

"This letter is not to condemn you nor accuse you, it is rather, again the attempt at coming to the resolve of a middle ground between us and establishing from this point on what we want and expect of one another and to clarify any confusion, misunderstanding and preconceived ideas we hold. Not tryna play guessing games no more neither can I expect you to have the ability to read my mind."

"Like I said, I have my opinions and ideas, but am unsure how they will be viewed. Especially at this point where so much is bottled up emotions, the good kind, because an obstruction in any and all our attempts for forward progress. But we must start somewhere and that's where we are now in our respective places with all its conditions and circumstances to make it all work. It's not going to be every and it's never been, but we can either pick it up and carry it or drop it and walk away. Trust must be restored. The task is a great one, my troubles have doubled and you're a burden much. I'm truly sorry for this. I recognize I have treated two of you unfairly, which pains me. Moreover, I am learning that you ladies were just the casualty of a war that I've been battling within. If there's any pain I've inflicted, as, I indeed have, upon your physical beings, and damages upon your soul; I've done so only to my demise. Forgive me, if what I am about to say sounds arrogant and selfish, but the consequences of my actions, I technically speaking, alone suffers."

"I had no intention of writing or calling you ever. Only because I felt hurt and we weren't getting nowhere in our conversation, moreover, except I develop an astronomical amount of faith and/ or come up with a practical plan, whereby, I can acquire the monies to pay a private attorney than the prospects of me having here anytime soon is slim. So, with that I concluded why even bother, "if there isn't any operation in setting forth the effort to get me out. What is there to talk about." Of course, this thinking is ruled by fear, and a number of other negative emotions. I want to change that. So, I forgive you, but the fact remains that I am here and you're out there, now what?"

P.S. "I am so delighted that my daughter is morphing into a little woman (ouch!) Saddens me that I am here. Feel like my bond is broken with her and there's so much I can teach her and show her, and she can even teach me and show me. I recommend you read "Think and Grow Rich" and thank you for the pictures."

Love,

- Toussaint
May 29, 2019

<hr />

"My Dear,

"Everytime, I view a picture of Jay-Z and Beyonce I think of us - I think of where we could be or should be at this point. A power couple - a dynamic duo on the conquest of personal achievement while impacting the world around us. I love you're my darling and will always be. You are bright although you tend to shy away from allowing your light to shine. You are capable of all things demanding your role as a leader, if only, you'd believe in your abilities more. Highly intelligent, this you are, but learning does not end with school. It's been a lonely world without you - I've been a fool without you - Sorry I ever doubted you. I know you've been doubted much throughout life. Sorry your father left you; I didn't mean to bring back upon you this curse of abandonment. I swear there's not another like you, this I assure you - you are unique. From your smile, to the showing of your teeth all the way to the shape of your eyes at the raising of your cheeks."

"You have a great sense of taste and an amazing sense of style, everything about you is posh, this just comes natural to you. It soothes me to hear your always possibly, the first quality about you that I fell in love with.

Secondly, your gentle and gracious tongue has been more sweet to me than honey can ever be!"

"Thank you forever for believing in me. You've been my cheerleader and have made me proud - you've also been my pride and my joy, succeeding in making my heart smile. Your past means nothing to me, only that it's brought you to me. You are strong - a woman distinguished amongst the rest of them - you never had to stoop to their level in emulating them all you have to do is take lead in yourself and be you and the rest will follow suit. I've always regarded you as sacred to me. I've always thought it my duty to protect you even if that meant it would cost me life or death, jail, or liberty. You've not yet reached your potential so don't stop now. The evolution of amazing women. I met, and fell in love with is still in there, and is herself waiting to be set free. Beaming in you is your own personal sun attempting to crack through your stormy clouds; weather it. I always believed with the two of us together, we could accomplish any task we set our minds to and be successful - if we exercise practical methods and sound judgment. When I was hustling, I wouldn't involve you much, except for keeping work in the house and driving with it in the car because I was afraid of putting you in harm's way. I even, which was one of my greatest fears - of getting arrested for dealing, knowing it would separate us. I wanted out long time ago, but I was limited in my thinking of exploring available options - that will produce as much. My pride for the most part with the barriers my record brought on, prevented me from opting for a regular nine to five. All I'm saying is if we would set aside our fears, and in a cooperation and concerted effort we could've then make a better analysis of our situation and probably have become the MOB by now having successfully run a drug enterprise - which branched off to legitimate businesses (MOB WIFE). Anything we desire to do, and we do together we can attain the object in back of it. I Love You and Happy Belated B-Day!!!"

"With Best Wishes, Believe Me Cordially Yours"

- Toussaint
June 6, 2019 (7:00am)

"My Dear,

"Our marriage was not motivated by wealth, neither of us possessed. It was our love, honor, and a connection and collaboration to accumulate a Fortune and have a will to acquire and maintain a commitment to each other legally - and through other methods of support to grow together our passion and loyalty for one another, lead us to seek a legal bond. When we first met you were just a young lady trying to get through nursing school - obviously not your passion and probably the influence of just a college student trying to decide a major out of the fear of just not having a clear vocation, job, or career upon graduation or it may have been the option for some women select to work in healthcare as a career path. As for me, a hustler by circumstances; my cash flowed from the commercial activities surrounding the underworld, but I've always been a dreamer-like yourself-and had the aspirations of becoming a "Musical Artist".

"You may wonder, where am I going with this? Just brace yourself for a minute and hear or read me out. When our union was finally sealed, together the thoughts of our minds were enlarged this expanding our initial aspirations to greater inspirations and loftier ideals. We envisioned, unconsciously at the time of becoming entrepreneurs - serial entrepreneurs - with dreams of owning multiple businesses and engaged in philanthropic activities allowing for us to be of the utmost service in providing jobs and creating opportunity for thousands if not millions of others. This vision was and still is depicted on a piece of construction paper we crafted together-symbolizing for us the 'Tree of Life - Our Life - Our Family'. The rendering of that design pointed us in a direction of success. It meant for us, improved circumstances and conditions, leisure and luxury, security, and comfort, and ultimately a unique way of life distant from the moves we make be inherited by our offsprings. That point was the mark of our "Economic Conquest", our escape from adverse conditions - poverty, misery, want and disease. Somewhere along the lines our effort was thwarted - our personal crisis and economic conditions has extended now for too long of a period. I take accountability - my charting back into the past isn't to condemn or criticize you, but rather it is in effort to analyze and closely examine the outcome of our current state of condition. So, in remembrance of that piece of paper in the moment we signed together - I found therein lies the root of the issues; and led to information that was missed by being shortsighted - that allowed for our marriage to be seen as if it was illusionary and the appearance of failure - I, now, refer to it as "temporary defeat". So fundamental is that thing that we missed, if we were to grasp it today then we can easily make up for our last financially - unfortunately, we can never make up for lost times."

"I've had a "Moment of Clarity "? This for me - not realizing then - indicates many things but of the most fundamental, practical, and profound thing that echoes to me now is Baby Steps", like an embryo goes through developmental stages of maturity (as all living organisms) so to, does a business - or any form of a relationship. Our dreams are so massive that at the sign of defeat we slowly lose hope - not maintaining faith. In the Outset of our Marriage, we never sat down and outlined a blueprint - to discuss issues firmly in all aspects - neither did we have an outline to a business plan or blueprint that would guide us along our adventures. We neglected the opportunity to equip ourselves with the necessary education and skills that would have thoroughly prepared us for any personal and business undertakings. I designed a definite plan, purpose, goal, and objectives. You speak of your wish of my presence- when meeting these men who seem to have accomplishments by boasting of their personal achievements. Well, the truth is I am with you in all that you do and before all whom you encounter. I am living vicariously through you. You are my eyes, my ears, and my mouth. What will I have to do or say or look for? Mind control is the result of self-discipline and habit. You either control your mind or it controls you. There is no half-way compromise. The most practical of all methods for controlling the mind is the habit of keeping it busy with a definite purpose, backed by a definite plan. Exercises your control over your own mind and directs it towards the attainment of definite objectives."

"The females you say that are clinging to you- let them cling - in fact, you'll be surprised of the power you can foster by being of 'service' to them. As for you, focus on your personal service and marketing your current occupation, developing skills such as pole dancing, etiquette and developmental classes, leadership qualifications, establishing yourself as an authority figure, and mind your conduct and actions before them. Naturally, they'll look to find where you are weak, but blindly they'll follow. You are the grand daughter of a general, a descendant of Ancient Nobility. Your social and economic status today isn't permanent. I have faith in myself and faith in the infinite. This lifestyle has its highs and its lows. Is chicks put themselves at anyone's mercy by disclosing their fragility and vulnerabilities, prevent from being too talkative, conceive false and empty promises, fueled by flattery and sorority; remember these men you meet are customers, clients, patients, and your involvement with them is exclusively Business. You must be placed at a premium - you aren't to accept any personal engagements except if it be business requirements. They must know you are about your business "Cash is King'. Don't just hand over your money without examining what alternatively could be done. Guard your mind from the susceptibility of negative influence. Don't teach your mind to be open to the negative influence of other people. If you must be careless with your possessions, then it is useless with material to others. Your mind is your spiritual state. Protect and use it with the cares in which the divine royalty is entitled. You were given a "Will-Power" for this purpose."

- Toussaint
June 10, 2019 (Time 6:45am)

"Would you tell me, please which way I ought to go from here?"

"That depends a good deal on where you want to get to," said
the Cat." - Lewis Carrol, Alice's Adventure in Wonderland

"Ja'Faith, what you do today will count for the morrow what you fail to do today you'll still be left with to do come the morrow. What do mean by that? Today's work is for the morrow's leisure; you can never relax until you have sufficiently fulfilled 'day's work'. Now what in the heck do I mean by that? Faith, carefully observe your habits today, your hobbies today, and your interest today because this may be what contributes to your success tomorrow or just may be the reason for your downfall. You have a dream to be a singer - well sing on today and bring the distant future in the here and now. Sing-sing-sing... write-write-write, do it only because you love it and it makes you feel alright. The world is a grand stage, and we are all merely performers; assuming many different roles, playing many different characters. You can choose to be whatever and whoever you'd like to be, but if you honor my opinion, the best role - is to simply be yourself. Then is it real-then is it authentic- then are you original and reassured greatly as a class act. Why wait for a coach, why wait to be implicated in a talent show only to be brought before judges imbued with bias and prejudice that would automatically disqualify you unless you've paid the ransom. Consequently, disparaging your true talent. Why- let the people vote - grab a camera. Get in front of the computer screen - showcase your talent and devise a theme."

"The most successful people in life are those who begin early in the fundamental lessons of getting money. What is money- money is an idea- money is a medium of exchange - wait go back - did you say money is an idea?"

"Well, I have plenty of ideas! What are you waiting for to put your ideas to work for you so that you can get the results you're looking for? A lemonade stand begins as an idea by the time it's taken from the mind and is what you see in the physical world (it materializes) the money or currency begins to flow towards it or you. But the earliest product or service you can provide is something that either solves a problem or fulfills a need. Whatever it is that you decide to do my dear. First, do your research like a little mad scientist - dig deep and scratch the surface - so that you know and understand everything that is required of you before you start."

"If you fail and you don't succeed, get back up and try again! Read everything that you can possibly get your hands on the subject of interest. If it's money, study the way accounting works, financing, etc. If it's acting learn all that you can about that-read or watch videos of the stars that came before you. My point is this: whatever you desire to be the best at it and do your best; know everything there is to know about it and know that "no man is an island", get the best people to help you."

"P.S. I am terribly sorry for my absence and hope that even with this handicap, you can translate it into a source of strength."

"I Love You!"
    Dad!

-Toussaint
August 26, 2019

"COMING THROUGH THE FIRE"

"Although believers we have victory in Jesus, although we have the power in Him to triumph in every situation, sometimes things got tough"

"Sometimes we encounter troubles and trials that drag on... and on... and on (despite our desperate prayers for relief) until we want to say what the Old Testament prophet Habakkuk said in the Bible: "O Lord, how long shall I cry for help and you not hear? Or cry out to you of violence and you will not save?" (Habakkuk 1:2) Almost every person on earth has been tempted to ask such questions at one time or another. It might have been because they needed healing and prayed for it for weeks, months or even years without seeing any results. It might have been because they were struggling with family issues or financial challenges they couldn't seem to receive. In those kinds of situations, we can all make the mistake Habakkuk did. We can be tempted to give in to the pressure of the devil, point the finger of blame of God and way, "Why

Although as belle - Is this taking so long? Aren't You listening to me?" But that is exactly the wrong thing to do. The trouble in our belief is that wins or victories are never God's fault. He is never behind it. When we ain't seem to opt answers to our prayers. He is not the problem; the problem is always on our end".

"Habakkuk can confirm it. He learned that lesson well when God answered all his questions with one simple statement. "The Just Shall Live by His Faith" (Habakkuk 2:4), or as the Amplified Bible puts it: "The Just and the (UNCOMPROMISING) righteousness shall live by faith and in his faithfulness".

"In a nutshell, that's where Habakkuk missed it. He'd been complaining up a storm to the Lord, pleading with him to fix the mass around him, but he hadn't been operating by faith. God works with faith and Habakkuk hadn't given Him anything to work with. The same can sometimes be said of us. Whenever we aren't getting the results we want from God, it's not because God is failing to do His part. It's because we're missing it where our faith is concerned. We aren't doing our part to receive the victory He has already provided. "But Honey," you might say, I've been walking by faith for years. I know how to do my part!" That might be true, but no matter how much you know, you can let things slip if you don't stay on top of them. What's more, every one of us is still learning. No one has arrived yet. Taking a faith refresher course is always a good idea. Especially when we're handling them the way God expects - not like Habakkuk did, but like Shadrach, Meshach, and Abednego. They went through a time of trouble the likes of which most of us will never experience. They were literally thrown into a raging inferno simply for refusing to worship a King's idol! Talk about a fiery trial! Shadrach, Meshach, and Abednego really went through it! But they know what to do. They lifted up their faith shield and quenched all the fiery darts of the devil (Ephesians 6:16). They not only survived the fire, they came out of it unharmed. "Not a hair on their heads was singed, and their clothing was not scorched. They didn't even smell of smoke" (Daniel 3: 27) All because they lived by faith."

> "Our lives have been put together by God and He wants
> us to live abundantly, so let's do it! Let's live by Faith."

"A substance more precious than Gold. What, exactly, is faith? It's believing what God says, regardless of what we might see, feel, or hear in this natural world. It's believing His word without compromise. It's being so confident God will fulfill His promise that no matter how much trouble the devil brings our way, we can say like Shadrach, Meshach, and Abednego did, "Our God whom we serve... Will deliver us" (Daniel 3:17, Amp)! According to the Bible, faith is "The substance of things hoped for, the evidence of things not seen" (Hebrews 11:1) "The victory that over cometh the world", (1 John 5:4)

"A force so powerful it will move the mountains in our lives. (Mark 11:23) so valuable, it is truly "more precious than Gold" (1 Peter 1:7) But it doesn't become ours simply because we want it. You can't just decide", I'm going to live by faith," and let that be the end of it. You have the backup to make a clear decision with action. You have to open up your Bible and see what God has to say, because "faith cometh by hearing, and hearing by the word of God" (Romans 10:17). Anyone who spends enough time in the world can be a faithful person. I could give a Bible to a beggar on the street and if he would read it, meditate on it and act like what it says is true, he could prosper. By this time next year, his poverty trial could be over. He and his circumstances could be so completely transformed that he wouldn't even seem like the same person, such transformations don't take place, however, just because someone needs an occasional scripture now and then. They don't happen to people who just have an easy-going, take-it-or-leave-it kind of attitude toward the Bible. They only happen in the lives of people who are seriously committed to knowing and doing what God says. "For thus says the Lord... seek me (inquire for and of me and require me as you require food) and you will live!" (Amos 5:4, Amp) This is the first key to overcoming any trouble you'll ever face. It's primary secret to overcoming faith: make God and His Word as important to you as the physical food you eat. Most likely, you rarely go very long without eating natural food. You're very diligent about it. I am too. At dinner time, "Where are you?" If I'm not there!" That's the way all of us born-again believers should be about the Word of God. We should be about the Word of God. We should be as loyal to it as we are to the dinner table. After all, God's Word is Spiritual Food! It nourishes our body. In nature humans can't go far physically without 'food' and you can't go far spiritually without spending time in the word. Like 'The Goat', you need to be feeding on it everyday! When you're going through a fiery test or trial, you should feed on the Word as often as possible all day long. Instead of wasting time watching secular television or doing some other silly thing, you should get into the Word and stay there. If you'll do that, you'll be well on your way to walking in victory, because when you require the Word the same way you require physical food, God says, "You Shall Live"?"

"God is your deliverer. James 1:7; "Every good gift and every perfect is from above, and cometh down from the father of lights, with whom there is no variableness, neither shadows of turning".

"Don't take the Road of Least Resistance "But I have been spending time in the Word, "you might say," and nothing has changed yet!" Well, just stick with it. Don't quit now! If you quit, you won't have any hope at all. Keep giving God something to work with. Stay in faith - and while you're at it, make sure your behavior matches your believing. That's what Shadrach, Meshach, and Abednego did. They not only believed God's Word in their hearts, but they also honored Him with their actions. They obeyed God's commands and became living illustrations of Isaiah 33: 14 15: "Who among us can dwell with that disastrous fire? He who walks righteously and speaks upright". If you work to be a person who comes through the 'fire' without getting burned, you must do the same. You must not only believe right on the inside, you must do right on the outside. You must be obedient to the Lord's commands. "But I thought you said faith is what matters!" It is - and obedience is inseparable from faith. Think about it, if we believe what God says, we're going to do what He tells us to do. We're going to walk upright and talk uprightly, even when we're faced with trying situations like sickness, poverty, or persecution. Don't misunderstand me. I'm not suggesting that as faith people we never stumble or miss it. I'm just saying that when we do, we are quick to repent. We don't try to hide from God or Justify our disobedient actions, we just say. "Lord, I was wrong. Please forgive me. I bleed the blood of Jesus and receive it, cleaning power. I ask you to help me and give me grace, so I'll never do that again. "Then we got back on track. We go back to walking and talking in line with God's Word. As a result, when trials do come, we have the confidence we need to stand against the devil, who is the one behind them. We can shake our fingers in his face and tell him to get his hands off our health, our finances, and our families for His name's sake! If the devil does not listen to you? Then you need to study what the New Testament says about the subject. It teaches that as born-again believers we have authority over the devil, and whom we have authority over the devil, and when we resist him, he flees from us (James 4:7). It also says that we're the ones responsible to keep the devil out of our lives and give him no place (Ephesians 4:27). Of course, even people who know those things sometimes get lazy and fail to act on them. I was reminded of this a few years ago when I was on the road. We'd finished ministering in Detroit and had arrived in Milwaukee where we were scheduled to minister again. When we got to the hotel on Saturday night, I was rather tired. So, I got into my pajamas and climbed into bed. "I'm taking the road of least resistance!" said. As I spoke these words, I realized that's what many people do when it comes to dealing with the devil. They take the road of least resistance. When sickness tries to come on them or they're faced with some other kind of trial, they just put on their 'spiritual Jammies', climb into the bed. They just hide under the covers and hope God will do something to help. That's a recipe for failure! The devil is the thief. He comes into our lives "to steal, and to kill, and to destroy". Jesus come that we might have life, and that (we) might have it more abundantly" (John 10:10). If we want to enjoy the abundant life Jesus has provided, we must receive it by faith, stand up to the devil and resist.

"He works with your faith, " Habakkuk 2:4 "The Just Shall Live by His Faith".

"We must say "No, you don't thief! You're not coming into my family. You're not stealing on my account. You're not destroying my health. I will not tolerate you in any part of my life. In the name of the Savior, I ease you out! Now Go!"

"Do you know whose voice you hear when you say those things? The one whipped him in the pit of hell. Jesus is the one who "having spoiled principalities and powers, he made a show of them only, triumphing over them in it" (Colossians 2:15). Jesus is the one who stripped the devil of all his power and left him with absolutely nothing, and gave us His Name to use! All the devil has to use against us now is lies! He doesn't have any power that we don't give him. So don't give him anything to work with. Don't give him your words. Don't give him your actions. Don't yield to him. Instead give it all to print. Give God everything to work with in your life and give no place to the devil! I will warn you though, in spite of the fact that the devil is a major loser, he does have one thing going for him. He is persistent. He's not triumphant but he is tenacious. You have to be aggressive with seeking God's promise, I used to illustrate this by describing how my mother would have reacted if an old slop hog had ever gotten into her living room. That was always easy for me to envision because my mother was a bold woman and she had white living room furniture. If some filthy hog had ever dared to poop near that furniture, she would have kicked it out of the house fast! She wouldn't have talked softly to it. She wouldn't have gently asked it to leave."

"She would have gone after it tooth and nail. She not only would have, should have, she would have grabbed the broom and beaten the shit out of that hog. We ought to be the same way. After all, spiritually speaking, we have a white living room, too. We've been washed clean by the blood of Jesus and made white as snow. Our lives have been put together by God and he wants us to live abundantly. So let's do it! Let's live by faith, take authority over the devil and triumph over every trouble. Let's come through every fiery trial like Shadrach, Meshach, and Abednego - unharmed and smelling like a rose!"

"Faith and obedience are inseparable, so believe right and do right. Isaiah 33:14-15: "who among us can dwell with that devourous fire? Who among us can dwell with these everlasting burnings? He who walks righteously and speaks uprightly..."

"Living the Spiritual life is not a piece of cake. Anyone who says it isn't telling you the whole story".

"Be diligent to stand against the devil. James 4:7 "submit yourselves therefore to God, Resist the devil, and he will flee from you."

- Toussaint
September 19, 2019

"If I have seen further than others it is by standing on the shoulders of giants" - Isaac Newton

"Faith,

You're an amazing beautiful human being. I thought you should know. Despite what anyone may think, not that their opinions matter - you are genius enough and perfect enough for me. Even my praises, you may reason, is to be expected as part of the typical intercourse between parent-child relationships, this isn't quite so! A Lot of parents, you'll find that are mostly in depressed circumstances having a poor mental constitution - do the opposite - they project their negative feelings and energy onto their children. Regardless of this fact - whether I praise you (motivate/ encourage) or not, the difference is in what you think of yourself although the influence of your immediate environment will have its bearing on your mind. With that being said, you don't need anybody's permission to be independent minded. It's ok to think differently, form your own opinion, express your unique views - after all its what freedom is all about!"

"Really quickly, to follow up on my last letter in reference to 'setting goals', realize the example I gave about the iPhone was just that an example. It doesn't have to be taken literally obviously there are variables to consider when planning the purchase of a merchandise such as the iPhone - like do you have to buy it brand new? Could you buy it refurbished at a discount? If you decide to buy it now, then can you put down a fraction of the price and arrange to make monthly payments on it? My point is to introduce you to the concept of setting goals, so that you may apply it in your daily life, setting daily, weekly, and monthly goals. Also, making sure that your goals are realistic, attainable, and worth pulling the effort towards. The lesson here is for you to begin practicing to be better organized, more efficient, and maximize and manage both your potential and time."

"Notice I have enclosed with this letter an article I tore out of the WASHINGTONIAN publication about a young girl Naiomi Wadler. I recommend you read it - it's truly an inspiring piece. If for any reason you have a tough time either understanding my handwriting or a word, I used that you're unfamiliar with, consult the dictionary! Expanding your vocabulary can be one of the most important things you can do to improve your literacy and articulation skills. I promise. Remember, I Love You and more so for being you. Stay true to yourself and you won't have to worry about impressing anyone - else."

Dad

- Toussaint
October 8, 2019

"There are two kinds of people in this World: *a leader* and *a follower* - choose which one you are."

"Ja'Faith,

It's me again, your father, by the grace of some unseen force I will make it out of this bind and when I do, I am coming to be by and on your side. This, I not only promise to you, but I promise to myself I've made the vow to God Heaven. How I feel, your Love for me is pure and unconditional. You find no fault with me even when I am honest with you, in sharing the lessons of my mistakes and weaknesses. As I told you on the phone, you're my motivation for waking up with the right attitude of mind, knowing "this too shall pass". Welcoming the day when we shall skate or love tag again. If you've suddenly lost interest in those activities - that's ok! Because there's a world of activities we can get into and am perfectly down with whatever makes you happy."

"I encourage you to read. Read all that you can get your hands on and put your eyes to, you will find that New Worlds are opening up to you."

"If you want to hide anything from a man, hide it in a book because he'll almost never pick it up". Remember that the best education is self-education! Opportunity comes to those who create it. You are the captain of your soul and the Master of your Fate'. The genius is within you - follow your spirit guide - it inspires you, gives you ideas and sends you haunches. Don't be afraid to act on it. You're a child of Heaven (that Gods) be not distracted by the devil and his/ her tools. Remember the devil isn't some red human figure with sharp pointy ears, long tail, and a pitchfork; the devil comes in many shapes, forms, and sizes. The devil can even possess you if you let it in. So therefore, always be on guard of your mind. You must be on point of the kind of "friends" ('so-called-friends') you choose to befriend - not everyone you meet and share a few seemingly pleasurable moments with these considered 'friend' - in fact misery does love company - so misery would be the first to call you out to play. More so, in life, you'll find as you get older that everyone whom you encounter today that was given the title of a friend will be your enemy tomorrow or a stronger one. In other words, it's a waste of time hoping to make friends - building smart and strategic relationships or alliances is different because it promotes your cause. For example, the young lady whom you associate with when you've said that her mother organizes the Girl Scouts, which led to you becoming a member of, is a strategic alliance because it's profitable and useful for you in many ways."

"This doesn't necessarily mean that you should go around using people - no, but you should definitely analyze who you associate with as they're energy, reputation, and image can strongly reflect on you. There's a saying "birds of a feather flocks together, "who are you flocking with? Trust no one but yourself. No man is your friend, no woman is your enemy, but all are your teachers".

"You Are Gifted - It's not your first Worldly Experience"

P.S. "Genuine/ jèny-yoo-in/ adj.1) really coming from it's stated, advertising or reputed source 2) properly so called; not sham 3) sincere; authentic, veritable, real, bonafide, legitimate."

Love You

-Toussaint,
October 17, 2019 (4:00AM)

·+————————◆————————+·

"Great love has no one that this, that someone lay down his life for his friends" -Yeshua (Jesus)

"Ja'Faith,

The letter I previously wrote you, in the paragraph - concerning "Friends", please allow me to correct that statement. 'You must stay open to making new friends. But always, always set your boundaries with them otherwise you'll risk leaving room for disrespect; you must stay open minded to who you work with; open to criticism and open to new ideas because, when you close your mind to those opportunities, you are also closing the door on your ability to get the most out of life. I personally have had bad experiences with friends throughout my life - probably because I've failed to set boundaries which has shaped my attitude towards these types of companions. Now I don't mean to sound hypocritical, but it has cost me a lot of pain, time, and energy to have learned that "no man is my enemy, no man is my friend, but all are my teachers. "However, despite that saying, "I today am ever more vigilant about who is counted as a friend. For you, however, don't allow my misdirected energy to dictate your ability to skilfully make friends. Your experiences contextually would be different then mine, however, the lessons and the wisdom will remain the same. At the end of the day, it's all about attracting the right energy - good positive vibes. People who are trustworthy, respectful, principled, civilized, that you can build on a strong, lasting, healthy relationship with will aid in the progress of your evolution (growth)."

"P. S - A true friend is not just there for you in the good times, fun, pleasurable moments and laughter, but is also there for you in your most trying times. That Book "Think and Grow Rich", I think that you'd take the time and initiative to read it. Read it every chance you get until you've completed it. In the morning before you go to school, on the bus ride to school, during intermission periods in school and before you go to bed at night! Take notes, have a dictionary handy in case there's words you don't know and want to find the meaning. Also, utilize Google to research some of the great contributors mentioned in the book. Familiarize yourself with greatness so that you too can be great. The Book may be a bit of a challenge because it's a little above your reading level, but who says lol! You' are intelligent, competent and you are competent and can comprehend any literary work placed in front of you. Do it for Daddy, do it for Mommy do it for yourself"

- Toussaint
October 21, 2019 (4:00am)

"Jenny,

I appreciate the poem, it was sweet; and thank you for the photos. It never fails to move me. I thank the good graces of Heaven for your role in mothering this single child of mines and I pray (not in a transitional sense) that she'll forever remain your top priority no matter what!"

"On a different note, it's not necessary that you share with me the highlight of your day - frankly. I am hardly concerned with your whereabouts or the company you keep more than I am of your safety and well being; Plus, I don't get why you felt the need to share the piece of information with me - you're doing you out there. I prefer you not tell me what you think I want to here because I am at this point hardly soothed by much or anything and anyone except having a daughter and even that's discomforting because I'm in here, when I had the chance to be there for her deferred for personal reasons, but I won't get into that now. I've listed to your sentiments, I've felt your resistance, I've sensed the resentment and it's ok you needed the justification, you needed your reasoning and license to be involved and more aloof, an excuse to drink and smoke and turn it loose. You got that! You got me. Tables turn. You Win!"

"The difference is I'm out of the game! I'm not for the arguing, the fighting and the 'cat and mouse games. I'm going to get out of here and take care of my business (whatever that is). Today you aren't here for me, with the examples of the four letters and dozens of pictures, and the handful of phone calls out of the 15 months of me being down?"

"At least to your credit, more involvement than I expected. I think I've apologized enough for the demons I had weighing me down and damages I've caused, and I find it difficult to rest in peace when I am constantly persecuted and made to feel quitted by 'All of the World'. I take mothers into my own bonds. I forgive myself. I'll continue to survive off nothing like I have been in the past 15 months. Sure, I'll be the nigga who appears to have no one's support. Don't be hungin'-up on me, I ain't stopping you from being all you can be - you can be - you need my permission? Flourish Succeed. Your still my sister, my African Queen (at least in my eyes), I wish to always be tight with ya. Yeah, I'm mad for various reasons, too but it's a purifying mad. Not a I want to hurt you type mad or assault you type mad. Love in the first pause probably is mind-boggler. In itself or at least mature love - and maybe you feel like I feel or maybe you don't but in reality - I now question who and what's real. You may question my integrity and doubt my abilities, but you won't be the first and you won't be the last. I'm used to it. I'm just going to live my truth. I don't have you - I do love you - but I don't think I know how to love - I've been a failure at it, and it feels like it's failed me too. As it never fails, I don't doubt my words here will be misunderstood."

'The Man You Claim to Love',

- Toussaint
October 24, 2019

"If I have seen further than others, it is by standing upon the shoulders of giants" - Isaac Newton

"Faith,

Your poem was remarkably beautiful and reassuring. Thank you so much. My god - have mercy - you are steadily growing. Such an unpleasant feeling for me to miss out on some of the most defining moments of your life. Sure, there will be better days to come. Hopefully by now you received my previous letter with the book. Think And Grow Rich enclosed! I really wish that you'd take the time out to read that book, it's really inspiring. Anyways, once again thank you."

"P.S Tell the world what you intend on doing but first you must show it" -J.E.T

LOVE DAD,
- Toussaint
October 24, 2019

'KNOW THYSELF'

Jenny,

"Whoa! First of all, I appreciate the gesture. That letter looks like it took quite some time to copy-ouch. If you value your time and it is at a premium - as I suspect if, to be - and you desire to work smarter not harder than I will give you this advice: Next time just print the darn article on notebook paper! It's so much more convenient and easier. Now I respect and admire your intentions with this letter - the information contained within - however, song writing or aspiring to be some famous rapper still no longer occupy any real estate in my heart and mind. The spark has blown over - I may infrequently toy with the idea - but it's never taken seriously anymore. It's a bigger Utopia - back when I was a younger man influenced by the "Culture". Now, I am much more mature having gained the wisdom I currently possess from my life experiences - understanding textures - I understand I must move on from dreams not meant for me but for someone else. Yes, maybe in part I have a role to play in the music industry, the movement of the "culture" or Entertainment in General but it won't be me rapping. My interest has evolved. The roles in business, entrepreneurship and investing industries differ across industries. All along making music - the idea behind all industries. I still entertain the idea of an Entertainment Company or Record label where I can manage Variety of Talents (artist, actors, comedians, etc)"

"Perhaps you had the right plan but the wrong idea - writing me might have been the right plan but the wrong idea - writing me might have been the right plan and the wrong idea - well of course it's the subject I suspended I'd be understood in. Though you meant well therefore I appreciated it, but I just feel it strays away from the care of the conversation we should be having and the questions that should be asked and addressed. It's like that proverbial elephant in the room that no one speaks on or of."

"If you wish to connect with me, then forget me when you desire to speak. We can't keep avoiding important issues and expect them to be dissolved or resolved with impersonal correspondence. It may be possible that you either lack the skills to communicate or are experiencing some blockage of energy, but has it dawned on you that you probably thought you knew me? And I can say the same about you. Yes habits die hard, therefore your character and personality is "generally" set in stone but the truth is the mind makes up the whole of your being - and you don't know where my mind is at these days and I don't know where yours is either. I hope in essence we still are the ones but nowadays I question everything, even the one."

Love One,

- Toussaint
November 1, 2019 (Time 4:31am)

"Everyone holds his fortune in his own hands, like a sculptor the raw material he will fashion into a figure. But it's the some with that type of artistic activity as with all others: We are merely born with the capability to do it. The skill to mold the material into what we want must be learned and attentively cultivated." - Johann Wolfgang von Goethe,

"Jenny,

"It's like human nature to always remember the bad things one has done unto them instead of the good. To this I can admittingly say I am guilty of. That's not all am quality of I've committed among offenses you can possibly indict me on - but most of all I am guilty of loving you. In time pass and still today you have been an Immense force in my life to which extent the polarity being even. Never-the-less, despite my less than intimate and affectionate forms of expression throughout the periods of us being together, I do deep down inside care and Love You. There's a lot on my heart that I must let go but something just isn't quite that easy. I'm in a very tough spot right now in my life, which I realize is reflective of a family dynamic. Not only am I locked up - 30 years old - can't afford an attorney - support base very minimal - but the very thing I've come to live for, I've secretly fought for and now will one day die for is beyond my reach - and that's to lead my family into a better life. Obviously I've since demonstrated this hope - that purpose poorly however my life mission has been to retire my parents, treat them to the good life, pay off all their debt and renovate their home - now it's looking like my mother is not likely to live to see her son attain high - level of achievement due to her condition; and as for my pops he'd continue to have the burden of drudgery into old age. The prospects are not looking good".

"Every young boy I'd like to think who has been raised by his parents - or guardian - has dreamed of taking their mother and or father out of the struggle and I now feel I am distant from reaching that possibility. Further, growing up not only had I not imagine it but I suspected I was the least of candidates to get married, settle down and build a family; Then when it happened although I'm prepared, a greater sense of urgency reached me - no longer was it to set the standard in my family while opening doors for the younger members to enter but now I had a family of my own and I wanted more than anything to be a model African - Haitian - American - Citizen with a strong support base, a beautiful wife and children who have reached the upper ranks of American Society. Though my utopia has become more challenging to fulfill and afraid not all will share in this dream - this vision".

"To get right to the point. It kills me for you to be living in your mother house with a child, without a vehicle and no steady income of course I feel totally responsible! It's unpleasant to hear you had to short sell the house - When with a little more effort and support you could have resorted to better options. It's saddening to hear that you threw five thousand dollars into a venture you struggled to launch all because of a few inefficiencies. Yes, if I was there and more attentive to your dreams, your dreams, your plans and your goals then circumstances would be different but I'm not, and it hurts. What hurts worse is the fact, although I have a strong sense that you've been doing your thing", it hurts me to also feel you feel you are ultimately bound to me therefore have to wait around for me. Now, so ask that it'll be but selfish of you to expect this."

"No, I don't agree with you going around as some weakling looking for an external source to fill your void neither should you turn to pleasure - indulgence and intemperance due to some emotional disparity. I think you should seriously take a step back - look at your life - see where it is you wish to be and head there along the way to acquire the necessary skills in support of your efforts. Then I think you should just move on- emotionally, find you somebody successful, decent, with strong values, morals, principals - who has a pleasant character, good spirited, and an exceptional personality. If I were you I'd not fall for what is being told to me but the proof and the evidence of the standard that you have set, low key screen to ask the right questions, look for the proper signals and red flags, or cues."

"Ultimately you need somebody who is not only financially secure but will also help you to be financially independent of him. Beware of one who tries to control you by this m measure. I don't know how long I'm going to be here, but if things don't turn out in my favor considering my own attorney is working against me, I can be looking at the most doing seven to five years. With that I say live your life. Save yourself and that daughter of mine - please don't lose yourself to the elements, you can do so much better - you can reach so much higher. I'll I'm still writing and calling from time to time. And will look forward to pictures every now and then of you - the family and Ja'Faith! I won't hate you for anything you do from here on out unless you let yourself down. You're my sister, my closest companion and forever a soulmate. You have my blessings! and if our legal moral status poses an obstacle later, we can resolve it then."

P.S "Judge no one based on appearance. It shouldn't matter as to the individual's race, as long as he can help you reach where you're trying to get to".

'Truly Yours Believe Me, I Love You'

- Toussaint
November 19, 2019

"It's easier to destroy an enemy who is divided and unsure of themselves than that which is united and confident of their efforts.

"Send the attorney an email requesting a copy of the discovery to be mailed to your address - with priority mail (email for evidence of transcript) (priority mail for a receipt). When you meet with him ask him what's his theories and strategies of your case and has, he a defense? If so, what is it? Also ask him all very candidly and assertively."

- What are all your options, be sure to take notes?
- Does Faith's school not have athletic programs she can enroll in? Plays, drama classes, musical instrument lessons, or things of the arts?

"Where does she balance the feeling of being overwhelmed by academics? If they do, wouldn't they provide transportation? Instead of her receiving useful objects for Christmas and her birthday from her loved ones couldn't a request be made to put the money towards paying on instructor to teach her a new language, play an instrument/ purchase one, enroll in some form of art, karate, acting etc - and couldn't you research whether those entities will either come to you or offer some form of transportation? Is there not a Boyz N Girls Club or YMCA in your area? I'm sure there is a way there is a will. Arrangements can be made to work and fit around everyone's schedule collectively."

"P.S. Oh and a tutor(s) to help her improve in key areas!

'Peace'
- Toussaint,
November 19, 2019

"Jah Jah,

Just want to share some money principles with you.

#1 Watch your ideas

#2 Watch what you say

#3 Watch whose giving you the idea

✓ Money is an immensely powerful tool. If you use it well it will make you rich, if you abuse it; it will make you poor.

✓ Money don't make you rich

✓ What makes you rich, poor, or middle class is how you handle your problems. Everyone has many problems both 'Rich and Poor' either too much or too little.

✓ Manage money well

✓ Having money comes down to a fundamental choice. The moment you say you can't afford something it becomes your reality. It's the power of the spoken word. Never say you can not do something, ask yourself how can you?

✓ Money is an idea, a concept.

✓ Change your ideas about the subject of money.

✓ Money is a mindset. It's your Attitude About Money!"

Love You

- Toussaint
December 10, 2019

"There are 25,550 days in 70 years - make each day count because tomorrow isn't promise to you" - Dad

"Ja'Faith

My Dear baby girl - My first and my only. I love you. Today is the day that magic has made, so rejoice and be glad in it. All that you can ever wish for or to be or to possess you have already. Look no further than yourself for love is within, peace is within, and joy is within. Nothing or person can ever bring about complete satisfaction, on this day. I this moment you have the best and the most incredible gift that anyone passing it up and failing to embrace it can wish for and that's the breath of Life. You are living and that's wonderful. You are witnessing the manifestations of light and life all around you and that's Fantastic. Yes, life can sometimes seem unfair; yes there are so many things that'll just get in your way but remember it's all a part of the process, it's all for the betterment of you. Stay strong my dear and stay woke-focus-pay attention or attention will pay you. Choose life. Choose peace, Choose Love, Choose Contentment. Choose wisely and Choose You. You Are #1"

'Love You Always and Forever, Dad'

-Toussaint,
December 13, 2019 (Song Dedication: Aaliyah «I Miss You»

"For the unbelieving husband is made holy because of his wife, and the unbelieving wife is made holy because of her husband."

"Baby,

I apologize if I fail to realize that you're still, today, the same gentle soul that captured my heart yesterday. It's a strong possibility that the lenses I am using to view you and the rest of the world around me have been distorted by many negative experiences - to which I am sure you can relate. I'm hurt - though not completely ruined, should you know, what would that change? My failures, my mistakes, and my wrongs have only been met with contention, 'reproachment', and rejection. Yeah, you can tell me you love me and write me on occasion many inspiring things but... you know what scratch that - I'm grateful for having you in my life please excuse my ignorance, my immorality and that's all I can really say."

"I guess it's because I've lost touch like lost the feeling because of the disconnect. I've floated away and lost gravity. Life, it all just seems, maybe I'm disillusioned to think nothing lasts anymore. A perennial chill courses through my veins, of course, I get hot flashes of emotions when I miss the love I have for my daughter and the warmth I once felt from her mother, but the climate encircling me is still on ice. It's like I've been haunted for life and making you my wife was my hope to escape the very evils I am hunted by and am forever fleeing from. Poison by the elements in my environment has done a lot to shape my mortality, attitudes, values, and beliefs. I feel so alone, I have no family or friends around me for comfort, although it's as though that kind of affection has never been offered, but the more presence of familiar persons I've taken for granted. I wish you could save me but you're worse as I am."

"P.S. The roles have surely reversed, I wonder which one of us is the greater believer and what is it that we believe in exactly?"

- Toussaint
December 19, 2019 (Time 2:15 am)

"Greatness is a Habit, Be Great"!

"Faith,

That "What is a Dad" poem was sweet. I really liked it. In fact, I loved it. Nearly brought me to my knees. Also, it appears that your handwriting is improving. Keep it up - yours as sure as hell, be, as sure as heaven, and be better than mine. Mommy on the other hand has us both beat, she deserves an award for best handwriting in the USA. Anyway, what I can say is that you both look equally amazing in the recent photos sent to me. I so badly desire to hold you both in my arms for a long pause out from life's fast-moving pace."

"Happy Holidays! Muah!"

- Toussaint
December 19, 2019 (Time 2:35 am)

APPRECIATED

"It may have been a challenge to live with you, but I can't live without you" - J.E.T.

"It grieves me darling to hear of your unfortunate encounter with law enforcement officers. I feel less than a man how I've not been there to protect and provide for you. I am blameworthy and tender tears. If not for my irresponsibility the event/ incident could have been avoided all together. I'm sorry those sexist, misogynist bastards put their filthy paws on you. I'm ashamed and hope that I am able to fully forgive myself. Nobody, not even I, have the right to put their hands on you to inflict intentional pain. I know life has treated you unfairly and you have suffered abuse in the hands of men since the departure of your Father, but I urge you baby to continue to be bold and fearless and not compromise your womanhood in a world ruled predominantly by men".

"Truly Yours,

Side Note: Read up on this young woman Megan Williams; Shani Baraka and her Partner Rayshon Holmes. Watch this documentary film with Faith: No! by Aishah Shahidah Simmons and Beyond Beats and Rhymes by Byron Hurts also for Faith's physical wellness and overall being, enroll her in some kind of physical activity such as soccer, volleyball, softball, figure skating, karate, something she would enjoy!"

- Toussaint
January 6, 2020 (Time 8:30am)

———————◆———————

"Great Power Comes with Great Responsibilities" -Spider-Man

"Jenny,

Why are you so afraid to live? What are your plans now going forward? You can't afford to sit and wait around; nothing will come to you that way. I strongly urge you get rid of that dreadful attitude and start making your efforts count. It's not what you do but the mindset in which you take it. You've sat back enough evaluated your situation - hope - and you know what you need to do or do you? Are you lost? Are you confused? Do you need guidance? Do you really? Would you act on sound advice if it was presented to you? What's got you? What's important to you? Why are you allowing whatever it is your emotions cloud your vision. Is it really that challenging for you to want to go back to Africa? You don't have the will to continue, the strength, the power to overcome. Is your spirit so broken that you'd prefer to sink deeper into the state of doubt you've notoriously cling to. You ain't see the bright side, are you so blind to miss the lessons in why things fail for you and what would work if you tried a different approach. Have you quit at the first signs of defeat and easily taken yourself out of the race? Where's your ambition; where's your drive? Are you that out of touch with inspiration - have no motivation? Why are you afraid to inquire about new skills, learn your industry, do your homework, become a mentor in your field, utilize free resources, take advantage of your charm? You didn't have to sell that property - you chose too, you didn't have to dissolve your efforts of building an e-commerce platform you choose too. You should try an exercise; write down all the reasons why you perceive things aren't wrong for you, for example: getting a job - your criminal history, then I want you to write on the opposite side of all your reasoning of why you had to sell the property, why the club thing didn't work out for ya. I want to know why I aid them, I want you to take a different approach and use yourself, why not? What different work approaches could you have taken? What haven't you done that you could have done? Moving forward. Sheesh being angry, bitter, and unforgiving, resentful' all that shit isn't going to get you nothing but what you've been getting. You're sending the wrong energy into the universe; therefore, you're reaping what you sow. Get off your pity potty and get your freaking life in order. You sleep more than you handle the defeats of your life as if you're in jail. No bullshit - I am - take the freaking lead Jeez, you have my permission. What role model are you to that little girl? What work ethic will you pass on to her, what characteristics, traits she will inherit from you, her biggest influence. What can she grow up with and will carry her for the rest of her life. What values, principals are you teaching her? In your presence, can only demonstrate her mother. Don't be imprisoned in your mind, break the shackles and chains!"

-Toussaint,
January 9, 2020 (Time 6:20 am)

"I need you to let me in, baby. I can't breathe in the outer space that I am in. At least I can be comforted knowing that I can live vicariously through you. Should I stop? If I'm sounding stupid weak, let me know, I'll fall back."

"P.S. FYI THE NAME OF MY ATTORNEY - STATE PAID ATTORNEY

"Take advantage of your position and be careful to make choices to advance your financial status. We do have many plans together. Do we stop now or do we use our intellectual energy to devise a definite plan?"

Still Down,

-Toussaint,
January 9, 2020

———◆———

"In order for things to change, you must be willing to change first."

"Jenny,

My sweetest obsession, I miss you girl. I really do. I just do this time with grace in letting you be because I know I brought this upon myself. There really aren't any words that I can say that will improve things. I keep my peace. Although there's this ever widening quiet between us, the love I have for you deep within will always serve as the bridge where we meet. I don't pity myself. I'm actually free from much of my past burdening thoughts and actions. I would negatively affect me, as it does to hear of your continuing struggles, regression, arrest, and the police's use of excessive force on you after being in a car accident that totaled your car. Not a good feeling for a man or one who calls himself a man with a wife and child. It makes me feel terrible about the stress you are under. The pressures that lead one to turn to disruptive behavior, drugs and alcohol is concerning. What a curse upon my life! As I am in no physical position to help you improve your condition. It is my hope that you will become the SuperWoman in your life and transform things. You can not be afraid to make moves out there; you just got to make smart moves. You must have a simple purpose where all your moves align with that purpose. I love you girl."

Yours Truly,
Toussaint
February 10, 2020 (Time 5:15 am)

"Jenny,

My Dear, it's on you to improve conditions. It sucks that I need you bad right now and you aren't in position to assist me. I know you can say some. But I have my hands tied - no liberty to act on my own free will. Hindsight is 2020 moving forward. We meant to act with foresight. I understand it's all frustrating and difficult and is easier said than done. But we are often setback by our expectations. You have many roles to play out there that you must put into practice and compartmentalize; you're a mother, still a wife, an aspiring entrepreneur, a caretaker, and a female Hustler also known as Diva. All these roles are cohesive but must be played separately in otherwise balanced. Like a trained actress starring in multiple films at a time playing diverse roles. You got to learn to be versatile. Not allowing your work to get in the way of your mommy duties. Yes, got to know how to get into charter, some roles if not must require severe discipline. Live with purpose. Outline your plan and goals. Tackle them one at a time. Set your standards high but sometimes you may have to go low to go higher but keep your mind on keeping your eyes on the prize -vision.

Some acts go against your morals and values - and cause you to fool, dirty or shame but if you Act in terms of profit, benefits and getting things done, then you can be restored of your spirit. Pay attention to the details they matter in the grand scheme of things."

'Love'

- Toussaint
February 11, 2020 (11:05am)

"Faith,

My baby girl - now my little lady - I miss you too much, my eyes fill with tears even as I write this letter. I won't bore you with it though. I know for certain you have other preoccupations. Faith there's so much I want and can say to you, but I don't know what matters much anymore. Honestly, I feel defeated however temporary –– nonetheless defeated still. I'm sorry I'm not there to protect you, keep yourself safe and provide for you the things you need and want. I know your Mommy's there but it's my responsibility too. I pray you don't grow to hate me. God knows I wanted better for all of us. Now do what's best for you and if you can help it never lose respect for your Mommy no matter what. Anyways I won't preach to you or lecture you or tell you what to do or how to do it. This is your life I just helped you get here. So whatever you do, be the best at it. I don't know if I'll ever see you again at least not this world - remember this when things get hard and things get difficult and become challenging, take some time out to yourself, go to a place where you can go undisturbed, then silence your thoughts, breathe and get back to it. I love you, never let yourself go. You're beautiful and bright. Prove it to yourself. Take care of yourself little lady and take care of all of what was given to you freely!"

P.S. "Thank You for believing in me and loving me unconditionally."

Sincerely Yours,

- Toussaint
October 20, 2021

To: "Mum"
From: J.E.T.
Date: November 15, 2021
Subject: RE: Response Letter

"Well,

Mother, first and foremost, thank you for taking out the time from your busy schedule to write to me, I thought for one, not expecting a response, nevertheless, I appreciate the courtesy. I too am mutually glad to hear from you and feel a sense of reprieve to know that you still genuinely care. I love you too, again thank you for the kind words and you're still believing in me. That really means a lot coming from you; And of course, I care for you. Inadvertently, your family has put me in touch with a sense of myself I've only before time read in the diluted pages of history books. I can humbly say it's been a most meritorious experience shared in every moment. Yes! not only is it a man's prerogative to provide for his family but to protect and secure his family as well. I'm afraid over the years my many efforts to provide, protect and to secure my family has been seriously weakened by many elements and factors. I want to get into the politics and manifold attacks upon the family unit. Stemming from economic pressures and social conditions because it's been engineered that way but on account of myself, I have my own character flaws and defects to blame. It's too easy to blame others. I must live with myself and the consequences of my actions. I take full accountability. In retrospect, (hindsight is 20/20) I regret how I've handled certain conflicts..."

"Nevertheless, in exercising my strong will I am trying my best not to beat myself up too much. It's easier to forgive others quicker than it is myself. But I shall be fine. As you say the past is the past and we can't get that back. Moving forward my release is inevitable. I just pray it's sooner rather than later and that I am free of all their implements and imposition of restricted conditions. Once this system has a grip on, ya great is the task of removing their claws".

"I'm happy to hear that Ja'Faith is doing well. Sadly, before I was taken in, I began saving money for her in an investment account that would grow on interest overtime. There was $18,000 in the account before I gave the only reason, I was able to make contact with at the time-because my circumstances precluded me from access to my phones; and he later then cut off my communication with him and accessed all my accounts. One day he shall pay. Anyhow, I hope Jenny is doing equally as well, in every aspect, I wish her the best in everything. If it's not too much to ask because you say that you will be visiting Florida in your birthday month, does that mean Ja'Faith is still here in the States? Also, has she taken that miserable microbe of a vaccine? God forbid! If you can, may you please send me some photos of her? I will tell you how: Download this add free prints select the photos from your camera roll, upload it on the app, input my information and I should receive the photos within a few days."

"Now that I have your contact, I will reach out to you at some point and time, after I've believed that you are in receipt of this letter. I appreciate your offer to assist me, if not by divine providence, then I am otherwise made to feel, not just by my own private thoughts, but with humanity; have to respect such an offer as not to burden or be of inconvenience to another, all things I've considered. Even so far you, much more so them for my immediate relative, whom I have made a very awkward minimal contact with. However, in all honesty the resources, power, energy, and the abundance of things that are directed from here is good and a blessing and is from the source. Last but not lease, in terms of you paying me a visit: For your information, they are no longer at this present time allowing family and friends to visit in person, instead one can visit remotely by registering and creating an account at the Miami Dade Govt site. Wait to be approved then schedule a visit with their loved ones. I would have to put you on the list. However, again it was great to hear from you and I wish you well and good fortune."

Love,

- James Toussaint
November 15, 2021

"Dear Faith,

Your birthday is coming up in a few days. It's a special day for me more for you than anything, sorry I'm not physically there to celebrate with you I pray the Universe delivers to you the wishes you can bear. Hope to see you soon again...

Happy Born Day
Merry X-MAS
Happy New Years

P.S: You should do your best in periodically contacting the other half of your family they Love you too and would love to hear from you."

Love Your Father

- Toussaint
December 13, 2021

"Hi,

How are you Faith? I miss you dearly-it hurts. I am paying for my mistakes and poor decisions while you suffer. I hope and pray you'd live life fully, fearlessly, wisely and make better choices. I hope that you are remaining active and creative, constantly learning new things, and achieving remarkable things. I cannot tell you what to do - though I can only advise you at this point because I am not there to guide you but in you there is something there that is great beyond measure, I pray by the grace of the almighty that you'd realize it, awaken it and discover it. You're different and it's ok. What doesn't kill you will make you stronger. Your life, your story will help to heal many others. Challenges are meant to be overcome."

Love Always,
Dad

- Toussaint
May 4, 2022

———————•———————•———————

"Hey, my little Big Love,

What a breath of fresh air to have finally heard from you. You inspire me and give me the drive I need to continue with courage through the valleys of the shadows of darkness. I want you to know that I am exceedingly grateful to be your dad and I appreciate your existence. I salute the divinity in you Peace, Love, and Joy Always

Heartily Yours,
DAD"

- Toussaint
May 13, 2022

———————•———————•———————

"Yesterday I was clever, so I wanted to change the world. Today I am wise, so I am changing myself" - Rumi

"Faith,

Hell is not real, nor does it exist except for in the mind. That which "we" refer to as the Devil has no physical appearance. In fact, it takes on many forms. It consists of negative energy and lives in the minds of people who fear it. It also occupies one-half of every atom of physical matter and every unit of mental and physical energy. Its nature is the negative portion of the atom. It is no beast with a formed tongue and a spiked tail..."

"Faith is extremely important that you heed my words. Society is transforming and a majority are asleep, and time is of the essence - so I need you to wake up and expand your consciousness unto infinite awareness. I need you to understand and know what reality is and who you are to get a greater understanding of why you're here and what is your definite purpose. I'm going to begin to share a series of information with you and give you some instructions - you must for the sake of your own soul, be open-minded and follow them."

"I will be sharing words for you to look up the definition and origin of them and I ask that you use and put them in proper context as it is critical you expand your vocabulary and learn the root of the words that are being used. I am going to recommend a series of movies, documentaries, songs, audiobooks, and books for you to read and watch."

"Following after that I'm going to ask that you either do a book report (if it's a book) or give me a summary of what it is that you watched highlighting the central point. This is so that you retain the information and learn how to organize and make practical use of facts. Faith, I encourage you to use your own mind. With that being said, I want to start by having you pull up YouTube and in the search bar type in 'Outwinning the Devil' by Napoleon Hill. I strongly urge you to listen to that audio until the point of completion. It's several hours long so it doesn't have to be in a day - maybe only about twenty minutes a day. Have with you a writing instrument and paper to take notes. Also, write down the words you don't understand and search for their definitions then write them down. From the time you get this letter, I'll give you a week, but please don't procrastinate or allow mental laziness to hinder you. Make no excuse as to why you hadn't gotten started or completed the audiobook. This is extremely important and if you don't follow suit your ignorance will be to your own destruction."

P.S. I believe in you Faith, don't get distracted by the culture, conduct, or misconduct and activities - extracurricular activities in school keep yourself pure and untainted. Resist the temptation! I love you, with all my heart, all my soul, and my might".

Daddy.

- Toussaint
July 11, 2022

"Faith,

What I want to write you today is something I've once read that a wise man said: "Hustle for your last name not your first". See with your first that's just about you, your last name that's about a generation of people, your kindred, your ancestors that have gone out into all of the worlds striving to live, work, and make something of themselves, passing along a great name, a great house, and legacy. You are just as much responsible as I am to carry that name into greatness - not just for you, for me, but for those after."

"I love how when you don't know something or the meaning of a word, you stop and ask the meaning of it. Keep that up! Always be anal in your requirement of clarity and understanding of things and communications with others. We want no confusion, mitigate the misunderstandings and miscommunication but absolute clarity. Start your morning with prayer my dear. Keep a to-do list, write down your goals, write down your plans".

"If you're going to be a stage manager and an actor-manager then be the damn best at it. Become an expert at it. Study your craft, know the history and best of all have a vision and see how far it can take you. Do what's necessary and required of you in your new experience. You get to fine-tune yourself and develop a new skill that can be added to your repertoire. As you evolve and travel through time, you'll learn the many stages that are set for you according to your use or misuse of your gift and talent. I'm in this program called Heroes 2nd Chance Father Hood Initiative brought on by a gentleman named Jack Brewer, hence the Jack Brewer Foundation given his namesake, is an eXNFL player who started this Christian-based program or non-profit organizations which goes around to prisons and offer fathers hope. Better persons, better men, and better fathers".

"I'm not present to do this with you or make the arrangements on your behalf, but I strongly suggest you study to become financially literate. It's essential to have the proper foundation for the success of your future. Learn bookkeeping, and personal finance - how to budget or create a budget and those basic financial principles. By simply searching YouTube, and Udemy you can find online covers, tutorials, and how-to guides on there. Also, you can ask your educators about learning bookkeeping and personal finance on the side and would they be so kind as to point you in the right direction. Do not take no for an answer. Never tolerate any disrespect from no man. Act like a lady, carry yourself well and respect yourself. You are of High Value and Worth. Never lower your standards, set them high. You're a young lady, a young black girl prove yourself how great you are, then prove to the world your greatness. Live Life Intentionally with Purpose. Cherish every moment. Waste no time."

Love You Always,

- Toussaint
December 10, 2023

"Family First"!

The first time Mumi & Dadi visited me in prison after three years I was at Moore Haven Correctional Facility in Florida. It felt good to see them both. I never felt so much love from them and how much they cared for me until that point. Love You Jah"

-Toussaint,
December 23, 2023

"La Familia,

"As much as I have to be there for you whew, I get out I will have to be there for these two lovely poor folks who has throughout my entire life been there for me through thick and thin; good or bad - no matter what! Standing Tall in the Face of Defeat"

'Love Dad'

-Toussaint,
January 13, 2024

✦

YOU GOT THIS

Jeremiah 1:5 "Before I formed you in my belly, I knew you; and before you came forth out of the womb, I sanctified you"

"Jah Jah,

How do you know when you hear the voice of God? How is it God even speaks to you? Have you been reading your bible? Do you know about the story of Job in the bible? He was a wealthy, noble, and honorable man, in whom God had tested and the devil having God's permission - tempted. Job lost everything - his children (sons and daughters in a disaster), his cattle (sheeps, cows, pigs, etc) were consumed by a fire even his servants were killed. Nevertheless, it was him and his wife remaining. The devil wanted to get Job to curse God, so the devil figured that he could bring upon Job all these adversities or problems that held eventually lose faith, doubt God, and live life carelessly and recklessly cursing God. God allowed those things to occur because God has confidence in Job. Job was a faithful servant of God upon the earth and Job wanted to prove to Satan not only could he not destroy the spirit and faith of one who believes and Job wanted to show the devil, neither did it have any real power except for which man gives it. Nevertheless, even when Job fell ill with boils covering his skin, he still would not curse God. Even his wife who lost faith and grew tired

with everything told him to forget all his Godly ways, still Job refused. In the Tenth Chapter 4th verse questioning God, asked, have you eyes of flesh? Or do you see as man sees? Are your days as the days of man? Are your years as man's years? God is omnipresent - meaning God is everywhere; omniscient meaning knows all things; omnipotent meaning God has unlimited power and authority. God says in the Book of Isaiah Chapter 55:8 for my thoughts are not your thoughts, nor are your ways, My ways; Verse 9; for as the heavens are higher than the earth, so are My ways higher than your ways, and My thoughts than your thoughts. My love, God speaks to us in many forms because God can assume what form it Wills - people, animals, stars, televisions, phones, SSM, music, etc. But we must be attuned with God to hear and see. Often, we are so distracted by the noise surrounding us in the world that we cannot hear or see who or what is guiding us along our journey. God especially uses your consciousness but again, this requires peace within a peace of mind to be still and hear.

In the book of Hosea, 4:6 says, "My people are destroyed from a lack of knowledge, do yourself a favor baby girl seek knowledge, find understanding, and get wisdom so that your days may be long and sleep sweet and your life blessed and prosperous. Read the bible and continue to be a lifelong learner. Daddy's proud of you and all that you are doing and who you are becoming. Be Great!"

Love You,

Your Father

P.S. "I've made several attempts to call you. Your Mom told me about your encounter with a politician, last man Raskin. I want a picture. Email it to me please! Thank You"

- Toussaint
February 5, 2024 (13:21)

———————◆———————

"JAH,

Peace GRACE to you and PEACE from God our Father and the Lord Jesus Christ."

"A new commandment I give you, that you love one another, as I have loved you, that you also love one another…" John 13:34

"You shall love the Lord your God with all your heart, with all your soul, and with all your strength" Deuteronomy 7:10

"My child, Daddy loves you dearly. Give all you got in all that you do. Never give up and never compromise your good and high moral standards for nothing."

- Toussaint
February 10, 2024

———————◆———————

CHAPTER

14

Educated from a Cell: General Educational Development Program

"All individual advancements commence with a shift in convictions. How do we initiate this transformation? The optimal approach involves linking substantial discomfort to existing beliefs. Internalize, at your core, that this belief not only brought past pain but continues to inflict present suffering, and inevitably promises future anguish. Subsequently, attach immense joy to embracing a fresh, empowering belief." -J.E.T. <eye3i>

"We need to shift our focus from treating disease to generating health..." - Imhotep (Ancient African Egyptian, The God of Medicine)

"Ancient African medicine was founded upon wholistic spirituality and Ma'at. This pre-Egyptian medical science is between 20,000 and 100,000 years old. In fact, it is the oldest medicinal science on this planet. The Westcar Papyrus (1550 B.C.) of the 18th Dynasty has stories from the early empires, which date before the Great Pyramid and they make reference to priest/ herbalist doctors of King Khufu (Cheops) of the 4th Dynasty (3800 B.C.)."

"The African Rhind mathematical papyrus (1650 B.C) is the oldest text on mathematics. The Medical writings of Imhotep (Egyptian God of Medicine) are the oldest medical documents written. Imhotep's books were stolen from Africa and are presently at Karl Marx University in Leipzig, Germany. Imhotep wrote over ten volumes on holistic treatments, diets and foods over 2,000 years before Hippocrates (European Father of medicine) was born."

"The food you eat can either be the safest and most powerful form of medicine or the slowest form of poison." - Ann Wigmore

"**GREEN** is not something you can buy
GREEN is a way of Life; Treasure Everything
Think permaculture; live sustainably in
all ways. Make it, grow it, build it yourself.
Do all you can with what you have."

EAT FIVE TIMES A DAY

Eating a good breakfast is important for blood sugar regulation, adrenal health, and immune system health. You've just woken up from fasting for eight hours and your body needs nourishment. Have some protein, carbohydrates, and fats for breakfast. Give your body some good calories, vitamins, minerals and take your supplements at that time.

✓ Eating a good lunch is also important since you have half of the day left. A good salad or healthy sandwich is a clever idea at this time.

✓ Have a small afternoon snack around 3 or 4pm to combat the afternoon blues. An apple, some nuts and water!

✓ Have a small dinner. We, in this society, focus on dinner as a main meal of the day. The problem is your digestive system would like to slow down at that time of day and here we are livening it up with a big meal. You can have your meat, salad, veggies or whatever you usually have just eat and half the size you usually eat.

✓ Then for some people, a snack before bed keeps their blood sugar stable while they sleep. This would be something like toast with nut butter. You will get some sleep if you eat this way because your body will be able to slow down more at night.

HOW TO REDUCE CHOLESTEROL

Latest research suggests that cholesterol lowering foods such as avocados, almonds, olive oil, soybeans, garlic, shiitake mushrooms, chili peppers, oat bran, beans (kidney, pintos, black beans, navy beans, etc.), onions, fatty fish, and flax seed play a crucial role in lowering LDL (low-density lipoprotein) and sometimes raising HDL (high-density lipoprotein) levels.

✓ Fitting in the recommendation 5 servings of fruits and vegetables (2 of one group and 3 of the other) helps take the place of some of the more processed snacks which contribute to high cholesterol.

✓ Fruits and vegetables are mostly fat free. Ingredients in cigarette smoke are extremely oxidizing. High cholesterol is particularly dangerous when it is oxidized. Smokers have a much higher need for antioxidants.

✓ The B Complex vitamins, including 2 forms of vitamin B3 can reduce nicotine craving.

SAVE BERRIES FROM MOLDING: WASH THEM WITH VINEGAR

When you get your berries home, prepare a mixture of one part vinegar (white or apple cider probably work best) and ten parts water. Dump the berries into the mixture and swirl around. Drain, rinse if you want mold spores and other bacteria that might be on the surface of the fruit and voila! Raspberries will last a week or more, and strawberries go almost two weeks without getting moldy and soft. So go forth and stock up on those pricey little gems, knowing they will stay fresh as long as it takes you to eat them. It also gets the pesticides off.

You're so berry welcome!

FOODS MENTIONED FOR NATURAL DETOX AND CLEANSING:

1. **Turnip Greens** - activate detox enzymes.
2. **Red Bell Pepper** - rich in vitamin C for toxin digestion.
3. **Citrus Fruits** - high in vitamin C for toxin breakdown.
4. **Mung Beans** - absorb toxic residue from intestines.
5. **Walnuts** - provide omega-3 oils for detox.
6. **Sunflower Seeds** - boost liver's detox capabilities.
7. **Watercress** - fights free radicals, energizes liver enzymes.
8. **Turmeric** - stimulates liver function for detox.
9. **Whole Grains** - high in fiber, essential for detox.
10. **Artichokes** - increase bile production, aid digestion.
11. **Lentils** - high fiber, aids toxin elimination and balances blood sugar.
12. **Garlic** - stimulates the liver to produce detox enzymes.
13. **Broccoli** - delivers vitamins while neutralizing toxins.
14. **Grapefruit** - lowers cholesterol, aids digestion.
15. **Cucumber** - high water content flushes toxins, alkalizes the body.

*Recommendation: Purchase **organic** because of commonly excessive amounts of trace **pesticides** on conventionally grown products.*

TEN WAYS TO GET RID OF TOXINS

Spring is traditionally the time of new beginnings. People like to use this time homes and personal spaces to make space for new things to come. Just like your home, your body needs some cleaning up, too. You've spent months absorbing toxins and pollutants through your skin, the air you breathe, the foods you eat. Your body is designed to want to shed toxins and other debris that have accumulated throughout the cold months due to reduced physical activity, and you can help your body do just that. A thorough spring cleanse can also help you regain much-needed energy, clear your skin, and improve digestion. You don't have to starve or drink just lemon water to accomplish this. Even with the busiest of schedules, there are a few things that you can incorporate into your routine to help you cleanse and get your body ready for summer. For the next few weeks, try following two or more of these tips:

1. **Get rid of gluten and processed foods** - Processed foods have been stripped of nutrients, leaving you with mostly artificial stuff left to eat. Most of these, including gluten (the protein of wheat that is also present in a lot of processed foods), cause a sluggish metabolism and the accumulation of toxins in the body.

2. **Have green grapes everyday** - Grapes have a lot of detoxifying qualities and consuming them at this time of the year can help you draw out toxins from your organs and dump them into your intestines for elimination. Grapes are rich in fiber, so drinking a lot of water is necessary in the detox process.

3. **Take a daily detox tea** - Goldenseal, dandelion and neem are some of the best-known detox herbal teas on the market today. You can also make tea with turmeric powder, a well-known herb used in many Indian dishes. If you prefer supplements in pill, you can try milk thistle.

4. **Avoid sugar** - especially the refined kind, is exceedingly difficult to digest, and messes around with your blood sugar levels. It will be hard to kick the sugar habit but try to stay away from refined sugars and artificial sweeteners.

5. **Stretch** - Stretching will kick your detox efforts up a notch. As you stretch, you allow oxygenated blood gets to all the nooks and crannies of your body, carrying toxins out with it. Exercises like yoga and tai ci are great activities to do in the springtime.

6. **Make teas from herbs in your pantry** - In addition to herbs like turmeric, you can make teas of bitter herbs available in your pantry or refrigerator. Endive, romaine, mustard green, gentian chamomile and goldenseal are but a few examples of herbs you can create tea concoctions with as they will detoxify, improve circulation, and increase your metabolism.

7. **Take deep breaths** - Most of us underestimate the cleansing power of breath, and most of us forget to breathe deeply and consciously. First thing in the morning, take a few minutes to breathe deeply 8 to 10 times. It will be invigorating and cleansing.

8. **Make sure you evacuate** - If you remove dirt and debris from your organs but don't eliminate them properly, your efforts could be futile. In fact, you could be doing more harm than good. Having two to three bowel movements each day is key in the cleansing process.

If you're not doing this, you may consider mild harm supplements like magnesium, trehala or Cascara Sagrada to assist you. And don't forget to drink water!

9. **Drink water, lemon, cayenne, and vinegar** - Speaking of water, a large glass of filtered water with the juice of 1/2 a lemon 1/2 teaspoon of apple cider vinegar and a pinch of cayenne pepper before breakfast will increase your energy and metabolism and will clear mucus and toxins from your vital organs. Drink it every day as long as you like.

10. **Sweat it out** - Your skin is your largest organ and one of the primary organs of elimination. Saunas, baths, and steam rooms are great detoxification aids, as they'll help you sweat, thus helping you eliminate up to 20% of toxins and debris from your body through your skin.

TOP FOODS HIGHEST IN LYCOPENE

Lycopene is currently the most powerful antioxidant which has been measured in food and is thought to pay a role in preventing cancer and heart disease. How large a protective role lycopene plays is a controversial issue which is still under scientific study. Lycopene is a carotenoid that gives many fruits and vegetables are their red color, eating lycopene in excess amounts can cause the skin and liver to have a yellow color. Unlike other carotenes, lycopene does not get converted into vitamin A.

#1 Guavas - an average guava contains only 37 calories and half a gram of fat

#2 <u>Watermelon</u> - a wedge of watermelon contains 86 calories and less than half a gram of fat

#3 <u>Tomatoes</u> (Cooked) - a cup of raw cherry tomatoes provided 3834µg (microgram) lycopene and cup of raw, chopped tomatoes provided 4631µg (microgram) lycopene.

#4 <u>Papaya</u> - A small papaya contains only 68 calories and less than half a gram of fat.

#5 <u>Grapefruit</u> - Half an average grapefruit contains only 41 calories and virtually no fat.

#6 <u>Sweet Red Peppers</u> (Cooked) - Half a cup of chopped, sauteed red peppers contain 71 calories.

#7 <u>Asparagus</u> (Cooked) - Half a cup of cooked asparagus contains only 20 calories and 0.2 grams of fat.

#8 <u>Red</u> (<u>Purple</u>) <u>Cabbage</u> - A cup of chopped raw cabbage contains only 28 calories and 0.14 grams of fat.

HEALTH RECOMMENDATIONS: DIARY

Eliminating dairy from your diet is advocated for several reasons:

1. **<u>High Fat and Cholesterol</u>:** Cheese and ice cream, common dairy products, are rich in fat and cholesterol.

2. **<u>Iron Deficiency</u>:** Dairy's low iron content may lead to deficiencies, especially noted in infants.

3. **<u>Diabetes Association</u>:** Some studies link dairy consumption to insulin-dependent childhood diabetes.

4. **<u>Ovarian Cancer Risk</u>:** Excessive galactose from dairy could triple the risk of ovarian cancer in certain cases.

5. **Cataract Connection**: Galactose breakdown from lactose in dairy might contribute to the development of cataracts.

6. **Lactose Intolerance**: Many, especially Asians and Africans, may experience lactose intolerance with dairy, causing digestive issues.

7. **Allergy Triggers**: Dairy products may trigger respiratory problems, canker sores, and skin conditions, often unnoticed.

8. **Toxin Concerns:** Dairy products can be contaminated with antibiotics and pesticides, affecting overall health.

9. **Osteoporosis Myth**: Despite common beliefs, dairy doesn't prevent osteoporosis; regions with high dairy intake often have higher osteoporosis rates.

10. **Colic in Babies**: Cows' milk can cause colic in infants, and breastfeeding mothers consuming dairy may pass antibodies to their contributing to colic.

WHOLE MILK IS:

87% Water
3.25% Fat
4% Casein
4.75% Other Proteins (pus)

Content in Milk: Most milk's protein, about 80%, is casein, a strong binding agent found in plastics, glue, and many processed foods.

ALLERGENIC AND MUCUS PRODUCTION

✓ Casein, being a robust allergen, triggers histamine release leading to increased mucus production.

✓ Somatic Cells and Bacteria in Milk: A single cubic centimeter of commercial cow's milk is permitted to contain up to 750,000 somatic cells ("PUS") and 20,000 live bacteria before being withdrawn from the market. This amounts to 20 million bacteria and up to 750 million pus cells per liter.

✓ Nutritional Benefits of Bulgur Wheat (Tabouli): Tabouli, with bulgur wheat, offers a meal rich in fiber, protein, and essential minerals such as iron, phosphorus, zinc, manganese, selenium, and magnesium. The insoluble fiber promotes quicker waste elimination, contributing to heart disease, diabetes, and cancer prevention.

WHY DRINK WATER

✓ We all know that water is good for us, but often the reasons are a little fuzzy. And even if we know why we should drink water, it's not a habit that many people form.

✓ But there are some immensely powerful reasons to drink lots of water everyday, and forming the habit isn't hard, with a little focus.

✓ The thing about it is, we do not often focus on this habit. We end up drinking coffee, and lots of soda, and alcohol, not to mention fruit juices and teas and milk and a bunch of other possibilities. Or just as often, we do not drink enough fluids, and we become dehydrated -- and that isn't good for our health.

I've made drinking water a daily habit, although I will admit that a couple of years ago, I was more likely to drink anything but water. Now I don't drink anything but water, except for a cup of coffee in the morning and once in awhile a beer with dinner. I love it!

Here are **NINE** powerful reasons to **drink water** (with tips on how to form the water habit afterwards):

1. **Weight Loss** - Water is one of the best tools for weight loss, first because it often replaces high-calories. But it's also a great appetite suppressant, and often when we think we're hungry, we're actually just

298 | JENNY TOUSSAINT

thirsty. Water has fat, no calories, no carbs, no sugar. Drink plenty to help your weight-loss regimen.

2. **Heart Healthy** - Drinking a good amount of water could lower your risks of a heart attack. A six-year published in the May 1,2002 American Journal of Epidemiology found that those who drink more than 5 glasses of water a day were 41% less likely to die from a heart attack during the study period than those who drank less than two glasses.

3. **Energy** - Being dehydrated can sap you energy and make you feel tired -- even mild dehydration of as little as one or two percent of your body weight. If you're thirsty, you're already dehydrated -- and this can lead to fatigue, muscle weakness, dizziness and other symptoms.

4. **Headache cure** - Another symptom of dehydration is headaches. In fact, often when we have headaches it's simply matter of not drinking enough water. There are lots of other causes of headaches of course, but dehydration is a common one.

5. **Healthy skin** - Drinking water can clear up your skin and people often report a healthy glow after drinking water. It won't happen overnight, of course but just a week if drinking a healthy amount of water can have good effects on your skin.

6. **Digestive problems** - Our digestive systems need a good amount of water to digest food properly. Often water can help cure stomach acid problems, and water along with fiber can cure constipation (often a result of dehydration).

7. **Cleansing** - Water is used by the body to help flush out toxins and waste products from the body.

8. **Cancer Risk** - Related to the digestive system item above, drinking a healthy amount of water has also been found to reduce the risk of colon cancer by 45%. Drinking lots of water can also reduce the risk of bladder cancer by 50% and potentially reduce the risk of breast cancer.

9. **Better exercise** - Being dehydrated can severely hamper your athletic activities, slowing you down and making it harder to lift weights. Exercise requires additional water, so be sure to hydrate before, during and after exercise.

AVOCADO NUTRITION - Avocados are a reliable source of fiber potassium, and vitamin C, K, folate, and B6. Half an avocado has 160 calories, 15 grams of heart-healthy unsaturated fat, and only 2 grams saturated fat. Half an avocado has 160 calories, 15 grams of heart-healthy unsaturated fat, and only 2 grams saturated fat.

HUMMUS - Preparation Time 10 minutes

Ingredients:

2 tablespoons (sesame seeds)
1 can chickpeas/ garbanzo beans (15 oz.)
2 tablespoons roasted garlic
1/2 tablespoon lemon juice
1 tablespoon olive oil
1/2 teaspoon oregano

ALOE VERA - This amazingly nutritious plant has been used for over 2000 years. The juice of Aloe Vera may be extracted by cutting the leaf in half, dropping it in a pitcher of water for 8+ hours before drinking it. The juice has several advantages when drunk. This can be partially because of the very fact that it contains twelve vitamins (including A, B1, B6, B12, C, and E), nineteen amino acids and over twenty minerals, most being essential to the body. It is good for your digestive tract: Aloe Vera juice encourages the bowels to move and helps with elimination if a person is constipated. And if you have diarrhea, it will help slow it down - amazing, right?

✓ Assists the immune system: Aloe Vera juice is especially great for those who have chronic immune disorders like fibromyalgia since the polysaccharides in aloe vera juice stimulate macrophages, the white blood cells that fight viruses.

✓ Pain reliever and reduces inflammation: Aloe Vera juice improves joint flexibility and comes filled with mucopolysaccharides - the amino sugars needed for the regeneration of body cells.

✓ It strengthens joint muscles: which therefore reduces pain and inflammation in weakened or aged joints.

WHEATGRASS

✓ Wheatgrass is used to help the body heal itself in cases of disease, injury, toxification, etc. Some animals are observed to eat grasses when injured or ill, but not when in good health.

✓ Wheatgrass juice is an excellent healer because it acts to produce an unfavorable environment for bacterial growth.

✓ The main ingredient is "crude" chlorophyll. It also contains over 100 elements including vitamin A, B, C, E and K.

✓ A few of the minerals it contains are Calcium, Magnesium, Iron, Phosphorus, Potassium, Sodium, Sulphur, Cobalt, Zinc, etc.

✓ Drinking wheatgrass and other green sprouted juices helps your body to build red blood cells which carry oxygen to every cell.

✓ Chlorophyll helps wash drug deposits from the body, purifies the blood and organs, and counteracts toxins.

✓ Wheatgrass helps remove toxic heavy metals (lead, mercury, and aluminium) that have become stored in the tissue.

✓ Wheatgrass juice helps to increase the enzyme level in our cells, aiding in rejuvenation of the body.

Calcium Replacements

- ✓ Sesame Seeds - A quarter cup of sesame seeds has 351 mg calcium

- ✓ Spinach - A cup of boiled spinach has 245 mg

- ✓ Collard Greens - A cup of boiled collard greens has 266 mg

- ✓ Blackstrap Molasses - One teaspoon has about 137 mg

- ✓ Kelp - One cup of raw kelp has 136 mg

- ✓ Tahini - Two tablespoons of raw tahini (sesame seed butter) have 126 mg

- ✓ Broccoli - Two cups of boiled broccoli have 124 mg

- ✓ Swiss Chard - One cup of boiled char has 102 mg

- ✓ Kale - One cup of boiled kale has 94 mg

- ✓ Brazil Nuts - Two ounces of Brazil nuts (12 nuts) have 90 mg

- ✓ Celery - Two cups of raw celery have 81 mg

- ✓ Almonds - One ounce of almonds (23 nuts) has 75 mg

TOP 10 SUPERFOODS FOR EXCEPTIONAL HEALTH

We've all heard of "superfoods" - those foods packed with so many nutrients that eating them regularly might actually change your life. Of course, everyone's favourite superfoods are different - and there are plenty that did not make this list. But one thing is certain - adding any of these foods to your diet can improve your health. So, here's our first. We hope it helps you decide which superfoods might suit you best.

1. ACAI
- Source: South American palm tree
- Rich Ingredients: Antioxidants, Healthy fats, Dietary fibre
- Potential Benefits: Battles free radicals, Cardiovascular health, Digestive Health
- Super tip: Consider beauty products that contain acai oil for antioxidant benefits

2. CACAO
- Source: Bean from South and Mesoamerica
- Rich Ingredients: Antioxidants, Magnesium, and Lipids
- Potential Benefits: Battles free radicals, Aids depression, Cardiovascular health
- Super tip: Choose dark chocolate made from raw cacao for maximum benefits

3. COCONUT OIL
- Source: Dried Coconut meat
- Rich Ingredients: Lactic acid, Dietary fibre
- Potential Benefits: Digestive health, Cardiovascular health, Weight loss, Immune function
- Super tip: Coconut oil can be used topically, and may help treat infections

4. KELP

- Source: Shallow saltwater, kalp forests
- Rich Ingredients: Vitamins, Calcium, Iodine
- Potential Benefits: Cellular metabolism, Cardiovascular health, Thyroid function,
- Super tip: Adequate iodine intake may help protect against radiation poisoning.

5. MANUKA HONEY
- Source: New Zealand bees that pollinate the manuka bush
- Rich Ingredients: Enzymes, Hydrogen peroxide, proteins

- Potential Benefits: Wound healing, relieves stomach ulcers, soothes heartburn
- Super tip: A spoonful can help treat a sore throat, and it can be applied to mouth ulcers.

6. BEE POLLEN
- Source: Collects on the bodies of bees
- Rich Ingredients: Vitamins, Carbohydrates, Lipids
- Potential Benefits: Digestive health, Combats fatigue, helps asthma, and allergies, increased energy
- Super tip: Don't heat pollen, heating will destroy precious nutrients

5. CHIA SEEDS

- Source: Central American plant (part of the mint family)
- Rich Ingredients: Fatty acids, Calcium, Protein
- Potential Benefits: Increases energy, Digestive health, Cholesterol levels
- Super tip: Soak in water to create a gel that can replace eggs in some recipes

6. GOJI BERRIES

- Source: Chinese shrub
- Rich Ingredients: Amino acids, Antioxidants, Vitamins
- Potential Benefits: Immune function, Mental function, Cardiovascular health
- Super tip: Skip the orange juice - goji berries have more vitamin C by weight than any other food.

7. MACA ROOT
- Source: Tuberous Peruvian vegetable
- Rich Ingredients: Amino acids, Vitamins, Enzymes
- Potential Benefits: Hormonal function, boosts libido, mental function, increase energy
- Supertip: Add maca root powder to your morning smoothie or cereal for an energy boost

8. SPIRULINA
- Source: Blue - green algae
- Rich Ingredients: Antioxidants, Vitamins
- Potential Benefits: Increases energy, Immune function, weight loss
- Super tip: Safe for use during pregnancy and breastfeeding and may boost fertility

WHAT TO DO TO GET SUGAR AND TOXINS OUT OF THE BODY?

If you value your health, then eliminate foods that are damaging your body. That includes all carbonated beverages, alcohol (beer especially) sugar or "sugar-free" drinks that contain both real and artificial sweeteners, white sugar, white flour, and cow's milk. Besides the problems stated above, bacteria in the body thrives on sugar, so if you suffer from constant illness, eliminating sugar will starve the bacteria into submission. Start adding raw, fresh food that is as close to nature as possible... Fruits, vegetables, and meats. Although organic is better, it is also more expensive. Your local grocery stores now carry many healthy foods.

"The practice **of oil pulling**, rooted in ancient Ayurvedic traditions, serves as a method for oral health and detoxification. This technique employs pure oils to extract harmful bacteria, fungi, and organisms from the mouth, teeth, gums, and throat.

- ✓ Enhances the overall strength of teeth, gums, and jaws.
- ✓ Guards against gum and mouth diseases, including cavities and gingivitis.
- ✓ Acts as a preventive measure for bad breath.
- ✓ Offers a potential holistic solution for bleeding gums.
- ✓ Avert dryness of the lips, mouth, and throat.
- ✓ Serves as a possible holistic approach for temporomandibular joints (TMJ) and alleviates general soreness in the jaw area."

HOW DOES OIL PULLING WORK?

The oil lubricates the inner lining of the mouth. Oil, though the process of selective solvent extraction, extracts out all the toxic waste from the mouth into the oil. All harmful toxins, microorganisms, and viruses are oil soluble. Pathogens cannot grow in an oily medium. The swishing activates enzymes and draws toxins from the oral cavity lining through the saliva. The swirling of the tongue activates all the vital organs mapped on the tongue and thus improves their functioning. Oil-pulling therapy mitigates headaches, bronchitis, tooth pain, root canal, thrombosis, eczema, ulcers, intestinal diseases, heart and kidney disease, encephalitis, and women's diseases. Within two weeks of oil pulling, you will notice an improvement in your strength and vitality. You will feel refreshed and will sleep calmly. Aches and pains from the body will disappear.

THE OIL PULLING PROCEDURE

The procedure for Oil Pulling is simple and easy to follow. Take a tablespoon of any edible cooking oil, although Coconut oil or Sesame oil are recommended. Place the oil in your mouth and pull and swirl the oil in your mouth through your teeth for 5 minutes to twenty minutes. Gargle the mouth with the oil without swallowing it in a controlled swirling manner. It should be done first thing in the morning, before eating or drinking. When the viscosity of the oil decreases due to its uniform mixing with saliva of the mouth, be ready to spit it out. The oil should appear milky white. If it is yellow, it indicates insufficient swishing. Rinse your mouth well and brush your teeth. Drinking a cup of warm water with or without fresh lemon juice completes the procedure.

ANEMIA

Anemia is the reduced number of circulating red blood cells, hemoglobin, and volume in the blood. It is not a dis-ease, but a symptom of various diseases. The disease may develop slowly, and the person may adjust to it and function with irritability, loss of appetite, constipation, problems concentrating and headaches. The noticeable symptoms are drowsiness, slight fever, pale fingernail beds, dizziness, sore tongue, angina, pectoris, loss of sexual interest, fast heartbeats, menstruation may stop, indigestion, paleness under the eyelid, depression, and weakness. Anemia can be caused by hormonal disorders, liver damage, radiation, ulcers, drugs, surgery, hemorrhoids, heavy bleeding during menstruation or between menstruation cycles, infections, diverticular disease, thyroid disorders, bone marrow disease, rheumatoid arthritis and/ or repeated pregnancies.

SUPPLEMENTS

- ✓ Iron (vegetable source; suggested dose 15-65mg; easily absorbed)
- ✓ Liquid Iron (vegetable source; suggested dose 2 tsp daily; easily absorbed)
- ✓ Magnesium (as directed; converts to iron)
- ✓ Blackstrap Molasses (1 tbsp twice daily for adults; for children and babies, add 1 tsp. to vegetable milk; has iron and essential B vitamins)
- ✓ Brewer Yeast (as directed on label, rich in basic nutrients)
- ✓ Copper Plus (2mg daily; copper is used in red blood cell production)
- ✓ Zinc (30 mg daily)
- ✓ Raw Spleen Concentrate (as directed)
- ✓ Vitamin A plus (10,000 IV daily; essential for the production of red blood cells)
- ✓ Beta-Carotene (15,000 IV daily)
- ✓ Vitamin E emulsion (700 IV daily or take in capsule form; take emulsion for easier assimilation; helps utilize red blood cells)
- ✓ Folic Acid (800 mcg, twice daily, 300mcg, twice daily; essential for the production of red blood cells)
- ✓ Vitamin B12 (2,000 mcg., 3 times daily injections are the most effective or take in sublingual form; essential for the production of blood cells)

✓ Vitamin B Complex with extra pantothenic acid (B5) - (50mg to 100mg of each 3 times daily - pantothenic acid and pyridoxine build red blood cells)
✓ Vitamin B6 (Pyridoxine) - (50 mg; 3 times daily - pantothenic acid and pyridoxine build red blood cells)
✓ Vitamin C - (3,000 mg - 10,000 mg daily after meals - needed for iron absorption; helps assimilate iron and B12)
✓ Betaine Hydrochloride (after meals helps assimilate iron and B12)

GLANDULARS

✓ **Raw Liver** - 300mg., twice daily - acid red blood cell production

AMINO ACIDS

✓ **Methionine** - use as directed, cleanses the liver

HERBS

✓ Alfalfa
✓ Barberry
✓ Comfrey
✓ Dandelion
✓ Elecampane
✓ Milk Thistle
✓ Mullein
✓ Nettle
✓ Oregon Grape
✓ Red Raspberry
✓ St. John wort
✓ Thyme

FOODS

✓ Apples
✓ Apricot
✓ Beets

- ✓ Blackberries
- ✓ Broccoli
- ✓ Cabbage
- ✓ Cauliflower
- ✓ Cherries
- ✓ Currants
- ✓ Collards
- ✓ Dandelion Greens
- ✓ Dates
- ✓ Endive
- ✓ Figs
- ✓ Grapefruit
- ✓ Guava
- ✓ Kale
- ✓ Macadamia Nuts
- ✓ Mustard Greens
- ✓ Peppers
- ✓ Turnip Greens
- ✓ Raisins

HOMEOPATHIC: China 4 - as directed; used for skin diseases

TISSUE SALTS: Ferum Phosthorium - as directed, essential for iron anemia

"I love you and I want you to love you; don't neglect your body because of problems that lies outside of you, be healed Daughter of the Most High God"

MARIJUANA
(Cannabis Sativa)

Marijuana is a plant in the grass family and is classified as a weed. It has some limited curative properties and as a curative, it must be drank as a tea, used as poultice or eaten raw. Interesting to note, as a food, raw marijuana is difficult to digest because people are not natural grass eaters. However, the plant mineral content is good for lung dis-eases. When marijuana is burnt and smoked, it is transformed into a processed toxic chemical with concerns deadly oils. The synthetic chemical droplets in marijuana smoke are a depressant. They depress the bodily function and motor activity, lessens heart action, dull thinking, lessons muscle contraction, lessens frequency and depth of breathing, decreases gland secretions (prostrate, thyroid, pituitary, etc.) and increases the aging process. Tiny droplets of chemicals in the smoke of Marijuana directly weaken the liver, brain, eyes, and sex organs.

It alters the breath and the rhythm of internal organs. Marijuana synthetic chemicals disorientate cellular control of the body. In The Low-Fat Way to Health Hazard by Dale Dominy, M.D., the subject is scientifically reviewed. The tiny droplets of chemicals in Marijuana, smoke reduce the sperm count and damages the nerve receptor site. The tiny droplets of chemicals in smoke contain more cancer-causing chemicals than tobacco smoke. Emphysema, lung cancer, bronchitis and related diseases that once only affected tobacco smokers are common in Marijuana smokers. The chemicals in Marijuana smoke can cause scarring of the lung tissue and the oily droplets of chemicals in the smoke clogs the lungs. This reduces oxygen to the cells. Tissue and organs such as liver. Reduced oxygen to the liver causes weak digestive enzyme fluid, reduces mineral absorption, disrupts hormone balance, weakens the pancreas and thyroid, and decreases the nutrients to the brain. The bitter oils stimulate the appetite. The new hi-tech plants contain 200% more tetrahydrocannabinol (THC). It is not the same marijuana of twenty or thirty years ago. It is a cloned and hybridized plant conduction. It is not natural. Those that grow their own plants do not research the origin of the cloned seeds. They grow them in synthetic fertilized soil or nutrient depleted soil. The private growers do not test the soil and ground water for contamination or toxic chemicals. Marijuana is deliberately bred to be addictive and can result in mind, severe, or delayed withdrawal symptoms. Some of the symptoms of withdrawal are chills, anxiety, food craving (related to liver damage), headaches, temper tantrums, diarrhea, hot flashes, apathy, family and relationship problems, hypersensitivity, mood swings, tremors, excessive talking, sleeplessness, and illusions about self worth.

TREATMENT: The detoxification of the body is a gradual process. It is suggested that detox should span over a two-to-four-week period. The suggested remedies should be taken daily. Supplements with meals and amino acids between meals or on an empty stomach.

SUPPLEMENTS

- ✓ Multiple Vitamin and Minerals (as directed, provided nutrients)
- ✓ Digestive Enzyme (as directed, improves digestion)
- ✓ Vitamin A (25,000 IU - strengthens tissue)
- ✓ Beta Carotene (20,000 IU - enhances immunity)
- ✓ Vitamin C (buffered) (10,000 mg - combats infection)
- ✓ Vitamin E (25,000 IU - aids circulation and immunity)
- ✓ Lecithin Capsules (1,000 mg - 4,000 mg - used for depression and nerves)
- ✓ Garlic Capsules (2 capsules three times daily - purifies blood)
- ✓ GABA (1,000 mg - 5,000 mg - stabilizes nerves)
- ✓ Pantothenic Acid (5 mg - 50 mg - reduces stress)
- ✓ Calcium (2,000 mg - calms nerves)
- ✓ Lipoic Acid (100mg - 200mg - heals nerve damage)
- ✓ Plant Sterolins (as directed - helps defend the tissue)

GLANDULARS

- ✓ Raw Adrenal
- ✓ Raw Liver (as directed - relieves stress, neutralizes drugs)

AMINO ACIDS

- ✓ Tyrosine (1,000mg - 3,000mg; daytime energizer)
- ✓ Phenylalanine (1,000mg - 3,000mg; relieves stress and pain)
- ✓ 5 HTP (500mg - 2,000mg - relaxes, rest, sleep)
- ✓ Glutathione: (500mg - 3,000 mg - removes toxins)

✓ Glucosamine and Chondroitin: (1,000 mg - heals tissue and relieves pain)

MARIJUANA (CANNABIS SATIVA) HERBS:

✓ Pau D'Arco
✓ Echinacea
✓ Gotu Kola
✓ Goldenseal, Chaparral (combine and drink in glass daily)

STIMULATOR: *Yohimbe* and *Ephedra* (daytime - combination is believed to be a natural type of "high")

NERVOUSNESS

✓ Valerian
✓ Passionflower
✓ Skullcap
✓ Catnip
✓ Chamomile (sleep aid)

FOODS: Raw fruits and fruit juices, fresh vegetables. If animal flesh is eaten, it must be baked or broiled without added oil. Use raw almond butter, raw sesame butter, a vegetable protein drink and wheat, corn, or oat bran daily.

ADDICTION: The effect that smoke from burnt Marijuana gives is a chemically addicting state. The synthetic chemicals in the smoke cause SICK-ness and malnutrition of the body. Marijuana causes the body to malfunction and biochemistry to be sickly, blocks nerve receptor sites, decreases oxygen and increases waste in cells. The tiny poisonous oil droplets within the smoke gums the lymph fluid, hormones, red and white blood cells, and corpuscles. This self-induced sickness is called "feeling good". This malnutrition or disease state (depression) is commonly called a "high". The synthetic chemicals in Marijuana smoke creates mental, emotional, behavioral, and physical dependency. Dependency behavior can mean smoking once a day, once a week, once a month or once a year. The regularity of smoking the chemicals in Marijuana reflects the individuality of the addictive person. Synthetic chemicals made from Marijuana smoke are addictive and cause the Marijuana to freely control and alter the mind, mood, and behavior of the addict.

MARIJUANA EFFECTS ON THE SPIRIT: Burnt (cooked) Marijuana is a chemical that alters the attachment of the spirit to the breath. It causes the spirit to lose its guiding effect on the mind, mood, and body. It can alter or destroy levels of spirituality.

Establishing & Repairing Credit

If you want to pay off credit cards or loans which include interest or determine the amount to save on a home, in most cases, you can take the amount you want to save and divide by the number of months (time).

GOALS SHOULD BE:

✓ Specific: what is the goal?
✓ How much should I save?
✓ How long will it take me?
✓ Realistic expectations?

FINANCIAL GOAL MAY BE:

✓ Vacation
✓ College/ Education/ Training
✓ New Care
✓ Down payment for a house
✓ Paying off credit card debts

Writing down your financial goals is a great starting point

SHORT TERM GOAL (less than 1 year):

✓ Goal: pay off $1500 credit card balance (12% interest)
✓ When: within 12 months
✓ How much? 134 per month
✓ Realistic expectations?

MID TERM GOAL (1 to 3 years):

✓ Goal: $3,000 vacation
✓ When: in 18 months
✓ How much? $167 per month
✓ Realistic expectations?

LONG TERM GOAL (3 years or more):

✓ Goal: $15,000 for a downpayment on a home
✓ When: in 5 years (60 months)
✓ How Much? $250 per month
✓ Realistic expectations?

WHY DO BUDGETS FAIL?

✓ Negative Attitude
✓ Lack of Motivation
✓ Unrealistic Expectations

HOW TO SAVE...

✓ Pay yourself first!
✓ Use automatic transfers
✓ Use payroll deduction
✓ Take advantage of your employer's retirement plan

"And don't forget... A quick and effortless way to save a little money is to toss your spare change into a jar or piggy bank! I hope you found this to be helpful recommendations!"

"GREAT CREDIT MADE EASY"

1. Budgeting
✓ Journalize spending, distinguish between needs and wants.
✓ Analyze spending patterns and cut unnecessary expenses.
✓ Plan for short-term, medium-term, and long-term goals.
✓ Set up a safety net as the first financial goal.

2. Credit Score Basics
✓ Understand the components: payment history, amount owed, length of credit history, new credit, and types of credit.
✓ FICO scores range from 300 to 850.
✓ Credit score makeup: payment history (35%), amount owed (30%), length of credit history (15%), new credit (10%), types of credit (10%).

3. Building Credit
✓ Avoid subprime car loans, high-fee unsecured credit cards.
✓ Be cautious with payday loans, buy here pay here car loans, title loans, and rent-to-own.
✓ Choose credit cards wisely, read terms and conditions, consider a secured card for rebuilding credit.

4. Debt Management
✓ Settle debt using a DIY method, save half the debt amount.
✓ Understand credit card history, be aware of changes in agreement terms.
✓ Cosigning affects your credit as if the account is yours.

5. Credit Protection
✓ Do not waste money on credit insurance; normal life and disability insurance are more valuable.
✓ Monitor your credit report but knowing it every day won't improve your score faster.
✓ Freeze your credit report if concerned about identity theft.

6. Identity Theft Protection
✓ 60% of stolen information is used to access credit card accounts.
✓ Monitor your own credit, use free non-FICO scores for protection.

7. Debt Options: Consider debt management plans, debt settlement programs, or bankruptcy.

8. Staying Out of Trouble
✓ No government-backed stimulus for walking away from debt.
✓ Be cautious with debt settlement advertising claims.

9. Dealing with Collections
✓ Negative items may disappear after 7 years.
✓ Get agreements in writing, keep proof of payments.
✓ Understand rights under the Fair Debt Collections Practice Act.
✓ Consider the age of the negative account.

"Value and appreciate the people who sacrifice their 'something' for you, because maybe that 'something' was their everything."

"Ten Things You Must Give Up Moving Forward"

1. Letting Others' Opinions Control Your Life: Focus on your own self-perception and what is best for your life.

2. Shame of Past Failures: Your past does not define your future; concentrate on the present.

3. Indecision about What You Want: Decide where you want to be and pursue it passionately.

4. Procrastination on Important Goals: Choose to accept responsibility for changing conditions; act now.

5. Choosing to Do Nothing: Life is about choices; seize the opportunity to live each day.

6. Need to Be Right: Aim for success but acknowledge the value of being wrong for learning and growth.

7. Running from Problems: Confront and address issues, communicate, appreciate, forgive, and love.

8. Making Excuses Instead of Decisions: Long-term failures often result from excuses, not decisions.

9. Overlooking Positive Points: Happiness is tied to gratitude for the good things in your life now.

10. Not Appreciating the Present Moment: Life's greatness lies in the trivial things; appreciate the present moment.

GOAL SETTING

- ✓ Many people feel as if they're adrift in the world. They work hard, but they don't seem to get anywhere worthwhile. Akey reason that they feel this way is that they haven't spent enough time thinking about what they want from life and haven't set themselves formal goals. After all, would you set out on a major journey with no real idea of your destination? Probably not!
- ✓ Goal setting is a powerful process for thinking about your ideal future, and for motivating yourself to turn your vision of this future into reality.
- ✓ The process of setting goals helps you choose where you want to go in life. By knowing precisely what you want to achieve, you know where you must concentrate your efforts. You'll also quickly spot the distractions that can, so easily, lead you astray!

FRAGMENTS OF IDENTITY | 317

WHY SET GOALS?

✓ Goal setting is used by top-level athletes, successful businesspeople, and achievers in all fields.
✓ Setting goals gives you long-term vision and short-term motivation.
✓ It focuses your acquisition of knowledge and helps you to organize your time and your resources so that you can make the very most of your life.
✓ By setting sharp, clearly defined goals, you can measure and take pride in the achievement of the goals, and you'll see forward progress in what might previously have seemed a long pointless grind.
✓ You will also raise your self-confidence, as you recognize your own ability and competence in achieving the goals that you have set.

'Set out to succeed – Make sure your first step is the right step'!

GOAL SETTING PROCESS

✓ Your thoughts or ideas are your dreams and wishes
✓ Sorting out all the wants (brainstorming)
✓ Determining the HOW Strategic Planning
✓ Solving the Obstacles (Problem Solving)

TIP 1: Write down all the tasks that you need to complete. If they're large tasks, break out the first action step, and write this down with the largest task. (Ideally, tasks or action steps should take no longer than one to two hours to complete).

TIP 2: It's important to remember that failing to meet goals does not mean failure, just as long as you learn from the experience.

SETTING SMALLER GOALS

✓ Once you have set your lifetime goals, set a five-year plan of smaller goals that you need to complete if you are to reach your lifetime plan.

✓ Then create a one-year plan, six-month plan, and a one-month plan of progressively smaller goals. Each of these should be based on the previous plan.

✓ Then create a daily To-Do-List of things that you should reach to achieve your lifetime goals.

✓ At an early stage, your smaller goals might be to read books and gather information on the achievement of your higher-level goals.

✓ This will help you to improve the quality and realism of your goal setting.

✓ Finally review your plans, and make sure that they fit the way in which you want to live your life.

SETTING LIFETIME GOALS

- The first step in setting personal goals is to consider what you want to achieve in your lifetime (or at least, by a significant and distant age in the future).
- Setting lifetime goals gives you the overall perspective that shapes all other aspects of your decision making.
- To give a broad, balanced coverage of all key areas in your life, try to set goals in some of the following categories (or in other categories of your own, where these are important to you):

CAREER - What level do you want to reach in your career, or what do you want to achieve?

FINANCIAL - How much do you want to earn, by what stage? How is this related to your career goals?

EDUCATION - Is there any knowledge you want to acquire in particular?

What information and skills will you need to have in order to achieve other goals?

FAMILY - Do you want to be a parent? If so, how are you going to be a good parent? How do you want to be seen by a partner or by members of your extended family?

ARTISTIC - Do you want to achieve any artistic goals?

ATTITUDE - Is any part of your mindset holding you back? Is there any part of the way that you behave that upsets you? (If so, set a goal to improve your behavior or find a solution to the problem.)

PHYSICAL - Are there any athletic goals that you want to achieve, or do you want good health deep into old age? What steps are you going to take to achieve this?

PLEASURE - How do you want to enjoy yourself?

PUBLIC SERVICE - Do you want to make a better place? If so, how?

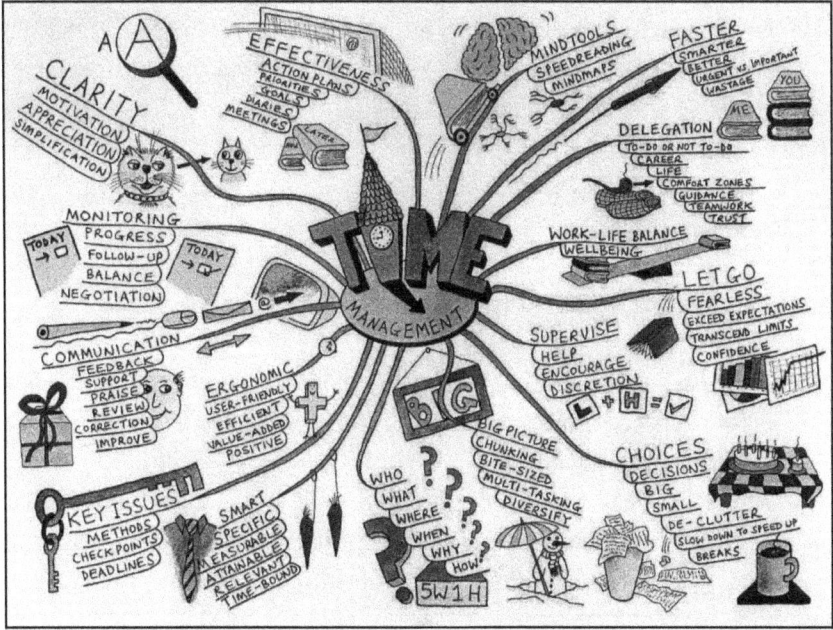

BRAINSTORMING Spend some time brainstorming these things, and then select one or more goals in each category that best reflect what you want to do. Then consider trimming again so that you have a small number of significant goals that you have a small number of significant goals that you can focus on. As you do this, make sure that the goals that you have set are ones that you genuinely want to achieve, not ones that your parents, family, or employers might want. (If you have a partner, you want to consider what he or she wants - however, make sure that you also remain true to yourself!)

GOAL SETTING IS AN IMPORTANT METHOD OF

✓ Deciding what you want to achieve in your life.
✓ Separating what's important from what's irrelevant, or a distraction.
  Motivating yourself.

✓ Building your self-confidence, based on successful achievement of goals.

✓ Set your lifetime goals first. Then, set a five-year plan of smaller goals that you need to complete if you are to reach your lifetime plan. Keep the process going by regularly reviewing and updating your goals. And remember to take time to enjoy the satisfaction of achieving your goals when you do so.

✓ If you don't already set goals, do so, starting now. As you make this technique part of your life, you'll find your career accelerating, and you'll wonder how you did without it!

YOU SET YOUR GOALS ON A NUMBER OF LEVELS

✓ First you create your "big picture" of what you want to do with your life (or over, say, the next ten years), and identify the large-scale goals that you want to achieve.

✓ Then, you break these down into smaller and smaller targets that you must hit to reach your lifetime goals.

✓ Finally, once you have your plan, you start working on it to achieve these goals.

✓ This is why we start the process of goal setting by looking at your lifetime goals.

✓ Then, we work down to the things that you can do in, say, the next five years, then next year, next month, next week, and today, to start moving towards them.

TEN STEPS TO ACHIEVING YOUR GOALS:

1. **SET A GOAL** that is believable to **YOU**
2. Select a target date
3. Identify the core reason you want it
4. Write a list of action steps that will get you to that goal
5. Seek partners to help you get there faster
6. Make it visual
7. Tap into the physiology of what if **FEELS** like to already have it
8. Read it, proclaim it, and visualize it daily

9. Feel grateful for achieving it
10. Celebrate and give thanks

GOALS SHOULD BE S-M-A-R-T:

Specific - can your goal be broken into smaller steps?

Motivational - Is it emotionally charged? Do you have the energy to carry out the goal?

Accountable - Can your goal be tracked and accounted for?

Responsible - Will it cost you friends? Respect from family? Your integrity?

Easy to respond to changes *IF* required?

Touchable - What will you have to hold as a completed result.

BUDGETING: CREATING A PERSONAL BUDGET

BALANCING INCOME & EXPENSES

- ✓ Start budgeting now - don't wait until you're finally "on your feet", to begin to beget.
- ✓ A budget is nothing more than the activity of balancing income versus expenses.

WHY BUDGET?

- ✓ Budgeting is the first step on the road to financial success.
- ✓ Controlling your day to day-to-day finances allows you to do things you want to do.

WHAT IS A BUDGET?

"A budget is a written record of the money that flows in and out of your household (or pocket) every month."

HOW TO START?

"If you haven't budgeted before, or feel at this point don't have a good idea of where your money is going...

✓ For the next month, write down EVERYTHING you spend money on and anything you receive money."
✓ *Monthly Tracking Sample*: Balance, Rent, Paycheck, Taxes, Dining Out, Phone Bill, Music, Car Repairs, Grocery, Clothes

CREATING A PERSONAL BUDGET

✓ Track your expenses.
✓ Figure out the amount of money you're spending.
✓ What do you have to spend?
✓ What are you spending that is not a necessity?

THERE ARE TWO TYPES OF EXPENSES:

✓ **Essential expenses - <u>HAVE</u> to have** in order to live
✓ **Non-essential expenses - <u>DON'T HAVE</u> to have** in order to live

EXPENSES / INCOME: What can you cut out? Dining Out or Buying Things you don't need?

BALANCING INCOME AND EXPENSES: At the end of the month, break everything down into categories. Is your income greater than your expenses?

If YES! Great = then you can save.
If NOT! There's a problem!

ESSENTIAL - FIXED - EXPENSES

- Mortgage or rent
- Insurance (auto and home)
- Car payments
- Taxes
- School loans

ESSENTIAL - VARIABLE - EXPENSES:

- Car maintenance
- Gas
- Food
- Electricity, heat
- Phone

NON-ESSENTIAL EXPENSES:

- Clothing
- Books
- Movies
- Video games
- Other items, you want, but don't need

SOME POSSIBLE EXPENSES...

- Housing
- Phone
- Magazine subscriptions
- Electricity
- Gas/ Electricity
- Water/ Sewer
- Garbage
- Pet Food
- Insurance
- Prescriptions
- Internet

- Movie Rentals
- Food
- Insurance
- Medical Bills
- Gym Membership
- Entertainment
- Toiletries
- Sundries
- Credit Cards
- Electricity
- Pet Food
- Movie Rentals
- Gym Membership
- Entertainment

TEN SECRETS TO SUCCESS

1. **How you think of everything**. Always be positive. Think of success, not failure. Beware of a negative environment.

2. **Decide upon your true dreams and goals**: Write down your specific goals and develop a plan to reach them.

3. **Take action**: Goals are nothing without action. Don't be afraid to get started. Just do it.

4. **Never stop learning**. Go back to school or read books. Get training and acquire skills.

5. **Be persistent and work hard**. Success is a marathon, not a sprint. Never give up.

6. **Learn to analyze details**. Get all the facts and input. Learn from your mistakes.

7. **Focus your time and money**. Don't let other people or things distract you.

8. **Don't be afraid to innovate**; be different. Following the herd is a sure way to mediocrity.

9. **Deal and communicate with people effectively.** No person is an island. Learn to understand and motivate others.

10. **Be honest and dependable; take responsibility.** Otherwise, #1-9 will not matter.

Proverbs 12:9 (New International Version) Better to be a nobody and yet have a servant than pretend to be somebody and have no food.

King James Bible - He that is despised, and hath a servant, is better than he that honoureth himself, and lacketh bread.

———◆———

Despite earlier setbacks of getting into the program earlier, J.E.T received his General Education Development (G.E.D) Certificate on April 25, 2016.

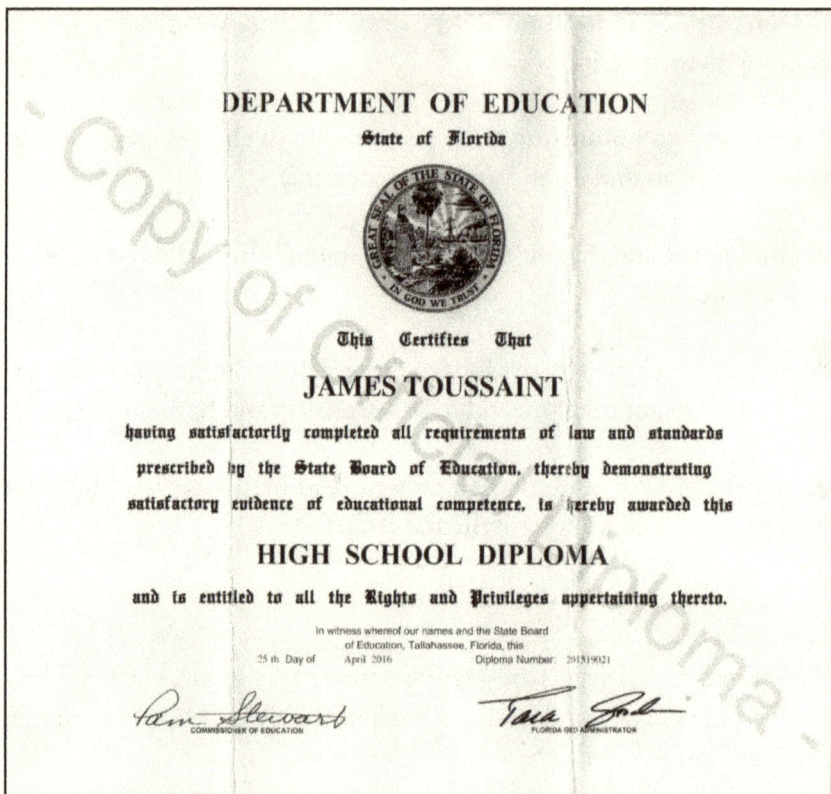

DEPARTMENT OF EDUCATION
State of Florida

This Certifies That

JAMES TOUSSAINT

having satisfactorily completed all requirements of law and standards prescribed by the State Board of Education, thereby demonstrating satisfactory evidence of educational competence, is hereby awarded this

HIGH SCHOOL DIPLOMA

and is entitled to all the Rights and Privileges appertaining thereto.

In witness whereof our names and the State Board of Education, Tallahassee, Florida, this

25 th Day of April 2016   Diploma Number: 201519021

COMMISSIONER OF EDUCATION   FLORIDA GED ADMINISTRATOR

"Commitment means staying loyal to what you said you were going to do long after the mood you said it in has left you."

"Don't Quit"

"When things go wrong, as they sometimes will,
When the road you're trudging seems all uphill,
When the funds are low and the debts are high,
And you want to smile, but you have to sigh.
When care is pressing you down a bit,
Rest, if you must, but don't you quit.

Life is queer with its twists and turns,
As every one of us sometimes learns, And many a failure turns about,
When he might have won had he stuck it out;
Don't give up though the pace seems slow -
You may succeed with another blow.

Often the goal is nearer than
It seems to a faint and following man,
Often the struggler has given up,
When he might have captured the victor's cup
And he learned too late when the night slipped down,

Success is failure turned inside out -
The silver tint of the clouds of doubt,
And you never can tell how close you are,
It may be near when it seems so far,
So stick to the fight when your hardest hit -
It's when things seem worst that you mustn't quit.
- J.E.T. <eye3i>

- Toussaint
April 25, 2016

———◆———

"Our profound apprehension doesn't stem from our inadequacy but rather from our untapped power. It is the brilliance within us, not our shadows, that often intimidates.
We question ourselves, asking, 'Why embrace brilliance, beauty, talent, and fabulousness?'

Yet, why not embrace them?
As a child of God, playing small doesn't benefit the world; there is no enlightenment in shrinking to ease others' insecurities. We are all meant to radiate, just as children naturally do.

Born to reveal the divine glory within, it extends to everyone, not just a chosen few.

By letting our light shine, we empower others to do the same. Liberated from fear, our presence becomes a catalyst for the liberation of others."

- Toussaint
April 25, 2016

"It's Time to Replace Some Bad Habits at Work"

I thought I might share this article with you to gain a perspective. With props to some of the advice we heard in 2015, here are ten reasonable goals for the upcoming year:

1. **Get to work early:** It's not a big deal if you walk into the office everyday on time

or even five or ten minutes late. It certainly doesn't impact your day of affect your relationship with co-workers but getting to work half an hour or so ahead of time, when the office is still empty, could greatly improve your at-work experience. You'll get the chance to go through e-mails, check your voice messages, grab a cup of coffee, take a look at some of your personal communications, create or update your to-do list and then ease into the day. It is much easier to get work done beginning at 9 a.m. if you already have a bit of momentum pushing you forward.

2. **Get up and walk around:** (Although your situation is different, and you are already up and mobile for the most part). Sure, the merits of leaving your desk for an occasional start around the cubicles is going for you physically and mentally, but it also good for your replication at the office. While it is certainly one way to get to know your co-workers, it also makes you a visible participant in the company's business. No longer confined to the carrier cubicle, your co-workers and managers will see you as an article participant in the day-to-day activities of your business.

3. **Know when I go:** while taking the above advice into account, don't be the person who overstays his or her welcome. Learn to read the signs of co-workers who has work to do or has simply finished talking about the weekend's game. If you see someone typing at her keyboard or looking at his phone while you're chatting away, it's a pretty god sign that it's time for you to get back to your desk.

4. **Eat better:** In addition to munching on healthy snacks throughout the day, maintain a simple breakfast and lunch to keep your energy level consistent throughout the day. Those post meal peaks and valleys can be incredibly disruptive to the workday, everyone jokes about the 15:00 crash but if you take a serious look at you productivity, you'll probably find that the days you chow down on that Italian beef and fries are the days you don't get much done in the afternoon.

5. **Prioritize your work:** you can find numerous. Strategies online and in your local bookstore that outlines how to maximize your productivity during the workday. One simple rule of thumb is to tackle the small tasks before moving on to the large ones. Answer emails that require less than five minutes of your time and you'll find yourself putting out small flames before they turn into unmanageable desires. Most importantly, find a workday and work, work. When do you do your best work? Pick up on these clues and come with a plan that works for you.

6. **Keep Learning:** Complacency can be a career killer. While you may be comfortable in your current position; you may not be fully aware of all the forces at work outside your station. Whether it's a pending buyout, upcoming layout or potential department reorganization, the only thing you can be sure of is your own work, so keep learning. Take seminars and classes when you can and be sure to attach yourself to key projects as well as the people who are doing the company's important work.

7. **Be ready to leave:** Always have a resume on hand and keep your social media profiles updated. You never know when a perfect opportunity may emerge at a friend's company or within a contact's division. The best way to move ahead is to always be ready. If someone mentions a job

that perfectly fits your skill set and experience, you can't take three days to put together your resume. It needs to be sent on the spot.

8. **Work well with others**: While most employees enjoy working alone, it is important to put extra effort into team projects. Don't worry so much about individual attention. If things go well, the entire group will benefit from the accomplishment. One way to keep co-workers on your side it is to be a productive and friendly member of any working team.

9. **Be nice: Make eye contact** with people in the hallways and say a brief hello when you see them on the elevators. And go ahead and make general small talk when standing next to each other at the copy machine. These things seem simple but plenty of careers have been sidetracked because of a perceived cold shoulder. You want your co-workers to think of you as friendly, engaged workers, not the grumpy curmudgeon who complains about his boss every chance he or she gets.

10. **Maintain your balance**. It's true "worklife" has become a bit of a corporate cliché, usually staked in the corporation's favor, but that doesn't mean you have to live your life by buzzwords. If you need to engage in an after-work activity or lunchtime workout to maintain your sanity, do so. Don't let the 'nine to five' section of your life define you. Instead, make it one aspect of your life, preferably one that enhances the other facets of you.

INTERNET APPENDIX

CITY AND NEIGHBORHOOD DATA:
www.census.gov
https://www.bls.gov
www.ojp.usdoj.gov/bjs

COMP SALES:
https://www.corelogic.com
www.latimes.com

CREDIT INFORMATION:
https://my.equifax.com
https://www.experian.com
www.myfico.com
www.creditinfocenter.com
www.fairisaac.com
https://www.credit.com

FINANCIAL CALCULATORS AND SPREADSHEETS:
https://www.mortgageretirementprofessor.com
https://www.hsh.com/

FORECLOSURES AND REPOS:
www.homesteps.com
www.hud.gov
www.va.gov
www.treas.gov
www.fanniemae.com
www.bankofamerica.com
www.viewforeclosurehomes.com
www.realtytrac.com

HOME IMPROVEMENT:
www.askthebuilder.com
www.kubus.com
www.bhg.com
www.doityourself.com
www.improvenet.com
https://dan.com

HOME INSPECTION:
www.homeinspector.org

HOMES FOR SALE:
www.realtor.com
https://go.crmls.org
www.cyberhomes.com

www.homes.com
www.ipix.com
www.owners.com
www.buyowner.com
www.fsbo.com
www.homegain.com
www.byowner.com
www.zillow.com
www.fsboguide.com
https://mobilehome.com

INSURANCE INFORMATION:
www.cpcu.com
www.statefar.com

LAW INFORMATION:
www.lectlaw.com
www.nolo.com

MORTGAGE APPLICATIONS:
www.interest.com
www.mortgagequotes.com
www.quickenloans.com
www.eloan.com

MORTGAGE INFORMATION:
www.mtgprofessor.com
www.hsh.com
www.homefair.com (house moving relocation calculators/ Real Estate
Mortgage Loans, Van Lines Apartments)

MORTGAGE PROVIDERS (UNDERWRITERS)
www.fanniemae.com
www.homesteps.com
www.va.gov
www.hud.gov

REAL ESTATE INFORMATION:

www.inman.com/bruss
www.ourfamilyplace.com
www.realtor.com
www.johntreed.com
www.arello.org

SCHOOL DATA:

www.schoolmatch.com

To make more informed investing and borrowing decisions we can start through the data overload that the web now offers. We must still beware; however, many sites do not provide accurate data, nor does the data necessarily relate to our specific needs. For example, neighborhood data and school data are plagued with inconsistencies, omissions, errors, and I'll define measures. Don't accept Web - based data as the last word. Check and verify all information (last updated 2/17/2024). The WebApp should not reduce our need to walk and talk the neighborhoods; visit schools, shops, parks other facilities; physically view comparable sales; and drive areas we might like to search out "For Sale" signs.

- Toussaint
April 25, 2016

CHAPTER

15

Navigating Maryland's Memories

I embarked on a transformative journey from the vibrant streets of Fort Lauderdale, the open road stretching before me like an unwritten chapter. Pursuing an old Dodge, the engine's familiar hum became a metaphor for a quest deeply rooted in the need for familiarity and connection. With Ja'Faith by my side, the drive from the sun-drenched landscapes of South Florida back to Maryland wasn't just a physical relocation; it was a symbolic journey toward regression. As the wheels rolled into Maryland, the atmosphere shifted. Tree-lined streets painted a picturesque scene, and the city embraced us with an eclectic charm, fostering a sense of community that stood in stark contrast to the urban buzz of Spring. It whispered promises of cultural events, local shops, and supportive outer community, a backdrop that set the stage. Returning to my home state was more than a mere logistical move; it was a strategic decision, a focused and purposeful approach to rebuilding my nursing knowledge. Enrolling in a nursing refresher course at Living Spring Institute became my commitment to overcoming life's obstacles. The resilient pursuit of passing the nursing state board exam on March 4th, 2014, became a pivotal moment, a symbol not only of dedication and resilience but also of opening doors to new horizons in my professional journey.

Meanwhile, Marie and her crew transitioned to a more spacious single-family house in Within the same area, a move that held promises of a fresh start and opportunities. As I successfully conquered the nursing state board exam, this achievement echoed through the narrative, validating my unwavering commitment to the nursing profession. The story unfolded like a symphony, each note resonating with a pivotal moment. Amid challenges in preparing for the NCLEX Exam in 2019, frustration fueled determination, leading to the birth of a website dedicated to hosting a nursing review course.

This venture, born from a desire to assist others in navigating the complexities of the nursing exam, further solidified my place in the nursing profession, creating a harmonious melody of dedication and resilience. Despite financial constraints, I defied the odds, breathing life into both a physical blueprint and a digital virtual classroom housing my invaluable nursing notes. However, the narrative took a poignant turn; September 2022, shrouded in adversity. The physical blueprint of my website, a tangible representation of my struggles and triumphs, was stolen from my bedroom in Marie's house. This loss, more than a minor setback, became a turning point, a stolen blueprint of my nursing website. The theft of the blueprint carried a weight beyond material loss; it became a discouraging force, casting a shadow over my aspirations for graduate school. This pivotal setback, orchestrated within the intricacies of Marie's involvement in my life, revealed her motives with a stark clarity — a motive rooted in exploiting me for her own gain, rather than supporting my pursuit. The stolen blueprint, more than a physical loss, symbolized the erosion of trust and the divergence of our paths, leading to a profound reconsideration of my academic endeavors.

To: Jenny
From: J.E.T.

"My Dear,

If you're planning on moving forward, you have to learn to let the past go. Learn from yesterday, benefit from yesterday, but not live in yesterday. Avoid being struck in time and prevented from making forward progress. Where you're going to be a lot bigger then where you were. What you do is -- have a funeral of your past, buy a coffin, if you will, and place everything of yesterday in it - the hurt, the pain, the disappointment, the losses, and the hang ups, then bury it in the dirt. Break the ties of yesterday. More importantly, moving forward, everything God has designed for you he's already given you; God gives what he intends for you before you get to it. It's a given but you must go get it - your future, the provisions sat for you, your earthly inheritance. Walk on it; claim it, you got to walk by Faith, lay hold of eternal life. If you want to rule your world you got to create the world you want to rule."

"Your idea to offer an online service teaching nursing students' concepts and strategies to help them pass the The National Council Licensure Examination (NCLEX) can only be made possible by you. I suggest you start establishing yourself as an expert in that space by starting your own little tribute online - offer tips on social media, start a blog - join discussions pertaining to the topic on blogs, offer articles, news, report or originate the reports, this way you develop your base, learn about potential customers amongst other potential information."

"P.S. Sit not idle, it's better to be an informed consumer. Educate yourself and gain insight on the things you are interested in obtaining, like buying a home there are programs or public events for first time home buyers - other seminars regarding finance. Check your local chamber of commerce, community section of your local newspaper, or the event section in the money section of the newspaper: I know you're waiting on me but don't wait to get insight. Especially J.E.T. What do we know about the Hair Care Market, the current trends in the industry, or the general economic climate?"

Love You,

- Toussaint
April 28, 2016

CHAPTER

16

Unveiling Deception

From the very essence of Marie stepping seamlessly into the role of my caregiver, she insidiously gained access to the core of my personal identity. Her influence, a subtle intrusion, transcended the boundaries of caregiving, extending into a realm where, with artful persuasion, she orchestrated the purchase of a vehicle for a sibling. This clandestine decision not only cast a looming shadow over my financial stability but etched indelible marks on my credit score, all transpiring without any consideration or discussion with my partner. I cannot pinpoint what I ever learned from Marie, it wasn't how to dress myself or even how to write, it wasn't how to cook a meal or even how to drive. These maneuvers, challenges of motherhood, and the relentless quest for self-identity became not just threads but pulsating veins of mystery and complexity entangled in the very tapestry of my narrative. Beyond the grim reality of financial abuse, the painstaking unwinding of paperwork revealed fragments of my past, concealed within a forgotten childhood photo and a birth certificate bearing conspicuous omissions. As these fragments unveiled, a protracted and intricate journey spanning many years unfurled before me.

In the quiet solitude of the old chimney adjacent amidst forgotten old and dusty bookshelf relics, I stumbled upon an artifact frozen in time, a photograph that whispered of untold stories. The pivotal moment, when

I laid eyes on that poignant photograph and of my birth certificate, marked a profound turning point in my soul. Memories surged forth, an unstoppable tide, prompting vivid recollections of Aunt Betty-Ann and her words of wisdom while styling my hair. In those cherished moments, she playfully hinted at a familial connection to the legendary Congolese Artist Jules Shungu, known as Papa Wemba, suggesting that he might be the missing link, a father lost to me.

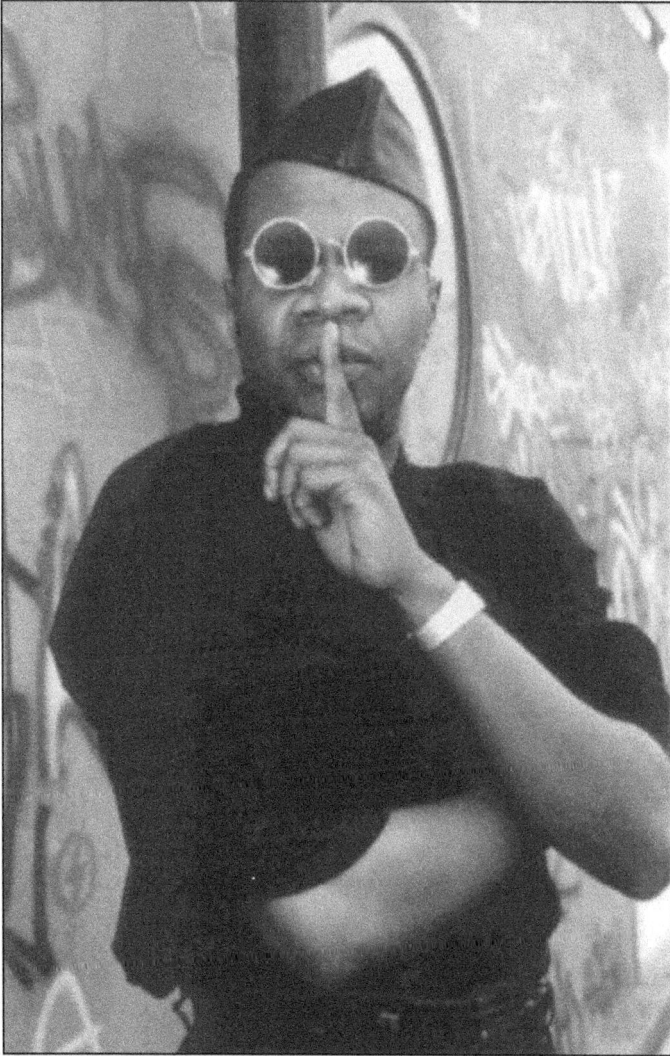

Drenched in the exploration of my biological roots, a profound connection to Papa Wemba, the 'King of Rumba Rock'; in the Congolese music and film industry, materialized. His legendary presence, an echo through time, resonated with my very essence. Acknowledged for his influential contributions to entertainment, Papa Wemba's impact was not just colossal but transcendent. In this revelatory moment, it felt as if the 'King of Rumba Rock' had, against all odds, discovered his long-lost Princess, a connection etched in the tapestry of my life, pulsating with an intensity only found in the deepest recesses of the heart.

The discovered photograph, adorned with the elegant inscription "Meilleurs Voeux", not only transports me to the festive Christmas of 1988 but serves as a poignant anchor, immersing me in the essence of that era. As I reflect on this captured moment, the profound legacy of Papa Wemba emerges as a potential key, weaving a familial connection that threads through my captivating journey of self-discovery. Each revelation deepens the mysterious link to Papa Wemba's tale, guiding me through the labyrinth of my past. Delving further into the enigma surrounding my birth and the elusive details on my birth certificate, the tantalizing possibility of being the missing Princess in Papa Wemba's narrative takes shape. Unraveling these cryptic clues transforms into a metamorphic journey, intricately intertwining the threads of my personal history with Papa Wemba's indelible impact on music and fashion. This journey parallels the exploration of Papa Wemba's influential work, *'Life Is Beautiful'* from 1987—a narrative that mirrors the complexities of my own journey. The film's profound exploration of love, ambition, and societal expectations resonates deeply within me, echoing the intricate layers of my identity. Another revelation surfaces as a photograph from April 1987, capturing me at just one year old. The inscription on the back, 'Avril 87 Jenny a 1 an Photo-Midi'; marks the passage of time and suggests a profound connection to Papa Wemba's fashion influence, binding my personal history to his iconic style. The fabric pattern in the photo transforms into a living representation of fashion, a poignant homage to Papa Wemba's enduring influence. As these threads gracefully entwine, the puzzle pieces seamlessly fit together, exposing the authentic narrative of my existence. Each revelation becomes an emotional landmark, a heartbeat in the symphony of my journey. Holding this additional photograph, a profound connection to my past and Papa Wemba's influence envelops me, deepening the emotional resonance of the moment. The culmination of these puzzle pieces heralds a profound moment of self-realization, an extraordinary act of embracing my true identity.

This additional context, interwoven with other clues in my journey, such as the Christmas photograph and my Aunt Betty-Ann's cherished memories, adds a chronological layer to my early years. It serves as a key, unlocking more details about my infancy, contributing to a richer understanding of my identity and its intricate ties to Papa Wemba's legacy. Having traversed the convoluted paths of my past, the realization of my true identity dawns upon me like clarity emerging from a foggy horizon. The meticulously pieced-together puzzle reveals the authentic narrative of my existence. In the collective pursuit of self-actualization, there exists a shared reverence, a common ground where diverse journeys converge, each individual weaving their unique tapestry of self-discovery and growth. As the puzzle pieces settle into place, the symphony of my identity finds its resounding harmony, echoing through the corridors of my past and present.

In the silent corridors of bureaucracy, an inconspicuous error reshaped the narrative of my family's history, the inadvertent transformation of 'Shungu' into 'Shunga', on my daughter's birth certificate. This subtle alteration set in motion unforeseen controversies and revelations, weaving a tapestry that extended beyond mere phonetics. As curious eyes from in-laws and newfound family members fell upon the altered name, it sparked confusion about my lineage. The significance of 'Shunga'; versus

'Shungu'; unraveled cultural differences embedded in our histories, taking me on a journey of self- discovery and familial connection through the corridors of correction. A decade later, the misspelled name echoed through time, revealing itself as whisper from the past. Papa Wemba's departure and shifts in the familial landscape added layers of meaning to the correction, transforming it into a bridge connecting generations. Navigating the bureaucratic labyrinth to rectify the misspelling, ancestral stories resonated in the echoes. The amended birth certificate became a testament to family ties, correcting not just letters but also a narrative that transcended time, a journey against the backdrop of shared stories, cultural nuances, and the resilience of identity.

The corrected document served as a reflective mirror, illuminating a lineage shaped by diverse roots. It became a symbolic cornerstone, celebrating the intricate interplay of heritage. The bureaucratic process mirrored our familial history's complexities, turning a correction into a profound exploration of self and a celebration of my identity's mosaic. Just as a birth certificate identifies a newborn to society, my suspicion about missing information in my own birth certificate evolved into a guiding compass for a deeper understanding of my roots. The journey, sparked by bureaucratic correction and my daughter's amended document, stands as a symbolic cornerstone, marking my place in a regal legacy that bridges generations. Now, as I reflect on my daughter's amended birth certificate, a stark realization dawned: the suspicious absence of such notes on my own birth certificate in America. In a country where even, the slightest alteration prompts an official record of correction, the absence of such documentation on mine adds an intriguing layer to my journey of self-discovery. The discovery of white-out traces on my birth certificate unveils a clandestine layer to my narrative. As if veiled by the hushed strokes of correction fluid, the obscured details beneath prompt a cascade of questions, adding an enigmatic dimension to my quest for understanding. Each whitened mark becomes a silent witness, inviting further exploration into the obscured chapters of my origin, propelling me deeper into the labyrinth of my own familial history. The faint whispers of white-out tell tales of hidden nuances, beckoning me to unravel the secrets concealed beneath its muted strokes.

CHAPTER

17

Rebuilding Foundations

As I embarked on the intricate journey of self-discovery, meticulously collecting the scattered dots that adorned my past experiences, it felt like assembling a puzzle with pieces that, once seemingly unrelated, now fit snugly together. Each moment held a unique fragment, a color in the larger canvas of my life. The tapestry of my true identity unfolded before me, revealing a rich mosaic woven from the threads of my unique story. It was a process of unraveling layers, peeling back the veneer of assumptions and societal expectations. This journey wasn't just about discovering a name or lineage; it was about understanding the very essence of my being. The revelations, though gradual, were profound, a kaleidoscope of colors and emotions that painted the canvas of my identity. In the quiet moments of reflection, I found myself revisiting pivotal memories, reexamining them through the lens of newfound awareness. In the quiet corners of my mind, where introspection and memories converged, I found myself revisiting pivotal moments with a newfound perspective. The nuances that once eluded me began to emerge, creating a narrative that resonated with authenticity. Each memory became a doorway to deeper self-understanding, and as I explored these corridors of my past, the shadows of uncertainty began to dissipate.

In connecting these dots, I not only uncovered the past but also forged a path towards a more authentic future. I could almost feel the texture of each thread as I moved through this profound journey, witnessing the tapestry slowly drapes over my shoulders. The sensation was akin to the gentle embrace of self-acceptance, as if the threads themselves whispered tales of resilience and growth. As the final pieces fell into place, a sense of completeness washed over me. The dots, once disconnected, now wove a tangible testament to the resilience found in understanding and embracing the intricacies of my true self. This was not just a conclusion but a new beginning, a chapter closing to make way for the unwritten pages of a more authentic and fulfilling future. Concluding this chapter, finding closure and peace becomes a poignant reflection on the transformative journey. Prioritizing emotional well-being is key, and seeking support from professionals or understanding individuals can offer valuable guidance. The echoes of self-discovery resonate not only within the confines of personal reflection but also extend into the broader context of mental and emotional health. It's a profound realization that the path to self-discovery is intertwined with the delicate threads of mental and emotional health. Recognizing the importance of mental and emotional health became a crucial aspect of self-care in my journey.

The labyrinth of emotions navigated during this exploration became a testament to the resilience found in understanding and embracing the intricacies of one's true self. Seeking support from professionals of various studies and backgrounds provided me with valuable insights and coping mechanisms to navigate the complexities of my past. The therapeutic dialogue became a bridge between unraveling the mysteries within and finding solace in the external world. The collaboration with mental health professionals added layers to my self-awareness, offering tools to navigate the intricate landscape of emotions. Understanding individuals, whether friends, family, or mentors, played a pivotal role in creating a support network. Their empathy, guidance, and non-judgmental stance offered a safe space to share my experiences and gain perspectives that contributed to my healing process. The act of opening up to others became a transformative step towards self-discovery and resilience. Embracing the concept of prioritizing emotional well-being and seeking support became not only a survival strategy but a profound testament to the strength found in vulnerability and connection. Navigating the depths of my emotions, I discovered that true healing arises not only from within but through the interconnected bonds forged with those who understand the intricate dance of the human soul. As the chapter concludes, the echoes of this transformative journey reverberate, leaving an indelible mark on the canvas of my evolving self. LOVE THY SELF!

www.ingramcontent.com/pod-product-compliance
Lightning Source LLC
Chambersburg PA
CBHW022113080426
42734CB00006B/114